Liquid Modernity

Liquid Modernity

Zygmunt Bauman

polity

First published in 2000 by Polity Press

Reprinted 2000, 2001, 2003, 2004 (twice), 2005, 2006 (three times), 2007, 2008, 2009, 2010 (twice), 2011, 2012, 2013 (twice), 2014, 2015

Polity Press
65 Bridge Street
Cambridge CB2 1UR, UK

Polity Press
350 Main Street
Malden, MA 02148, USA

ISBN 978-0-7456-2409-9
ISBN 978-0-7456-2410-5 (pbk)

A catalogue record for this book is available from the British Library and has been applied for from the Library of Congress.

Typeset in 11 on 13 pt Sabon
by Ace Filmsetting Ltd, Frome, Somerset
Printed in Great Britain by MPG Books Ltd, Bodmin

This book is printed on acid-free paper.
For further information on Polity, please visit our website www.politybooks.com

Contents

Foreword to the 2012 Edition

Liquid Modernity Revisited

When more than ten years ago I tried to unpack the meaning of the metaphor of 'liquidity' in its application to the form of life currently practised, one of the mysteries obtrusively haunting me and staunchly resisting resolution was the status of the liquid-modern human condition: was it an intimation, an early version, an augury or a portent of things to come? Or was it, rather, a temporary and transient – as well as an unfinished, incomplete and inconsistent – interim settlement; an interval between two distinct, yet viable and durable, complete and consistent answers to the challenges of human togetherness?

I have not thus far come anywhere near to a resolution of that quandary, but I am increasingly inclined to surmise that we presently find ourselves in a time of 'interregnum' – when the old ways of doing things no longer work, the old learned or inherited modes of life are no longer suitable for the current *conditio humana*, but when the new ways of tackling the challenges and new modes of life better suited to the new conditions have not as yet been invented, put in place and set in operation . . . We don't yet know which of the extant forms and settings will need to be 'liquidized' and replaced, though none seems to be immune to criticism and all or almost all of them have at one time or another been earmarked for replacement.

Most importantly, unlike our ancestors, we don't have a clear image of a 'destination' towards which we seem to be moving – which needs to be a model of *global* society, a global economy, global politics, a global jurisdiction . . . Instead, we react to the latest trouble, experimenting, groping in the dark. We try to diminish carbon dioxide pollution by dismantling coal-fed power plants and replacing them with nuclear power plants, only to conjure up the spectres of Chernobyl and Fukushima to hover above us . . . We feel rather than know (and many of us refuse to acknowledge) that power (that is, the ability to do things) has been separated from politics (that is, the ability to decide which things need to be done and given priority), and so in addition to our confusion about 'what to do' we are now in the dark about 'who is going to do it'. The sole agencies of collective purposive action bequeathed to us by our parents and grandparents, confined as they are to the boundaries of nation-states, are clearly inadequate, considering the global reach of our problems, and of their sources and consequences . . .

We remain of course as modern as we were before; but these 'we' who are modern have considerably grown in numbers in recent years. We may well say that by now all or almost all of us, in every or almost every part of the planet, have become modern. And that means that today, unlike a decade or two ago, every land on the planet, with only a few exceptions, is subject to the obsessive, compulsive, unstoppable change that is nowadays called 'modernization', and to everything that goes with it, including the continuous production of human redundancy, and the social tensions it is bound to cause.

Forms of modern life may differ in quite a few respects – but what unites them all is precisely their fragility, temporariness, vulnerability and inclination to constant change. To 'be modern' means to modernize – compulsively, obsessively; not so much just 'to be', let alone to keep its identity intact, but forever 'becoming', avoiding completion, staying underdefined. Each new structure which replaces the previous one as soon as it is declared old-fashioned and past its use-by date is only another momentary settlement – acknowledged as temporary and 'until further notice'. Being always, at any stage and at all times, 'post-something' is also an undetachable feature of modernity. As time flows on, 'modernity' changes its forms in the manner of the legendary Proteus . . . What was some time ago dubbed (erroneously) 'postmodernity', and what I've chosen to call, more to the point, 'liquid modernity', is the growing conviction that change is *the only* permanence, and uncertainty *the only* certainty. A hundred years ago 'to be modern' meant to chase 'the final state of perfection' – now it means an infinity of improvement, with no 'final state' in sight and none desired.

I did not think earlier and do not think now of the solidity versus liquidity conundrum as a dichotomy; I view those two conditions as a couple locked, inseparably, by a dialectical bond (the kind of bond François Lyotard probably had in mind when he observed that one can't be modern without being postmodern first . . .). After all, it was the quest for the solidity of things and states that most often triggered, kept in motion and guided their liquefaction; liquidity was not an adversary, but an effect of that quest for solidity, having no other parenthood, even when (or if) the parent might deny the legitimacy of the offspring. In turn, it was the formlessness of the oozing, leaking and flowing liquid that prompted the efforts at cooling, damping and moulding. If there is anything that permits a distinction between the 'solid' and 'liquid' phases of modernity (that is, arranging them in an order of succession), it is the change in both the manifest and the latent purposes behind the effort.

The original cause of the solids melting was not resentment against solidity as such, but dissatisfaction with the degree of solidity of the extant and inherited solids: purely and simply, the bequeathed solids were found not to be solid enough (insufficiently resistant or immunized to change) by the standards of the order-obsessed and compulsively order-building modern powers. Subsequently, however (in our part of the world, to this day), solids came to be viewed and accepted as transient, 'until further notice' condensations of liquid magma; temporary settlements, rather than ultimate solutions. Flexibility has replaced solidity as the ideal condition to be pursued of things and affairs. All solids (including those that are momentarily desirable) are tolerated only in as far as they promise to remain easily and obediently fusible on demand. An adequate technology of melting down again must be in hand even before the effort starts of putting together a durable structure, firming it up and solidifying it. A reliable assurance of the right and ability to dismantle the constructed structure must be given before the job of construction starts in earnest. Fully 'biodegradable' structures, starting to disintegrate the moment they have been assembled, are nowadays the ideal, and most, if not all structures, must struggle to measure up to this standard.

To cut a long story short, if in its 'solid' phase the heart of modernity was in controlling and fixing the future, in the 'liquid' phase the prime concern moved to ensuring the future was not mortgaged, and to averting the threat of any pre-emptive exploitation of the still undisclosed, unknown and unknowable opportunities the future was hoped to and was bound to bring. Nietzsche's spokesman Zarathustra, in anticipation of this human condition, bewailed 'the loitering of the present moment' that threatens to make the Will – burdened with the thick and heavy deposits of its past accomplishments and misdeeds – 'gnash its teeth', groan and sag, crushed by their weight . . . The fear of things fixed too firmly to permit them being dismantled, things overstaying their welcome, things tying our hands and shackling our legs, the fear of following Faustus to hell because of that blunder he committed of wishing to arrest a beautiful moment and make it stay forever, was traced by Jean-Paul Sartre back to our visceral, extemporal and inborn resentment of touching slimy or viscous substances; and yet, symptomatically, that fear was only pinpointed as a prime mover of human history at the threshold of the liquid modern era. That fear, in fact, signalled modernity's imminent arrival. And we may view its appearance as a fully and truly paradigmatic watershed in history . . .

Of course, as I've stated so many times, the whole of modernity stands out from preceding epochs by its compulsive and obsessive modernizing – and modernizing means liquefaction, melting and smelting. But – but! Initially, the major preoccupation of the modern mind was not so much the technology of smelting (most of the apparently solid structures around seemingly melted from their own incapacity to hold out) as the design of the moulds into which the molten metal was to be poured and the technology of keeping it there. The modern mind was after perfection – and the state of perfection it hoped to reach meant in the last account an end to strain and hard work, as all further change could only be a change for the worse. Early on, change was viewed as a preliminary and interim measure, which it was hoped would lead to an age of stability and tranquillity – and so also to comfort and leisure. It was seen as a necessity confined to the time of transition from the old, rusty, partly rotten, crumbling and fissiparous, and otherwise unreliable and altogether inferior structures, frames and arrangements, to their made-to-order and ultimate, because perfect, replacements – windproof, waterproof, and indeed history-proof . . . Change was, so to speak, a movement towards the splendid vision on the horizon: the vision of an order, or (to recall Talcott Parsons's crowning synthesis of modern pursuits) a 'self-equilibrating system', able to emerge victorious from every imaginable disturbance, stubbornly and irrevocably returning back to its settled state: an order resulting from a thorough and irrevocable 'skewing of probabilities' (maximizing the probability of some events, minimizing the likelihood of others). In the same way as accidents, contingencies, melting pots, ambiguity, ambivalence, fluidity and other banes and nightmares of order-builders, change was seen (and tackled) as a *temporary irritant* – and most certainly not undertaken for its own sake (it is the other way round nowadays: as Richard Sennett observed, perfectly viable organizations are now gutted just to prove their ongoing viability).

The most respected and influential minds among nineteenth-century economists expected economic growth to go on 'until such time as all human needs are met', and no longer – and then to be replaced by a 'stable economy', reproducing itself year by year with the same volume and content. The problem of 'living with difference' was also viewed as a temporary discomfort: the confusingly variegated world, continually thrown out of joint by clashes of difference and battles between apparently irreconcilable opposites, was to end up in the peaceful, uniform, monotonous tranquillity of a classlessness thoroughly cleansed of conflicts and antagonisms – with the help of a (revolutionary) 'war to end all wars', or of (evolutionary) adaptation and assimilation. The two hot-headed youngsters from Rhineland, Karl Marx and Friedrich Engels, watched with admiration as the capitalist furnace did the melting job that needed to be performed to usher us into just this kind of stable, trouble-free society. Baudelaire praised his favourite 'modern painter', Constantin Guys, for spying eternity inside a fleeting moment. In short, modernization then was a road with an *a priori* fixed, preordained finishing line; a movement destined to work itself out of a job.

It still took some time to discover or to decree that modernity without compulsive and obsessive modernization is no less an oxymoron than a wind that does not blow, or a river that does not flow . . . The modern form of life moved from the job of melting inferior solids that were not solid enough to the job of melting solids as such, unviable because of their excessive solidity. Perhaps it had performed this kind of job from the start (wise after the fact, we are now convinced that it did) – but its spokesmen would have hotly protested had that been suggested to them in the times of James Mill, Baudelaire or, for that matter, the authors of the Communist Manifesto. At the threshold of the twentieth century, Eduard Bernstein was shouted down by the Establishment Chorus of social democracy, and angrily excommunicated by the Socialist Establishment's Areopagus, when he dared to suggest that 'the goal is nothing, the movement is everything'. There was an essential axiological difference between Baudelaire and Marinetti, separated by a few decades – despite their apparently shared topic. And this precisely was the difference that made the difference . . .

Modernity was triggered by the horrifying signs and prospects of durable things falling apart, and of a whirlwind of transient ephemera filling the vacancy. But hardly two centuries later, the relation of superiority/inferiority between the values of durability and transience has been reversed. In a drastic turnaround, it is now the facility with which things can be turned upside down, disposed of and abandoned that is valued most – alongside bonds easy to untie, obligations easy to revoke, and rules of the game that last no longer than the game currently being played, and sometimes not as long as that. And we are all thrown into an unstoppable hunt for novelty.

The advent of 'liquid modernity', as Martin Jay justly insists, is anything but globally synchronized. In different parts of the planet, the passage to the 'liquid stage', like any other passage in history, occurs on different dates and proceeds at a different pace. What is also crucially important is that each time it takes place in a different setting – since the sheer presence on the global scene of players who have already completed the passage excludes the possibility of their itineraries being copied and reiterated (I'd suggest that the 'latecomers' tend on the whole to telescope and condense the trajectories of the pattern-setters, with sometimes disastrous and gory results). China is currently preoccupied with the challenges and tasks of the 'primitive accumulation of capital', known to generate an enormous volume of social dislocations, turbulence and discontent – as well as to result in extreme social polarization. Primitive accumulation is not a setting hospitable to any kind of freedom – whether of the producer or consumer variety. The course things are taking is bound to shock its victims and collateral casualties, and produce potentially explosive social tensions which have to be suppressed by the up-and-coming entrepreneurs and merchants, with the help of a powerful and merciless, coercive state dictatorship. Pinochet in Chile, Syngman Rhee in South Korea, Lee Kuan Yew in Singapore, Chiang Kai-shek in Taiwan, as well the present-day rulers of China, were or are dictators (Aristotle would call them 'tyrants') in everything but the self-adopted names of their offices; but they presided or preside over outstanding expansion and a fast-rising power of markets. All these countries would not be acclaimed as epitomes of 'economic miracles' today had it not been for the protracted dictatorship of the state. And, we may add, it's no coincidence that they have turned into such epitomes, and that they are now head-over-heels engrossed in the chase after an exquisitely 'liquid modern', consumerist form of life. Let me also add that the earlier 'economic miracles' in postwar Japan and Germany could to a considerable extent be explained by the presence of foreign occupation forces, which took over the coercive/oppressive functions of state powers from the native political institutions, while effectively evading all and any control by the democratic institutions of the occupied countries.

In a nutshell, if the freedom visualized by the Enlightenment and demanded and promised by Marx was made to the measure of the 'ideal producer', market-promoted freedom is designed with the 'ideal consumer' in mind; neither of the two is 'more genuine', more realistic or more viable than the other – they are just different, focusing attention on different factors of freedom: to recall Isaiah Berlin, on 'negative' freedom ('freedom from'), and 'positive' freedom ('freedom to'). Both visions present freedom as an 'enabling' condition, a condition enhancing the subject's capacity – but enabling them to do what, and stretching which capacity? Once you attempt in earnest to open those questions to empirical scrutiny, you'll inevitably discover sooner or later that both visions – producer-oriented and consumer-oriented – herald powerful odds standing in the way of their implementation in practice, and that the odds in question are in no way external to the programmes that the visions imply. On the contrary, those 'disabling' factors are, bewilderingly, the very conditions considered indispensable for putting the programme of 'enabling' into operation; and so having one without the other seems to be an idle dream and a doomed effort.

This is, though, a socio-political problem, not a metaphysical issue. An ideal and flawless freedom, 'complete freedom', enabling without disabling, is an oxymoron in metaphysics, just as it appears to be an unreachable goal in social life; if for no other reason than for the fact that – being inherently and inescapably a *social* relation – the thrust for freedom cannot but be a divisive force and any concrete application is certain to be essentially contested. Like so many ideals and values, freedom is perpetually in statu nascendi, never achieved but (or rather, for that very reason) constantly aimed at and fought for, and as a result an immense driving force in the never-ending experimentation called history.

The 'liquidity' of our plight is caused primarily by what is summarily dubbed 'deregulation': the separation of power (that means, the ability to do things) from politics (that means, the ability to decide which things are to be done) and the resulting absence or weakness of agency, or in other words the inadequacy of tools to the tasks; and also caused by the 'polycentrism' of action on a planet integrated by a dense web of interdependencies. To put it bluntly, under conditions of 'liquidity' everything could happen yet nothing can be done with confidence and certainty. Uncertainty results, combining feelings of ignorance (meaning the impossibility of knowing what is going to happen), impotence (meaning the impossibility of stopping it from happening) and an elusive and diffuse, poorly specified and difficult to locate fear; fear without an anchor and desperately seeking one. Living under liquid modern conditions can be compared to walking in a minefield: everyone knows an explosion might happen at any moment and in any place, but no one knows when the moment will come and where the place will be. On a globalized planet, that condition is universal – no one is exempt and no one is insured against its consequences. Locally caused explosions reverberate throughout the planet. Much needs to be done to find an exit from this situation, but remarrying power and politics, after the divorce, is undoubtedly a condition *sine qua non* of what one is inclined nowadays to think of as a 'resolidification'.

Another issue that has moved further to the fore since the first edition of *Liquid Modernity* is the unstoppably rising volume of 'uprooted' people – migrants, refugees, exiles, asylum seekers: people on the move and without permanent abode. 'Europe needs immigrants' was the blunt statement of Massimo D'Alema, currently president of the Foundation for European Progressive Studies, in *Le Monde* of 10 May 2011 – in direct dispute with 'the two most active European pyromaniacs', Berlusconi and Sarkozy. The calculation to support that postulate could hardly be simpler: there are today 333 million Europeans, but the present (and still falling) average birth rate means the number would shrink to 242 million over the next 40 years. To fill that gap, at least 30 million newcomers will be needed – otherwise our European economy will collapse, together with our cherished standard of living. 'Immigrants are an asset, not a danger,' D'Alema concludes. And so, too, is the process of cultural *métissage* ('hybridization'), which the influx of newcomers is bound to trigger; a mixing of cultural inspirations is a source of enrichment and an engine of creativity – for European civilization as much as for any other. All the same, only a thin line separates enrichment from a loss of cultural identity; for cohabitation between autochthons and allochthons to be prevented from eroding cultural heritages, it therefore needs to be based on respecting the principles underlying the European 'social contract' . . . The point is, by *both* sides!

How can such respect be secured, though, if recognition of the social and civil rights of 'new Europeans' is so stingily and haltingly offered, and proceeds at such a sluggish pace? Immigrants, for instance, currently contribute 11 per cent to Italian GNP, but they have no right to vote in Italian elections. In addition, no one can be truly certain about how many newcomers there are with no papers or with counterfeit documents who actively contribute to the national product and thus to the nation's well-being. 'How can the European Union', asks D'Alema all but rhetorically, 'permit such a situation, in which political, economic and social rights are denied to a substantial part of the population, without undermining our democratic principles?' And since, again in principle, citizens' duties come in a package deal with citizens' rights, can the newcomers seriously be expected to embrace, respect, support and defend those 'principles underlying the European social contract'? Our politicians muster electoral support by blaming immigrants for their genuine or putative reluctance to 'integrate' with the standards of the autochthon, while doing all they can, and promising to do still more, to put those standards beyond the allo-chthons' reach. On the way, they discredit or erode the very stand-ards they claim to be protecting against foreign invasion . . .

The big question, a quandary likely to determine the future of Europe more than any other, is which of the two contending 'facts of the matter' will eventually (yet without too much delay) come out on top: the life-saving role played by immigrants in a fast ageing Europe, a role few if any politicians so far dare to embroi-der on their banners, or the power-abetted and power-assisted rise in xenophobic sentiments eagerly recycled into electoral capital?

After their dazzling victory in the provincial elections in Baden-Württemberg in March 2011, replacing the Social Democrats as the alternative to Christian Democrats and for the first time in the history of the Bundesrepublik putting one of their own, Winfried Kretschmann, at the head of a provincial government, the German Greens, and notably Daniel Cohn-Bendit, are beginning to ponder the possibility of the German Chancellery turning green as soon as 2013. But who will make that history in their name? Cohn-Bendit has little doubt: Cem Özdemir, their current sharp-minded and clear-headed, dynamic, widely admired and revered co-leader, re-elected a few months ago by 88 per cent of the votes. Until his eighteenth birthday, Özdemir held a Turkish passport; then he, a young man already deeply engaged in German and European politics, selected German citizenship because of the harassment to which Turkish nationals were bound to be exposed whenever they tried to enter the United Kingdom or hop over the border to neighbouring France. One wonders: Who in present-day Europe are the advance messengers of Europe's future? Europe's most active pair of pyromaniacs, or Daniel Cohn-Bendit?

This is not, however, the last in the list of worries which are bound to hound our liquid modern form of life, as we are increas-ingly aware. As Martin Heidegger reminded us, all of us, human beings, live towards death – and we can't chase that knowledge away from our minds however hard we try. But a rising number of our thoughtful contemporaries keep reminding the rest of us that the human species to which we all belong is aiming towards extinction – drawing all or most of the other living species, in the manner of Melville's Captain Ahab, into perdition; though thus far they have failed to make us absorb that knowledge however hard they try.

The most recent announcement of the International Energy Agency – that world production of petrol peaked in 2006 and is bound to glide downwards at a time when unprecedented numbers of energy-famished consumers in countries like China, India or Brazil are entering the petrol market – failed to arouse public concern, let alone sound the alert, whether among political elites, men of business or opinion-making circles, and passed virtually unnoticed.

'Social inequalities would have made the inventors of the modern project blush with shame': so Michel Rocard, Dominique Bourg and Floran Augagneur conclude in their co-authored article 'The human species, endangered', in *Le Monde* of 3 April 2011. In the era of the Enlightenment, in the lifetimes of Francis Bacon, Descartes or even Hegel, there was no place on earth where the standard of living was more than twice as high as in its poorest region. Today, the richest country, Qatar, boasts an income per head 428 times higher than the poorest, Zimbabwe. And, let us never forget, these are all comparisons between averages – bringing to mind the proverbial recipe for the hare-and-horse pâté: take one hare and one horse . . .

The stubborn persistence of poverty on a planet in the throes of economic-growth fundamentalism is enough to make thinking people pause and reflect on the collateral casualties of progress-in-operation. The deepening precipice separating the poor and prospectless from the well-off, sanguine and boisterous – a precipice of a depth already exceeding the ability of any but the most muscular and least scrupulous hikers to climb – is another obvious reason for grave concern. As the authors of the quoted article warn, the prime victim of deepening inequality will be democracy, as the increasingly scarce, rare and inaccessible paraphernalia of survival and an acceptable life become the objects of a cut-throat war between the provided-for and the unaided needy.

And there is yet another, no less grave reason for alarm. The rising levels of opulence translate as rising levels of consumption; enrichment, after all, is a value worth coveting in so far as it helps to improve the quality of life, but in the vernacular of the planet-wide congregation of the Church of Economic Growth the meaning of 'making life better', or just rendering it somewhat less unsatisfactory, means to 'consume more'. For the faithful of that fundamentalist church, all roads to redemption, salvation, divine and secular grace, and immediate and eternal happiness alike, lead through shops. And the more tightly packed the shops' shelves waiting for the seekers of happiness to clear them out, the emptier is the earth, the sole container and supplier of the resources – raw materials and energy – needed to refill them: a truth reiterated and reconfirmed day in, day out by science, yet according to recent research bluntly denied in 53 per cent of the space devoted by the American press to the issue of 'sustainability', while the remainder neglects it or passes it by in silence.

What is passed by in a deafening, numbing and incapacitating silence is Tim Jackson's warning in his book *Prosperity without Growth*, published already two years ago, that by the end of this century 'our children and grandchildren will face a hostile climate, depleted resources, the destruction of habitats, the decimation of species, food scarcities, mass migration and almost inevitably war'. Our debt-driven consumption, zealously abetted, assisted and boosted by the powers that be, 'is unsustainable ecologically, problematic socially, and unstable economically'. Jackson has several other chilling observations, among them that in a social setting like ours, where the richest fifth of the world gets 74 per cent of annual planetary income while the poorest fifth has to settle for 2 per cent, the common ploy of justifying the devastation perpetuated by policies of economic growth by citing the noble need to put paid to poverty is clearly sheer hypocrisy and an offence to reason – this, too, has been almost universally ignored by the most popular (and effective) channels of information; or relegated, at best, to pages or times known to host and accommodate voices reconciled and habituated to their plight of crying in wilderness.

Jeremy Leggett (in the *Guardian* of 23 January 2010) follows Jackson's hints and suggests that a lasting (as opposed to doomed or downright suicidal) prosperity needs to be sought 'outside the conventional trappings of affluence' (and, let me add, outside the vicious circle of stuff-and-energy use/misuse/abuse): inside relationships, families, neighbourhoods, communities, meanings of life, and an admittedly misty and recondite area of 'vocations in a functional society that places value on the future'. Jackson himself opens his case with a sober admission that the questioning of economic growth is deemed to be an act of 'lunatics, idealists and revolutionaries', risking, fearing and expecting, not without reason, to fall into one or all three of those categories assigned by the apostles and addicts of the grow-or-perish ideology.

Elinor Ostrom's book *Governing the Commons* (1990) is ten times older than Jackson's, but already we could read there that the arduously promoted belief that people are naturally inclined to act for short-term profit and follow the principle of 'each man for himself and the devil take the hindmost' does not stand up to the facts of the matter. From her study of locally active small-scale businesses, Ostrom derives quite a different conclusion: 'people in community' tend to reach decisions that are 'not just for profit'. In conversation with Fran Korten last March she referred to honest and sincere communication inside communities, shaming and honouring, respecting the commons and open pastures, and other waste-free stratagems consuming virtually no energy, as quite plausible, almost instinctual human responses to life's challenges – none of them particularly propitious to economic growth, but all of them friendly to the sustainability of the planet and its inhabitants.

It is high time to start wondering: Are those forms of life-in-common, known to most of us solely from ethnographic reports sent back from the few remaining niches of bygone 'outdated and backward' times, irrevocably things of the past? Or is, perhaps, the truth of an alternative view of history (and so also of an alternative understanding of 'progress') about to out: that far from being an irreversible dash forward, with no retreat conceivable, the episode of chasing happiness through shops was, is and will prove to be for all practical intents and purposes a one-off detour, intrinsically and inevitably temporary?

The jury, as they say, is still out. But it is high time for a verdict. The longer the jury stays out, the greater the likelihood that they will be forced out of their meeting room because they have run short of refreshments . . .

June 2011

Foreword

On Being Light and Liquid

Interruption, incoherence, surprise are the ordinary conditions of our life. They have even become real needs for many people, whose minds are no longer fed . . . by anything but sudden changes and constantly renewed stimuli . . . We can no longer bear anything that lasts. We no longer know how to make boredom bear fruit.

So the whole question comes down to this: can the human mind master what the human mind has made?

Paul Valery

'Fluidity' is the quality of liquids and gases. What distinguishes both of them from solids, as the *Encyclopaedia Britannica* authoritatively informs us, is that they 'cannot sustain a tangential, or shearing, force when at rest' and so undergo 'a continuous change in shape when subjected to such a stress'.

This continuous and irrecoverable change of position of one part of the material relative to another part when under shear stress constitutes flow, a characteristic property of fluids, In contrast, the shearing forces within a solid, held in a twisted or flexed position, are maintained, the solid undergoes no flow and can spring back to its original shape.

Liquids, one variety of fluids, owe these remarkable qualities to the fact that their 'molecules are preserved in an orderly array over only a few molecular diameters'; while 'the wide variety of behaviour exhibited by solids is a direct result of the type of bonding that holds the atoms of the solid together and of the structural arrangements of the atoms'. 'Bonding', in turn, is a term that signifies the stability of solids – the resistance they put up 'against separation of the atoms'.

So much for the *Encyclopaedia Britannica* – in what reads like a bid to deploy 'fluidity' as the leading metaphor for the present stage of the modern era.

What all these features of fluids amount to, in simple language, is that liquids, unlike solids, cannot easily hold their shape. Fluids, so to speak, neither fix space nor bind time. While solids have clear spatial dimensions but neutralize the impact, and thus downgrade the significance, of time (effectively resist its flow or render it irrelevant), fluids do not keep to any shape for long and are constantly ready (and prone) to change it; and so for them it is the flow of time that counts, more than the space they happen to occupy: that space, after all, they fill but 'for a moment'. In a sense, solids cancel time; for liquids, on the contrary, it is mostly time that matters. When describing solids, one may ignore time altogether; in describing fluids, to leave time out of account would be a grievous mistake. Descriptions of fluids are all snapshots, and they need a date at the bottom of the picture.

Fluids travel easily. They 'flow', 'spill', 'run out', 'splash', 'pour over', 'leak', 'flood', 'spray', 'drip', 'seep', 'ooze'; unlike solids, they are not easily stopped – they pass around some obstacles, dissolve some others and bore or soak their way through others still. From the meeting with solids they emerge unscathed, while the solids they have met, if they stay solid, are changed – get moist or drenched. The extraordinary mobility of fluids is what associates them with the idea of 'lightness'. There are liquids which, cubic inch for cubic inch, are heavier than many solids, but we are inclined nonetheless to visualize them all as lighter, less 'weighty' than everything solid. We associate 'lightness' or 'weightlessness' with mobility and inconstancy: we know from practice that the lighter we travel the easier and faster we move.

These are reasons to consider 'fluidity' or 'liquidity' as fitting metaphors when we wish to grasp the nature of the present, in many ways *novel*, phase in the history of modernity.

I readily agree that such a proposition may give a pause to anyone at home in the 'modernity discourse' and familiar with the vocabulary commonly used to narrate modern history. Was not modernity a process of 'liquefaction' from the start? Was not 'melting the solids' its major pastime and prime accomplishment all along? In other words, has modernity not been 'fluid' since its inception?

These and similar objections are well justified, and will seem more so once we recall that the famous phrase 'melting the solids', when coined a century and a half ago by the authors of *The Communist Manifesto*, referred to the treatment which the self-confident and exuberant modern spirit awarded the society it found much too stagnant for its taste and much too resistant to shift and mould for its ambitions – since it was frozen in its habitual ways. If the 'spirit' was 'modern', it was so indeed in so far as it was determined that reality should be emancipated from the 'dead hand' of its own history – and this could only be done by melting the solids (that is, by definition, dissolving whatever persists over time and is negligent of its passage or immune to its flow). That intention called in turn for the 'profaning of the sacred': for disavowing and dethroning the past, and first and foremost 'tradition' – to wit, the sediment and residue of the past in the present; it thereby called for the smashing of the protective armour forged of the beliefs and loyalties which allowed the solids to resist the 'liquefaction'.

Let us remember, however, that all this was to be done not in order to do away with the solids once and for all and make the brave new world free of them for ever, but to clear the site for *new and improved solids*; to replace the inherited set of deficient and defective solids with another set, which was much improved and preferably perfect, and for that reason no longer alterable. When reading de Tocqueville's *Ancien Régime*, one might wonder in addition to what extent the 'found solids' were resented, condemned and earmarked for liquefaction for the reason that they were already rusty, mushy, coming apart at the seams and altogether unreliable. Modern times found the pre-modern solids in a fairly advanced state of disintegration; and one of the most powerful motives behind the urge to melt them was the wish to discover or invent solids of – for a change – *lasting* solidity, a solidity which one could trust and rely upon and which would make the world predictable and therefore manageable.

The first solids to be melted and the first sacreds to be profaned were traditional loyalties, customary rights and obligations which bound hands and feet, hindered moves and cramped the enterprise.

To set earnestly about the task of building a new (truly solid!) order, it was necessary to get rid of the ballast with which the old order burdened the builders. 'Melting the solids' meant first and foremost shedding the 'irrelevant' obligations standing in the way of rational calculation of effects; as Max Weber put it, liberating business enterprise from the shackles of the family–household duties and from the dense tissue of ethical obligations; or, as Thomas Carlyle would have it, leaving solely the 'cash nexus' of the many bonds underlying human mutuality and mutual responsibilities. By the same token, that kind of 'melting the solids' left the whole complex network of social relations unstuck – bare, unprotected, unarmed and exposed, impotent to resist the business-inspired rules of action and business-shaped criteria of rationality, let alone to compete with them effectively.

That fateful departure laid the field open to the invasion and domination of (as Weber put it) instrumental rationality, or (as Karl Marx articulated it) the determining role of economy: now the 'basis' of social life gave all life's other realms the status of 'superstructure' – to wit, an artefact of the 'basis' whose sole function was to service its smooth and continuing operation. The melting of solids led to the progressive untying of economy from its traditional political, ethical and cultural entanglements. It sedimented a new order, defined primarily in economic terms. That new order was to be more 'solid' than the orders it replaced, because – unlike them – it was immune to the challenge from non-economic action. Most political or moral levers capable of shifting or reforming the new order have been broken or rendered too short, weak or otherwise inadequate for the task. Not that the economic order, once entrenched, will have colonized, re-educated and converted to its ways the rest of social life; that order came to dominate the totality of human life because whatever else might have happened in that life has been rendered irrelevant and ineffective as far as the relentless and continuous reproduction of that order was concerned.

That stage in modernity's career has been well described by Claus Offe (in 'The Utopia of the Zero Option', first published in 1987 in *Praxis International*): 'complex' societies 'have become rigid to such an extent that the very attempt to reflect normatively upon or renew their "order", that is, the nature of the coordination of the processes which take place in them, is virtually precluded by dint of their practical futility and thus their essential inadequacy'. However free and volatile the 'subsystems' of that order may be singly or severally, the way in which they are intertwined is 'rigid, fatal, and sealed off from any freedom of choice'. The overall order of things is not open to options; it is far from clear what such options could be, and even less clear how an ostensibly viable option could be made real in the unlikely case of social life being able to conceive it and gestate. Between the overall order and every one of the agencies, vehicles and stratagems of purposeful action there is a cleavage – a perpetually widening gap with no bridge in sight.

Contrary to most dystopian scenarios, this effect has not been achieved through dictatorial rule, subordination, oppression or enslavement; nor through the 'colonization' of the private sphere by the 'system'. Quite the opposite: the present-day situation emerged out of the radical melting of the fetters and manacles rightly or wrongly suspected of limiting the individual freedom to choose and to act. *Rigidity of order is the artefact and sediment of the human agents' freedom.* That rigidity is the overall product of 'releasing the brakes': of deregulation, liberalization, 'flexibilization', increased fluidity, unbridling the financial, real estate and labour markets, easing the tax burden, etc. (as Offe pointed out in 'Binding, Shackles, Brakes', first published in 1987); or (to quote from Richard Sennett's *Flesh and Stone*) of the techniques of 'speed, escape, passivity' – in other words, techniques which allow the system and free agents to remain radically disengaged, to by-pass each other instead of meeting. If the time of systemic revolutions has passed, it is because there are no buildings where the control desks of the system are lodged and which could be stormed and captured by the revolutionaries; and also because it is excruciatingly difficult, nay impossible, to imagine what the victors, once inside the buildings (if they found them first), could do to turn the tables and put paid to the misery that prompted them to rebel. One should be hardly taken aback or puzzled by the evident shortage of would-be revolutionaries: of the kind of people who articulate the desire to change their individual plights as a project of changing the order of society.

The task of constructing a new and better order to replace the old and defective one is not presently on the agenda – at least not on the agenda of that realm where political action is supposed to reside. The 'melting of solids', the permanent feature of modernity, has therefore acquired a new meaning, and above all has been redirected to a new target – one of the paramount effects of that redirection being the dissolution of forces which could keep the question of order and system on the political agenda. The solids whose turn has come to be thrown into the melting pot and which are in the process of being melted at the present time, the time of fluid modernity, are the bonds which interlock individual choices in collective projects and actions – the patterns of communication and co-ordination between individually conducted life policies on the one hand and political actions of human collectivities on the other.

In an interview given to Jonathan Rutherford on 3 February 1999, Ulrich Beck (who a few years earlier coined the term 'second modernity' to connote the phase marked by the modernity 'turning upon itself', the era of the *soi-disant* 'modernization of modernity') speaks of 'zombie categories' and 'zombie institutions' which are 'dead and still alive'. He names the family, class and neighbourhood as the foremost examples of that new phenomenon. The family, for instance:

> Ask yourself what actually is a family nowadays? What does it mean? Of course there are children, my children, our children. But even parenthood, the core of family life, is beginning to disintegrate under conditions of divorce . . . [G]randmothers and grandfathers get included and excluded without any means of participating in the decisions of their sons and daughters. From the point of view of their grandchildren the meaning of grandparents has to be determined by individual decisions and choices.

What is happening at present is, so to speak, a redistribution and reallocation of modernity's 'melting powers'. They affected at first the extant institutions, the frames that circumscribed the realms of possible action-choices, like hereditary estates with their no-appeal-allowed allocation-by-ascription. Configurations, constellations, patterns of dependency and interaction were all thrown into the melting pot, to be subsequently recast and refashioned; this was the 'breaking the mould' phase in the history of the inherently transgressive, boundary-breaking, all-eroding modernity. As for the individuals, however – they could be excused for failing to notice; they came to be confronted by patterns and figurations which, albeit 'new and improved', were as stiff and indomitable as ever.

Indeed, no mould was broken without being replaced with another; people were let out from their old cages only to be admonished and censured in case they failed to relocate themselves, through their own, dedicated and continuous, truly life-long efforts, in the ready-made niches of the new order: in the *classes*, the frames which (as uncompromisingly as the already dissolved *estates*) encapsulated the totality of life conditions and life prospects and determined the range of realistic life projects and life strategies. The task confronting free individuals was to use their new freedom to find the appropriate niche and to settle there through conformity: by faithfully following the rules and modes of conduct identified as right and proper for the location.

It is such patterns, codes and rules to which one could conform, which one could select as stable orientation points and by which one could subsequently let oneself be guided, that are nowadays in increasingly short supply. It does not mean that our contemporaries are guided solely by their own imagination and resolve and are free to construct their mode of life from scratch and at will, or that they are no longer dependent on society for the building materials and design blueprints. But it does mean that we are presently moving from the era of pre-allocated 'reference groups' into the epoch of 'universal comparison', in which the destination of individual self-constructing labours is endemically and incurably underdetermined, is not given in advance, and tends to undergo numerous and profound changes before such labours reach their only genuine end: that is, the end of the individual's life.

These days patterns and configurations are no longer 'given', let alone 'self-evident'; there are just too many of them, clashing with one another and contradicting one another's commandments, so that each one has been stripped of a good deal of compelling, coercively constraining powers. And they have changed their nature and have been accordingly reclassified: as items in the inventory of individual tasks. Rather than preceding life-politics and framing its future course, they are to follow it (follow *from* it), to be shaped and reshaped by its twists and turns. The liquidizing powers have moved from the 'system' to 'society', from politics' to 'life-policies' – or have descended from the 'macro' to the 'micro' level of social cohabitation.

Ours is, as a result, an individualized, privatized version of modernity, with the burden of pattern-weaving and the responsibility for failure falling primarily on the individual's shoulders. It is the patterns of dependency and interaction whose turn to be liquefied has now come. They are now malleable to an extent unexperienced by, and unimaginable for, past generations; but like all fluids they do not keep their shape for long. Shaping them is easier than keeping them in shape. Solids are cast once and for all. Keeping fluids in shape requires a lot of attention, constant vigilance and perpetual effort – and even then the success of the effort is anything but a foregone conclusion.

It would be imprudent to deny, or even to play down, the profound change which the advent of 'fluid modernity' has brought to the human condition. The remoteness and unreachability of systemic structure, coupled with the unstructured, fluid state of the immediate setting of life-politics, change that condition in a radical way and call for a rethinking of old concepts that used to frame its narratives. Like zombies, such concepts are today simultaneously dead and alive. The practical question is whether their resurrection, albeit in a new shape or incarnation, is feasible; or – if it is not – how to arrange for their decent and effective burial.

This book is dedicated to this question. Five of the basic concepts around which the orthodox narratives of the human condition tend to be wrapped have been selected for scrutiny: emancipation, individuality, time/space, work, and community. Successive avatars of their meanings and practical applications have been (albeit in a very fragmentary and preliminary fashion) explored, with the hope of saving the children from the outpouring of polluted bathwaters.

Modernity means many things, and its arrival and progress can be traced using many and different markers. One feature of modern life and its modern setting stands out, however, as perhaps that 'difference which make[s] the difference'; as the crucial attribute from which all other characteristics follow. That attribute is the changing relationship between space and time.

Modernity starts when space and time are separated from living practice and from each other and so become ready to be theorized as distinct and mutually independent categories of strategy and action, when they cease to be, as they used to be in long premodern centuries, the intertwined and so barely distinguishable aspects of living experience, locked in a stable and apparently invulnerable one-to-one correspondence. In modernity, time has *history*, it has history because of the perpetually expanding 'carrying capacity' of time – the lengthening of the stretches of space which units of time allow to 'pass', 'cross', 'cover' – or *conquer*. Time acquires history once the speed of movement through space (unlike the eminently inflexible space, which cannot be stretched and would not shrink) becomes a matter of human ingenuity, imagination and resourcefulness.

The very idea of speed (even more conspicuously, that of acceleration), when referring to the relationship between time and space, *assumes* its variability, and it would hardly have any meaning at all were not that relation truly changeable, were it an attribute of inhuman and pre-human reality rather than a matter of human inventiveness and resolve, and were it not reaching far beyond the narrow range of variations to which the natural tools of mobility – human or equine legs – used to confine the movements of pre-modern bodies. Once the distance passed in a unit of time came to be dependent on technology, on artificial means of transportation, all extant, inherited limits to the speed of movement could be in principle transgressed. Only the sky (or, as it transpired later, the speed of light) was now the limit, and modernity was one continuous, unstoppable and fast accelerating effort to reach it.

Thanks to its newly acquired flexibility and expansiveness, modern time has become, first and foremost, the weapon in the conquest of space. In the modern struggle between time and space, space was the solid and stolid, unwieldy and inert side, capable of waging only a defensive, trench war – being an obstacle to the resilient advances of time. Time was the active and dynamic side in the battle, the side always on the offensive: the invading, conquering and colonizing force. Velocity of movement and access to faster means of mobility steadily rose in modern times to the position of the principal tool of power and domination.

Michel Foucault used Jeremy Bentham's design of Panopticon as the archmetaphor of modern power. In Panopticon, the inmates were tied to the place and barred from all movement, confined within thick, dense and closely guarded walls and fixed to their beds, cells or work-benches. They could not move because they were under watch; they had to stick to their appointed places at all times because they did not know, and had no way of knowing, where at the moment their watchers – free to move at will – were. The surveillants' facility and expediency of movement was the warrant of their domination; the inmates' 'fixedness to the place' was the most secure and the hardest to break or loose of the manifold bonds of their subordination. Mastery over time was the secret of the managers' power – and immobilizing their subordinates in space through denying them the right to move and through the routinization of the time-rhythm they had to obey was the principal strategy in their exercise of power. The pyramid of power was built out of velocity, access to the means of transportation and the resulting freedom of movement.

Panopticon was a model of mutual engagement and confrontation between the two sides of the power relationship. The managers' strategies of guarding their own volatility and routinizing the flow of time of their subordinates merged into one. But there was tension between the two tasks. The second task put constraints on the first – it tied the 'routinizers' to the place within which the objects of time routinization had been confined. The routinizers were not truly and fully free to move: the option of 'absentee landlords' was, practically, out of the question.

Panopticon is burdened with other handicaps as well. It is an expensive strategy: conquering space and holding to it as well as keeping its residents in the surveilled place spawned a wide range of costly and cumbersome administrative tasks. There are buildings to erect and maintain in good shape, professional surveillants to hire and pay, the survival and working capacity of the inmates to be attended to and provided for. Finally, administration means, willy-nilly, taking responsibility for the overall well-being of the place, even if only in the name of well-understood self-interest – and responsibility again means being bound to the place. It requires presence, and engagement, at least in the form of a perpetual confrontation and tug-of-war.

What prompts so many commentators to speak of the 'end of history', of post-modernity, 'second modernity' and 'surmodernity', or otherwise to articulate the intuition of a radical change in the arrangement of human cohabitation and in social conditions under which life-politics is nowadays conducted, is the fact that the long effort to accelerate the speed of movement has presently reached its 'natural limit'. Power can move with the speed of the electronic signal – and so the time required for the movement of its essential ingredients has been reduced to instantaneity. For all practical purposes, power has become truly *exterritorial*, no longer bound, not even slowed down, by the resistance of space (the advent of cellular telephones may well serve as a symbolic 'last blow' delivered to the dependency on space: even the access to a telephone socket is unnecessary for a command to be given and seen through to its effect. It does not matter any more where the giver of the command is – the difference between 'close by' and 'far away', or for that matter between the wilderness and the civilized, orderly space, has been all but cancelled.) This gives the power-holders a truly unprecedented opportunity: the awkward and irritating aspects of the panoptical technique of power may be disposed of. Whatever else the present stage in the history of modernity is, it is also, perhaps above all, *post-Panoptical*. What mattered in Panopticon was that the people in charge were assumed always to 'be there', nearby, in the controlling tower. What matters in post-Panoptical power-relations is that the people operating the levers of power on which the fate of the less volatile partners in the relationship depends can at any moment escape beyond reach – into sheer inaccessibility.

The end of Panopticon augurs *the end of the era of mutual engagement*: between the supervisors and the supervised, capital and labour, leaders and their followers, armies at war. The prime technique of power is now escape, slippage, elision and avoidance, the effective rejection of any territorial confinement with its cumbersome corollaries of order-building, order-maintenance and the responsibility for the consequences of it all as well as of the necessity to bear their costs.

This new technique of power has been vividly illustrated by the strategies deployed by the attackers in the Gulf and Jugoslav wars. The reluctance to deploy ground forces in the conduct of war was striking; whatever the official explanations might have implied, that reluctance was dictated not only by the widely publicized 'body-bag' syndrome. Engaging in a ground combat was resented not just for its possible adverse effect on domestic politics, but also (perhaps mainly) for its total uselessness and even counter-productivity as far as the goals of war are concerned. After all, the conquest of territory with all its administrative and managerial consequences was not just absent from the list of the objectives of war actions, but it was an eventuality meant to be by all means avoided, viewed with repugnance as another sort of 'collateral damage', this time inflicted on the attacking force itself.

Blows delivered by stealthy fighter planes and 'smart' self-guided and target-seeking missiles – delivered by surprise, coming from nowhere and immediately vanishing from sight – replaced the territorial advances of the infantry troops and the effort to dispossess the enemy of its territory – to take over the land owned, controlled and administered by the enemy. The attackers definitely wished no longer to be 'the last on the battlefield' after the enemy ran or was routed. Military force and its 'hit and run' war-plan prefigured, embodied and portended what was really at stake in the new type of war in the era of liquid modernity: not the conquest of a new territory, but crushing the walls which stopped the flow of new, fluid global powers; beating out of the enemy's head the desire to set up his own rules, and so opening up the so-far barricaded and walled-off, inaccessible space to the operations of the other, non-military, arms of power. War today, one may say (paraphrasing Clausewitz's famous formula), looks increasingly like a 'promotion of global free trade by other means'.

Jim MacLaughlin has reminded us recently (in *Sociology* 1/99) that the advent of the modern era meant, among other things, the consistent and systematic assault of the 'settled', converted to the sedentary way of life, against nomadic peoples and the nomadic style of life, starkly at odds with the territorial and boundary preoccupations of the emergent modern state. Ibn Khaldoun could in the fourteenth century sing the praise of nomadism, which brings peoples 'closer to being good than settled peoples because they . . . are more removed from all the evil habits that have infected the hearts of the settlers' – but the practice of feverish nation- and nation-state-building which shortly afterwards started in earnest all over Europe put the 'soil' firmly above the 'blood' when laying the foundations of the new legislated order and codifying the citizens' rights and duties. The nomads, who made light of the legislators' territorial concerns and blatantly disregarded their zealous efforts of boundary-drawing, were cast among the main villains in the holy war waged in the name of progress and civilization. Modern 'chronopolitics' placed them not just as inferior and primitive beings, 'underdeveloped' and in need of thorough reform and enlightenment, but also as backward and 'behind time', suffering from 'cultural lag', lingering at the lower rungs of the evolutionary ladder, and unforgivably slow or morbidly reluctant to climb it to follow the 'universal pattern of development'.

Throughout the solid stage of the modern era, nomadic habits remained out of favour. Citizenship went hand in hand with settlement, and the absence of 'fixed address' and 'statelessness' meant exclusion from the law-abiding and law-protected community and more often than not brought upon the culprits legal discrimination, if not active prosecution. While this still applies to the homeless and shifty 'underclass', which is subject to the old techniques of panoptical control (techniques largely abandoned as the prime vehicle of integrating and disciplining the bulk of the population), the era of unconditional superiority of sedentarism over nomadism and the domination of the settled over the mobile is on the whole grinding fast to a halt. We are witnessing the revenge of nomadism over the principle of territoriality and settlement. In the fluid stage of modernity, the settled majority is ruled by the nomadic and exterritorial elite. Keeping the roads free for nomadic traffic and phasing out the remaining check-points has now become the meta-purpose of politics, and also of wars, which, as Clausewitz originally declared, are but 'extension of politics by other means'.

The contemporary global elite is shaped after the pattern of the old-style 'absentee landlords'. It can rule without burdening itself with the chores of administration, management, welfare concerns, or, for that matter, with the mission of 'bringing light', 'reforming the ways', morally uplifting, 'civilizing' and cultural crusades. Active engagement in the life of subordinate populations is no longer needed (on the contrary, it is actively avoided as unnecessarily costly and ineffective) – and so the 'bigger' is not just not 'better' any more, but devoid of rational sense. It is now the smaller, the lighter, the more portable that signifies improvement and 'progress'. Travelling light, rather than holding tightly to things deemed attractive for their reliability and solidity – that is, for their heavy weight, substantiality and unyielding power of resistance – is now the asset of power.

Holding to the ground is not that important if the ground can be reached and abandoned at whim, in a short time or in no time. On the other hand, holding too fast, burdening one's bond with mutually binding commitments, may prove positively harmful and the new chances crop up elsewhere. Rockefeller might have wished to make his factories, railroads and oilrigs big and bulky and own them for a long, long time to come (for eternity, if one measures time by the duration of human or human family life). Bill Gates, however, feels no regret when parting with possessions in which he took pride yesterday; it is the mind-boggling speed of circulation, of recycling, ageing, dumping and replacement which brings profit today – not the durability and lasting reliability of the product. In a remarkable reversal of the millennia-long tradition, it is the high and mighty of the day who resent and shun the durable and cherish the transient, while it is those at the bottom of the heap who – against all odds – desperately struggle to force their flimsy and paltry, transient possessions to last longer and render durable service. The two meet nowadays mostly on opposite sides of the jumbo-sales or used-car auction counters.

The disintegration of the social network, the falling apart of effective agencies of collective action is often noted with a good deal of anxiety and bewailed as the unanticipated 'side effect' of the new lightness and fluidity of the increasingly mobile, slippery, shifty, evasive and fugitive power. But social disintegration is as much a condition as it is the outcome of the new technique of power, using disengagement and the art of escape as its major tools. For power to be free to flow, the world must be free of fences, barriers, fortified borders and checkpoints. Any dense and tight network of social bonds, and particularly a territorially rooted tight network, is an obstacle to be cleared out of the way. Global powers are bent on dismantling such networks for the sake of their continuous and growing fluidity, that principal source of their strength and the warrant of their invincibility. And it is the falling apart, the friability, the brittleness, the transience, the until-further-noticeness of human bonds and networks which allow these powers to do their job in the first place.

Were the intertwined trends to develop unabated, men and women would be reshaped after the pattern of the electronic mole, that proud invention of the pioneering years of cybernetics immediately acclaimed as the harbinger of times to come: a plug on castors, scuffling around in a desperate search for electrical sockets to plug into. But in the coming age augured by cellular telephones, sockets are likely to be declared obsolete and in bad taste as well as offered in ever shrinking quantity and ever shakier quality. At the moment, many electric power suppliers extol the advantages of plugging into their respective networks and vie for the favours of the socket-seekers. But in the long run (whatever 'the long run' means in the era of instantaneity) sockets are likely to be ousted and supplanted by disposable batteries individually bought in the shops and on offer in every airport kiosk and every service station along the motorway and country road.

This seems to be a dyotopia made to the measure of liquid modernity – one fit to replace the fears recorded in Orwellian and Huxleyan-style nightmares.

June 1999

1

Emancipation

Towards the end of the 'glorious three decades' which followed the end of the Second World War – the three decades of the unprecedented growth and entrenchment of wealth and economic security in the affluent West – Herbert Marcuse complained:

> As to today and our own situation, I think we are faced with a novel situation in history, because today we have to be liberated from a relatively well functioning, rich, powerful society . . . The problem we are facing is the need for liberation from a society which develops to a great extent the material and even cultural needs of man – a society which, to use a slogan, delivers the goods to an ever larger part of the population. And that implies, we are facing liberation from a society where liberation is apparently without a mass basis.[1]

That to emancipate, to 'liberate from society', we *ought* and *must* was not for Marcuse a problem. What *was* a problem – *the* problem specific to the society which 'delivers the goods' – was that for liberation there was no 'mass basis'. To put it simply: few people wished to be liberated, even fewer were willing to act on that wish, and virtually no one was quite sure in what way the 'liberation from society' might differ from the state they were already in.

To 'liberate', means literally to set free from some kind of fetters that obstruct or thwart the movements; to start *feeling* free to move or act. To 'feel free' means to experience no hindrance, obstacle, resistance or any other impediment to the moves intended or conceivable to be desired. As Arthur Schopenhauer observed, 'reality' is created by the act of willing; it is the stubborn indifference of the world to my intention, the world's reluctance to submit to my will, that rebounds in the perception of the world as 'real' – constraining, limiting and disobedient. Feeling free from constraint, free to act on one's wishes, means reaching a balance between the wishes, the imagination and the ability to act: one feels free in so far as the imagination is not greater than one's actual desires, while neither of the two reaches beyond the ability to act. The balance may therefore be established and kept unimpaired in two different ways: either by tapering, cutting down the desires and/or imagination, or by expanding one's ability to act. Once the balance is achieved, and as long as it stays intact, 'liberation' is a meaningless slogan, lacking motivational force.

Such usage allows us to set apart 'subjective' and 'objective' freedom – and so also the subjective and objective 'need of liberation'. It could be the case that the will to improvement has been frustrated or not allowed to arise in the first place (for example by the pressure of the 'reality principle' exerted, according to Sigmund Freud, on the human drive to pleasure and happiness); intentions, whether really experienced or just imaginable, have been cut down to the size of the ability to act, and particularly the ability to act reasonably – with a chance of success. On the other hand, it could be the case that through the direct manipulation of the intentions – some sort of 'brainwashing' – one could never put the 'objective' ability to act to the test, let alone find out what they really are, and therefore would set the ambitions below the level of the 'objective' freedom.

The distinction between 'subjective' and 'objective' freedom opened a genuine Pandora's box of vexing issues of the 'phenomenon vs. essence' kind – of varying, but on the whole considerable, philosophical significance and potentially huge political import. One such issue was the possibility that what feels like freedom is not in fact freedom at all; that people may be satisfied with their lot even though that lot were far from being 'objectively' satisfactory; that, living in slavery, they feel free and so experience no urge to liberate themselves, thus forsaking or forfeiting the chance of becoming genuinely free. The corollary of that possibility was the supposition that people may be incompetent judges of their own plight, and must be forced or cajoled, but in any case guided, to experience the need to be 'objectively' free and to muster the courage and determination to fight for it. A yet darker foreboding gnawed at philosophers' hearts: that people may simply dislike being free and resent the prospect of emancipation, given the hardships which the exercise of freedom may incur.

The mixed blessings of freedom

In an apocryphal version of the famous episode from the Odyssey ('Odysseus und die Schweine: das Unbehagen an der Kultur'), Lion Feuchtwanger proposed that the sailors bewitched by Circe and turned into hogs relished their new condition and desperately resisted Odysseus' attempt to break the spell and bring them back to human form. When told by Odysseus that he had found magic herbs able to dispel the curse and that they would soon be made human again, the sailors-turned-hogs ran to shelter with a speed their zealous saviour could not match. Odysseus managed in the end to trap one of the swine; once rubbed with the wondrous herb, the bristly hide let out Elpenoros – a sailor, as Feuchtwanger insists, by all accounts average and ordinary, just 'like all the others, neither distinguished in wrestling nor remarkable for his wits'. The 'liberated' Elpenoros was anything but grateful for his release and furiously attacked his 'liberator':

> So you are back, you rascal, you busybody? Again you want to nag us and pester, again you wish to expose our bodies to dangers and force our hearts to take ever new decisions? I was so happy, I could wallow in the mud and bask in the sunshine, I could gobble and guzzle, grunt and squeak, and be free from meditations and doubts: 'What am I to do, this or that?' Why did you come?! To fling me back into that hateful life I led before?

Is liberation a blessing, or a curse? A curse disguised as blessing, or a blessing feared as curse? Such questions were to haunt thinking people through most of the modern era which put 'liberation' on the top of the agenda of political reform, and 'freedom' at the top of its list of values – once it had become abundantly clear that freedom was slow to arrive while those meant to enjoy it were reluctant to welcome it. Two kinds of answer were given. The first cast doubt on the readiness of 'ordinary folks' for freedom. As the

American writer Herbert Sebastian Agar put it (in *A Time for Greatness*, 1942), 'The truth that makes men free is for the most part the truth which men prefer not to hear.' The second inclined to accept that men have a point when they cast doubt on the benefits which the freedoms on offer are likely to bring them.

Answers of the first kind prompt, intermittently, pity for the 'people' misled, cheated and deceived into surrendering their chance of liberty, or contempt and outrage against the 'mass' unwilling to assume the risks and the responsibilities which come together with genuine autonomy and self-assertion. Marcuse's complaint entails a mixture of both, as well as an attempt to lay the blame for the evident reconciliation of the unfree to their unfreedom at the door of the new affluence. Other popular addresses for similar complaints have been the 'embourgeoisement' of the underdog (the substitution of 'having' for 'being', and 'being' for 'acting', as the uppermost values) and 'mass culture' (a collective brain-damage caused by a 'culture industry' planting a thirst for entertainment and amusement in the place which – as Matthew Arnold would say – should be occupied by 'the passion for sweetness and light and the passion for making them prevail').

Answers of the second kind suggested that the sort of freedom eulogized by dedicated libertarians is not, contrary to their assertions, a warrant for happiness. It is likely to bring more misery than joy. According to this standpoint, libertarians are wrong when they aver, as does for instance David Conway,[2] restating Henry Sidgwick's principle that the general happiness is promoted most effectively through maintaining in adults 'the expectation that each will be thrown on his own resources for the supply of his own wants'; or Charles Murray,[3] who waxes lyrical when describing the happiness endemic to lonely pursuits: 'What filled an event with satisfaction is that *you* did it . . . with a substantial responsibility resting on *your* shoulders, with a substantial amount of the good thing being *your* contribution.' 'Being thrown on one's own resources' augurs mental torments and the agony of indecision, while 'responsibility resting on one's own shoulders' portends a paralysing fear of risk and failure without the right to appeal and seek redress. This cannot be what 'freedom' really means; and if 'really existing' freedom, the freedom on offer, does mean all that, it can be neither the warrant of happiness nor an objective worth fighting for.

Answers of the second kind stem ultimately from the Hobbesian gut-horror of the 'man on the loose'. They draw their credibility from the assumption that a human being released from coercive social constraints (or never subjected to them in the first place) is a beast rather than a free individual; and the horror they generate derives from another assumption, that absence of effective constraints will make life 'nasty, brutish and short' – and so anything but happy. It was the selfsame Hobbesian insight that was developed by Émile Durkheim into a comprehensive social philosophy, according to which it is the 'norm', measured by the average or the most common, and supported by harsh punitive sanctions, that truly liberates would-be humans from the slavery most horrid and most to be afraid of; the kind of slavery which does not lurk in any external pressure but inside, in the pre-social or asocial nature of man. Social coercion is in this philosophy the emancipatory force, and the sole hope of freedom that a human may reasonably entertain.

> The individual submits to society and this submission is the condition of his liberation. For man freedom consists in deliverance from blind, unthinking physical forces; he achieves this by opposing against them the great and intelligent force of society, under whose protection he shelters. By putting himself under the wing of society, he makes himself also, to a certain extent, dependent upon it. But this is a liberating dependence; there is no contradiction in this.[4]

Not only is there no contradiction between dependence and liberation; there is no other way to pursue the liberation but to 'submit to society' and to follow its norms. Freedom cannot be gained against society. The outcome of rebellion against the norms, even if the rebels have not been turned into beasts right away and so lost the power to judge their condition, is a perpetual agony of indecision linked to a state of uncertainty about the intentions and moves of others around – likely to make life a living hell. Patterns and routines imposed by condensed social pressures spare humans that agony: thanks to the monotony and regularity of recommended, enforceable and in-drilled modes of conduct, humans know how to proceed most of the time and seldom find themselves in a situation with no road markings attached, such situations in which decisions are to be taken on their own responsibility and without the reassuring knowledge of their consequences, making each move pregnant with risks difficult to calculate. The absence, or mere unclarity of norms – anomie – is the worst lot which may occur to people as they struggle to cope with their life-tasks. Norms *enable* as they disable; anomie augurs disablement pure and simple. Once the troops of normative regulation vacate the battlefields of life, only doubt and fear are left. When (as Erich Fromm memorably put it) 'each individual must go ahead and try his luck', when 'he had to swim or to sink' – 'the compulsive quest for certainty' takes off, the desperate search for 'solutions' able to 'eliminate the *awareness* of doubt' begins – anything is welcome that promises to 'assume the responsibility for "certainty"'.[5]

'Routine can demean, but it can also protect'; so states Richard Sennett, and then reminds his readers of the old controversy between Adam Smith and Dennis Diderot. While Smith warned against the degrading and stultifying effects of working routine, 'Diderot did not believe routine work is degrading . . . Diderot's greatest modern heir, the sociologist Anthony Giddens, has tried to keep Diderot's insight alive by pointing to the primary value of habit in both social practices and self-understanding.' Sennet's own proposition is straightforward: 'To imagine a life of momentary impulses, of short-term action, devoid of sustainable routines, a life without habits, is to imagine indeed a mindless existence.'[6]

Life has not reached yet the extremes which would render it mindless, but quite a lot of damage has been done, and all future tools of certainty, including the newly designed routines (unlikely to last long enough to turn into habits and probably resented and resisted if showing the sign of addiction) cannot but be crutches, artifices of human ingenuity which look like the real thing only as long as one refrains from examining them too closely. All certainty that comes after the 'original sin' of dismantling the matter-of-fact world full of routine and short of reflection must be a manufactured certainty, a blatantly and unashamedly 'made-up' certainty, burdened with all the inborn vulnerability of human-made decisions. Indeed, as Giles Deleuze and Felix Guattari insist,

> We no longer believe in the myth of the existence of fragments that, like pieces of an antique statue, are merely waiting for the last one to be turned up, so that they may all be glued back together to create a unity that is precisely the same as the original unity. We no longer believe in a primordial totality that once existed, or in a final totality that awaits us at some future date. [7]

What has been cut apart cannot be glued back together. Abandon all hope of totality, future as well as past, you who enter the world of fluid modernity. The time has arrived to announce, as Alain Touraine has recently done, 'the end of definition of the human being as a social being, defined by his or her place in society which determines his or her behaviour and actions'. Instead, the principle of the combination of the 'strategic definition of social action that is not oriented by social norms' and 'the defence, by all social actors, of their cultural and psychological specificity' 'can be found within the individual, and no longer in social institutions or universalistic principles'.[8]

The tacit assumption which underpins such a radical stand is that whatever freedom was conceivable and likely to be achieved has already arrived; nothing more is left to be done than clean up the few remaining cluttered corners and fill the few blank spots – a job bound to be completed soon. Men and women are fully and truly free, and so the agenda of emancipation has been all but exhausted. Marcuse's complaint and the communitarian pinings for the lost community may be manifestations of mutually opposite values, but they are equally anachronistic. Neither the rerooting of the uprooted nor the 'awakening of the people' to the unfulfilled task of liberation is on the cards. Marcuse's quandary is outdated since 'the individual' has already been granted all the freedom he might have dreamed of and all the freedom he might have reasonably hoped for; social institutions are only too willing to cede the worries of definitions and identities to the individual initiative, while universal principles to rebel against are hard to find. As to the communitarian dream of 're-embedding the disembedded', nothing may change the fact that there are but motel beds, sleeping bags and analysts' couches available for re-embedding, and that from now on the communities - more *postulated* than 'imagined' – may be only ephemeral artifacts of the ongoing individuality play, rather than the identities' determining and defining forces.

The fortuities and changing fortunes of critique

What is wrong with the society we live in, said Cornelius Castoriadis, is that it stopped questioning itself. This is a kind of society which no longer recognizes any alternative to itself and thereby feels absolved from the duty to examine, demonstrate, justify (let alone prove) the validity of its outspoken and tacit assumptions.

This does not mean, though, that our society has suppressed (or is likely to suppress, barring a major upheaval) critical thought as such. It has not made its members reticent (let alone afraid) of voicing it either. If anything, the opposite is the case: our society – a society of 'free individuals' – has made the critique of reality, the disaffection with 'what is' and the voicing of disaffection, both an unavoidable and an obligatory part of every member's life-business. As Anthony Giddens keeps reminding us, we are all engaged nowadays in 'life-politics'; we are 'reflexive beings' who look closely at every move we take, who are seldom satisfied with its results and always eager to correct them. Somehow, however, that reflexion does not reach far enough to embrace the complex mechanisms which connect our moves with their results and decide their outcomes, let alone the conditions which hold such mechanisms in full swing. We are perhaps more 'critically predisposed', much bolder and intransigent in our criticism than our ancestors managed to be in their daily lives, but our critique, so to speak, is 'toothless', unable to affect the agenda set for our 'life-political' choices. The unprecedented freedom which our society offers its members has arrived, as Leo Strauss warned a long while ago, together with unprecedented impotence.

One sometimes hears the opinion that contemporary society (appearing under the name of late modern or postmodern society, Ulrich Beck's society of 'second modernity' or, as I prefer to call it, the 'society of fluid modernity') is inhospitable to critique. That opinion seems to miss the nature of the present change by assuming that the meaning of 'hospitality' itself stays invariant over successive historical phases. The point is, however, that contemporary society has given to the 'hospitality to critique' an entirely new sense and has invented a way to accommodate critical thought and action while remaining immune to the consequences of that accommodation, and so emerging unaffected and unscathed – reinforced rather than weakened – from the tests and trials of the open-house policy.

The kind of 'hospitality to critique' characteristic of modern society in its present form may be likened to the pattern of a caravan site. The place is open to everyone with his or her own caravan and enough money to pay the rent. Guests come and go;

none of them takes much interest in how the site is run, providing
the customers have been allocated plots big enough to park the
caravans, the electric sockets and water taps are in good order and
the owners of the caravans parked nearby do not make too much
noise and keep down the sound from their portable TVs and hi-fi
speakers after dark. Drivers bring to the site their own homes
attached to their cars and equipped with all the appliances they
need for the stay, which at any rate they intend to be short. Each
driver has his or her own itinerary and time schedule. What the
drivers want from the site's managers is not much more (but no
less either) than to be left alone and not interfered with. In exchange, they promise not to challenge the managers' authority and
to pay the rent when due. Since they pay, they also demand. They
tend to be quite adamant when arguing for their rights to the
promised services but otherwise want to go their own ways and
would be angry if not allowed to do so. On occasion, they may
clamour for better service; if they are outspoken, vociferous and
resolute enough, they may even get it. If they feel short-changed or
find the managers' promises not kept, the caravanners may com-
plain and demand their due – but it won't occur to them to question
and renegotiate the managerial philosophy of the site, much less to
take over the responsibility for running the place. They may, at the
utmost, make a mental note never to use the site again and not to
recommend it to their friends. When they leave, following their own
itineraries, the site remains much as it was before their arrival,
unaffected by past campers and waiting for others to come; though
if some complaints go on being lodged by successive cohorts of
caravanners, the services provided may be modified to prevent repetitive discontents from being voiced again in the future.

In the era of liquid modernity society's hospitality to critique
follows the pattern of the caravan site. At the time when classic
critical theory, gestated by the experience of another, order-obsessed
modernity and thus informed by and targeted on the *telos* of emancipation, was put in shape by Adorno and Horkheimer, it was a
very different model, that of a shared household with its institutionalized norms and habitualized rules, assignment of duties and
supervised performance, in which, with good empirical reason, the
idea of critique was inscribed. While hospitable to critique after the
fashion of the caravan site's hospitality to the caravan owners, our
society is definitely and resolutely *not* hospitable to critique in the

mode which the founders of the critical school assumed and to which they addressed their theory. In different, but corresponding terms, we may say that a 'consumer-style critique' has come to replace its 'producer-style' predecessor.

Contrary to a widespread fashion, this fateful shift cannot be explained merely by reference to a changing public mood, a waning of the appetite for social reform, a fading interest in the common good and images of the good society, the falling popularity of political engagement, or the rising tide of hedonistic and 'me first' sentiments – though undoubtedly all such phenomena are indeed prominent among the marks of our time. The causes of the shift reach deeper; they are rooted in the profound transformation of the public space and, more generally, in the fashion in which modern society works and perpetuates itself.

The kind of modernity which was the target, but also the cognitive frame, of classical critical theory strikes the analyst in retrospect as quite different from the one which frames the lives of present-day generations. It appears 'heavy' (as against the contemporary 'light' modernity); better still, 'solid' (as distinct from 'fluid', 'liquid', or 'liquefied'); condensed (as against diffuse or 'capillary'); finally, systemic (as distinct from network-like).

That heavy/solid/condensed/systemic modernity of the 'critical theory' era was endemically pregnant with the tendency towards totalitarianism. The totalitarian society of all-embracing, compulsory and enforced homogeneity loomed constantly and threateningly on the horizon – as its ultimate destination, as a never-fully-defused time-bomb or never-fully-exorcized spectre. That modernity was a sworn enemy of contingency, variety, ambiguity, waywardness and idiosyncrasy, having declared on all such 'anomalies' a holy war of attrition; and it was individual freedom and autonomy that were commonly expected to be the prime casualties of the crusade. Among the principal icons of that modernity were the *Fordist factory*, which reduced human activities to simple, routine and by and large predesigned moves meant to be followed obediently and mechanically without engaging mental faculties, and holding all spontaneity and individual initiative off limits; *bureaucracy*, akin at least in its innate tendency to Max Weber's ideal model, in which identities and social bonds were deposited on entry in the cloakroom together with hats, umbrellas and overcoats, so that solely the command and the statute book could drive, uncontested, the actions of the insiders as long as they stayed inside; *Panopticon*, with its watch-towers and the inmates never allowed to count on their surveillants' momentary lapses of vigilance; *Big Brother*, who never dozes off, always keen, quick and expeditious in rewarding the faithful and punishing the infidels; and – finally – the *Konzlager* (later to be joined in the counter-Pantheon of modern demons by the Gulag), the site where the limits of human malleability were tested under laboratory conditions, while all those presumed not to be or found not to be malleable enough were doomed to perish of exhaustion or sent to gas chambers and crematoria.

Again in retrospect, we can say that critical theory was aimed at defusing and neutralizing, preferably turning off altogether, the totalitarian tendency of a society presumed to be burdened with totalistic proclivities endemically and permanently. Defending human autonomy, freedom of choice and self-assertion and the right to be and stay different was critical theory's principal objective. In the likeness of the early Hollywood melodramas, which presumed that the moment when the lovers found each other again and took their marriage vows signalled the end of the drama and the beginning of blissful 'living happily ever after', early critical theory saw the wrenching of individual liberty from the iron grip of routine or letting the individual out of the steely casing of a society afflicted with insatiable totalitarian, homogenizing and uniformizing appetites as the ultimate point of emancipation and the end to human misery – the moment of 'mission accomplished'. Critique was to serve that purpose; it needed to look no further, not beyond the moment of its attainment – nor had it time to do so.

George Orwell's *Nineteen Eighty-four* was, at the time it was written, the fullest – and canonical – inventory of the fears and apprehensions which haunted modernity in its heavy stage. Once projected upon the diagnoses of contemporary troubles and the causes of contemporary sufferings, such fears set the horizons of the emancipatory programmes of the era. Come the real 1984, and Orwell's vision was promptly recalled, expectably drawn back into public debate and given once more (perhaps for the last time) a thorough venting. Most writers, again expectably, sharpened their pens to set apart the truth from the untruth of Orwell's prophecy as tested by the stretch of time which Orwell allocated for his words to turn into flesh. No wonder, though, that in our times, when even the immortality of the crucial milestones and monuments of human cultural history is subject to continuous recycling and needs to be periodically brought back to human attention on the occasion of anniversaries or by the hype preceding and accompanying retrospective exhibitions (only to vanish from view and from thought once the exhibitions are over or another anniversary comes along to consume press space and TV time), the staging of the 'Orwell event' was not very different from the treatment accorded intermittently to the likes of Tutankhamun, Inca gold, Vermeer, Picasso or Monet.

Even so, the brevity of the 1984 celebration, the tepidity and fast cooling of interest it aroused and the speed with which Orwell's *chef d'oeuvre* sank back into oblivion once the media-led hype had ended, make one pause and think. That book, after all, served for many decades (and until just a couple of decades ago) as the most authoritative catalogue of public fears, forebodings and nightmares; so why no more than a passing interest in its brief resurrection? The only reasonable explanation is that people who discussed the book in 1984 felt unexcited and were left lukewarm by the subject they had been commissioned to discuss or ponder because they no longer recognized their own chagrins and agonies, or the nightmares of their next-door neighbours, in Orwell's dystopia. The book reappeared in public attention but fleetingly, accorded a status somewhere between that of Plinius the Elder's *Historia naturalis* and that of Nostradamus' prophecies.

One can do worse than define historical epochs by the kind of 'inner demons' that haunt and torment them. For many years Orwell's dystopia, alongside the sinister potential of the Enlightenment project unravelled by Adorno and Horkheimer, Bentham/Foucault's Panopticon or recurrent symptoms of the gathering totalitarian tide, was identified with the idea of 'modernity'. No wonder, therefore, that when the old fears were eased out from the public stage and new fears, quite unlike the horrors of impending *Gleichschaltung* and loss of freedom, came to the fore and forced their way into public debate, quite a few observers were quick to proclaim the 'end of modernity' (or even, more boldly, the end of history itself, arguing it had already reached its *telos* by making freedom, at least the type of freedom exemplified by the free market and consumer choice, immune to all further threats). And yet (credits go to Mark Twain) the news of modernity's passing away, even the rumours of its swan song, are grossly exaggerated: their profusion does not make the obituaries any less premature. It seems that the kind of society which has been diagnosed and put on trial by the founders of critical theory (or, for that matter, by Orwell's dystopia) was just one of the forms that versatile and protean modern society was to take. Its waning does not augur the end of modernity. Nor does it herald the end of human misery. Least of all does it presage the end of critique as an intellectual task and vocation; and by no means does it render such critique redundant.

The society which enters the twenty-first century is no less 'modern' than the society which entered the twentieth; the most one can say is that it is modern in a different way. What makes it as modern as it was a century or so ago is what sets modernity apart from all other historical forms of human cohabitation: the compulsive and obsessive, continuous, unstoppable, forever incomplete *modernization*; the overwhelming and ineradicable, unquenchable thirst for creative destruction (or of destructive creativity, as the case might be: of 'clearing the site' in the name of a 'new and improved' design; of 'dismantling', 'cutting out', 'phasing out', 'merging' or 'downsizing', all for the sake of a greater capacity for doing more of the same in the future – enhancing productivity or competitiveness).

As Lessing pointed out a long time ago, at the threshold of the modern era we have been emancipated from belief in the act of creation, revelation and eternal condemnation. With such beliefs out of the way, we humans found ourselves 'on our own' – which means that from then on we knew of no limits to improvement and self-improvement other than the shortcomings of our own inherited or acquired gifts, resourcefulness, nerve, will and determination. And whatever is man-made, men can un-make. Being modern came to mean, as it means today, being unable to stop and even less able to stand still. We move and are bound to keep moving not so much because of the 'delay of gratification', as Max Weber suggested, as because of the *impossibility* of ever being gratified: the horizon of satisfaction, the finishing line of effort and the moment of restful self-congratulation move faster than the fastest of the runners. Fulfilment is always in the future, and achievements lose their attraction and satisfying potential at the moment of their attainment, if not before. Being modern means being perpetually ahead of oneself, in a state of constant transgression (in Nietzsche's terms, one cannot be *Mensch* without being, or at least struggling to be, *Übermensch*); it also means having an identity which can exist only as an unfulfilled project. In these respects, there is not much to distinguish between the plight of our grandfathers and our own.

Two features, nonetheless, make our situation – our form of modernity – novel and different.

The first is the gradual collapse and swift decline of early modern illusion: of the belief that there is an end to the road along which we proceed, an attainable *telos* of historical change, a state of perfection to be reached tomorrow, next year or next millennium, some sort of good society, just society and conflict-free society in all or some of its many postulated aspects: of steady equilibrium between supply and demand and satisfaction of all needs; of perfect order, in which everything is allocated to its right place, nothing out of place persists and no place is in doubt; of human affairs becoming totally transparent thanks to knowing everything needing to be known; of complete mastery over the future – so complete that it puts paid to all contingency, contention, ambivalence and unanticipated consequences of human undertakings.

The second seminal change is the deregulation and privatization of the modernizing tasks and duties. What used to be considered a job to be performed by human reason seen as the collective endowment and property of the human species has been fragmented ('individualized'), assigned to individual guts and stamina, and left to individuals' management and individually administered resources. Though the idea of improvement (or of all further modernization of the *status quo*) through legislative action of the society as a whole has not been completely abandoned, the emphasis (together with, importantly, the burden of responsibility) has shifted decisively towards the self-assertion of the individual. This fateful departure has been reflected in the relocation of ethical/political discourse from the frame of the 'just society' to that of 'human rights', that is refocusing that discourse on the right of individuals to stay different and to pick and choose at will their own models of happiness and fitting life-style.

The hopes of improvement, instead of converging on big money in governmental coffers, have been focused on the small change in the taxpayers' pockets. If the original modernity was top-heavy, the present-day modernity is light at the top, having relieved itself of its 'emancipatory' duties except its duty to cede the business of emancipation to the middle and bottom layers, to which most of the burden of continuous modernization has been relegated. 'No more salvation by society', famously proclaimed the apostle of the new business spirit, Peter Drucker. 'There is no such thing as society', declared Margaret Thatcher yet more bluntly. Don't look back, or up; look inside yourself, where your own cunning, will and power – all the tools that life's improvement may require – are supposed to reside.

And there is no more 'Big Brother watching you'; it is now your task to watch the swelling ranks of Big Brothers and Big Sisters, and watch them closely and avidly, in the hope of finding something useful for yourself: an example to imitate or a word of advice about how to cope with your problems, which, like their problems, need to be coped with individually and can be coped with only individually. No more great leaders to tell you what to do and to release you from responsibility for the consequences of your doings; in the world of individuals, there are only other individuals from which you may draw examples of how to go about your own life-business, bearing full responsibility for the consequences of investing your trust in this example rather than another.

The individual in combat with the citizen

The title given by Norbert Elias to his last, posthumously published study, 'Society of Individuals', flawlessly grasps the gist of the problem which has haunted social theory since its inception. Breaking with a tradition established since Hobbes and reforged by John Stuart Mill, Herbert Spencer and the liberal orthodoxy into the *doxa* (the unexamined frame for all further cognition) of our century, Elias replaced the 'and' or the 'versus' with the 'of'; and by so doing he shifted the discourse from the *imaginaire* of the two forces locked in a mortal yet unending battle of freedom and domination, into that of 'reciprocal conception': society shaping the individuality of its members, and individuals forming society out of their life actions while pursuing strategies plausible and feasible within the socially woven web of their dependencies.

Casting members as individuals is the trade mark of modern society. That casting, however, was not a one-off act: it is an activity re-enacted daily. Modern society exists in its incessant activity of 'individualizing' as much as the activities of individuals consist in the daily reshaping and renegotiating of the network of mutual entanglements called 'society'. Neither of the two partners stays put for long. And so the meaning of 'individualization' keeps changing, taking up ever new shapes – as the accumulated results of its past history undermine inherited rules, set new behavioural precepts and turn out ever new stakes of the game. 'Individualization' now means something very different from what it meant a hundred years ago and what it conveyed at the early times of the modern era – the times of the extolled 'emancipation' of man from the tightly knit tissue of communal dependency, surveillance and enforcement.

Ulrich Beck's 'Jenseits von Klasse und Stand?' and a few years later his 'Risikogesellschaft: auf dem Weg in eine andere Moderne'[9] (together with Elisabeth Beck-Gernsheim's 'Ein Stück eigenes Leben: Frauen im Individualisierung Prozeß') opened a new chapter in our comprehension of the 'individualizing process'. These works presented this process as an ongoing and unfinished history with its distinct stages – though with a mobile horizon and an erratic logic of sharp twists and turns rather than with the *telos* or preordained destination. It can be said that just as Elias historicized Sigmund Freud's theory of the 'civilized individual' exploring civilization as an event in (modern) history, so Beck historicized Elias's account of the birth of the individual by re-presenting that birth as a perpetual aspect of continuous and continuing, compulsive and obsessive *modernization*. Beck also set the portrayal of individualization free from its time-bound, transient accoutrements, by now beclouding understanding more than they clarify the picture (first and foremost, free from the visions of linear development, a progression plotted along the axes of emancipation, growing autonomy and freedom of self-assertion), thereby opening to scrutiny the variety of historical tendencies of individualization and their products and allowing the better comprehension of the distinctive features of its current stage.

To put it in a nutshell, 'individualization' consists of transforming human 'identity' from a 'given' into a 'task' and charging the actors with the responsibility for performing that task and for the consequences (also the side-effects) of their performance. In other words, it consists in the establishment of a *de jure* autonomy (whether or not the *de facto* autonomy has been established as well).

As this happens, human beings are no more 'born into' their identities. As Jean-Paul Sartre famously put it: it is not enough to be born a bourgeois – one must live one's life as a bourgeois. (Note that the same did not need to be, nor could be said about princes, knights, serfs or townsmen of the pre-modern era; neither could it be said as resolutely about the hereditary rich and hereditary poor of modern times.) Needing to *become* what one *is* is the feature of modern living – and of this living alone (not of 'modern individual-ization', that expression being evidently pleonastic; to speak of individualization and of modernity is to speak of one and the same social condition). Modernity replaces the heteronomic deter-mination of social standing with compulsive and obligatory self-determination. This holds true for 'individualization' for the whole of the modern era – for all periods and all sectors of society. Yet within that shared predicament there are significant variations, which set apart successive generations as well as various categories of actors sharing the same historical stage.

Early modernity 'disembedded' in order to 're-embed'. While the disembedding was the socially sanctioned fate, the re-embedding was a task put before the individuals. Once the stiff frames of estates had been broken, the 'self-identification' task put before men and women of the early modern era boiled down to the challenge of living 'true to kind' ('up with the Joneses'), of actively conforming to the emerging class-bound social types and models of conduct, of imitating, following the pattern, 'acculturating', not falling out of step, not deviating from the norm. 'Estates' as the locations of inherited belonging came to be replaced by 'classes' as the targets of manufactured membership. While the first were a matter of ascription, the membership of the second contained a large measure of achievement; classes, unlike estates, had to be 'joined', and the membership had to be continuously renewed, reconfirmed and tested in day-by-day conduct.

It can be said in retrospect that the class division (or gender division for that matter) was a by-product of unequal access to resources required to render the self-assertion effective. Classes differed in the range of identities available and in the facility of

choosing and embracing them. People endowed with fewer resources, and thus with less choice, had to compensate for their
individual weaknesses by the 'power of numbers' – by closing
ranks and engaging in collective action. As Claus Offe pointed out,
collective, class-oriented action came to those lower down the
social ladder as naturally and matter-of-factly as the *individual*
pursuit of their life-goals came to their employers.

The deprivations 'added up', so to speak; and having added up,
they congealed in 'common interests' and were seen as amenable
solely to a collective remedy. 'Collectivism' was a first-choice strategy for those placed at the receiving end of individualization yet
unable to self-assert as individuals while limited to their own, individually owned, blatantly inadequate resources. The class-orientation
of the better-off was, on the other hand, partial and, in a sense,
derivative; it came to the fore mostly when the unequal distribution
of resources was challenged and contested. Whatever was the case,
however, the individuals of 'classic' modernity, left 'disembedded'
by the decomposition of the estate-order, deployed their new empowerment and the new entitlements of autonomous agency in the
frantic search for 're-embeddedment'.

And there was no shortage of 'beds' waiting and ready to accommodate them. Class, though formed and negotiable rather than
inherited or simply 'born into' as the estates used to be, tended to
hold its members as fast and as tight as the pre-modern hereditary
estate. Class and gender hung heavily over the individual range of
choices; to escape their constraint was not much easier than to
contest one's place in the pre-modern 'Divine chain of being'. To
all intents and purposes, class and gender were 'facts of nature' and
the task left to the self-assertion of most individuals was to 'fit in'
in the allocated niche through behaving as the other occupants did.

This is, precisely, what distinguished the 'individualization' of
yore from the form it has taken in *Risikogesellschaft*, in times of
'reflexive modernity' or 'second modernity' (as Ulrich Beck variously calls the contemporary era). No 'beds' are furnished for 're-
embedding', and such beds as might be postulated and pursued
prove fragile and often vanish before the work of 're-embedding' is
complete. There are rather 'musical chairs' of various sizes and
styles as well as of changing numbers and positions, which prompt
men and women to be constantly on the move and promise no
'fulfilment', no rest and no satisfaction of 'arriving', of reaching the

final destination, where one can disarm, relax and stop worrying. There is no prospect of re-embeddedment' at the end of the road taken by (now chronically) disembedded individuals.

Let there be no mistake: now, as before – in the fluid and light as much as in the solid and heavy stage of modernity – individualization is a fate, not a choice. In the land of the individual freedom of choice the option to escape individualization and to refuse participation in the individualizing game is emphatically *not* on the agenda. The individual's self-containment and self-sufficiency may be another illusion: that men and women have no one to blame for their frustrations and troubles does not need now to mean, any more than it did in the past, that they can protect themselves against frustration using their own domestic appliances or pull themselves out of trouble, Baron Munchausen style, by their bootstraps. And yet, if they fall ill, it is assumed that this has happened because they were not resolute and industrious enough in following their health regime; if they stay unemployed, it is because they failed to learn the skills of gaining an interview, or because they did not try hard enough to find a job or because they are, purely and simply, work-shy; if they are not sure about their career prospects and agonize about their future, it is because they are not good enough at winning friends and influencing people and failed to learn and master, as they should have done, the arts of self-expression and impressing others. This is, at any rate, what they are told these days to be the case, and what they have come to believe, so that they now behave as if this was, indeed, the truth of the matter. As Beck aptly and poignantly puts it, 'how one lives becomes a *biographical solution to systemic contradictions*'.[10] Risks and contradictions go on being socially produced; it is just the duty and the necessity to cope with them which are being individualized.

To cut a long story short: a gap is growing between individuality as fate and individuality as the practical and realistic capacity for self-assertion. (Better to be set apart from 'individuality by assignment', as 'individuation': the term selected by Beck to distinguish the self-sustained and self-propelled individual from a human being who has no choice but to act, even if counterfactually, as if the individuation has been attained.) Bridging this gap is, most crucially, *not* part of that capacity.

The self-assertive capacity of individualized men and women falls short, as a rule, of what a genuine self-constitution would require.

As Leo Strauss observed, the other side of unencumbered freedom is insignificance of choice, the two sides conditioning each other: why bother to prohibit what is, anyway, of little consequence? A cynical observer would say that freedom comes when it no longer matters. There is a nasty fly of impotence in the tasty ointment of freedom cooked in the cauldron of individualization; that impotence is felt to be all the more odious, discomfiting and upsetting in view of the empowerment that freedom was expected to deliver.

Perhaps, as in the past, standing shoulder to shoulder and marching in step would offer a remedy? Perhaps if individual powers, however feeble and impotent when single, are condensed into a collective stand and action, things will be done jointly which no man or woman could dream of doing alone? Perhaps . . . The snag is, though, that such convergence and condensation of individual grievances into shared interests and then into a joint action is a daunting task, since the most common troubles of individuals-by-fate are these days *non-additive*. They are not amenable to 'summing up' into a 'common cause'. They may be put beside each other, but they will not congeal. One may say that they are shaped from the beginning in such a way as to lack the interfaces allowing them to dovetail with other people's troubles.

Troubles may be *similar* (and the increasingly popular chat-shows go out of their way to demonstrate their similarity, while hammering home the message that their most important similarity lies in being handled by each sufferer on his or her own) but they do not form a 'totality which is greater that the sum of its part'; they neither acquire any new quality nor become easier to handle by being faced up to, confronted and tackled, together. The sole advantage the company of other sufferers may bring is to reassure each one that fighting the troubles alone is what all the others do daily – and so to refresh and boost once more the flagging resolve to go on doing just that. One may perhaps also learn from other people's experience how to survive the next round of 'downsizing', how to handle children who think they are adolescents and adolescents who refuse to become adults, how to get the fat and other unwelcome 'foreign bodies' 'out of one's system', how to get rid of addiction that is no longer pleasurable or partners who are no longer satisfying. But what one learns in the first place from the company of others is that the only service companies can render is advice about how to survive in one's own irredeemable loneliness, and that everyone's life is full of risks which need to be confronted and fought alone.

And so there is another snag as well: as de Tocqueville long suspected, setting people free may make them *indifferent*. The individual is the citizen's worst enemy, de Tocqueville suggested. The 'citizen' is a person inclined to seek her or his own welfare through the well-being of the city – while the individual tends to be lukewarm, sceptical or wary about 'common cause', 'common good', 'good society' or 'just society'. What is the sense of 'common interests' except letting each individual satisfy her or his own? Whatever individuals may do when they come together, and whatever other benefits their shared labours may bring, portends constraint on their freedom to pursue what they see fit for each separately, and will not help such pursuit anyway. The only two useful things one would expect, and wish, 'public power' to deliver are to observe 'human rights', that is to let everyone go her or his own way, and to enable everyone to do it in peace – by guarding the safety of her or his body and possessions, locking actual or would-be criminals in prisons and keeping the streets free from muggers, perverts, beggars and all other sorts of obnoxious and malevolent strangers.

With his usual, inimitable wit Woody Allen unerringly grasps the fads and foibles of the present-day individuals-by-decree, when browsing through imaginary advertising leaflets of 'Adult Summer Courses' of the kind which Americans would be eager to attend. The course in Economic Theory includes the item 'Inflation and Depression – how to dress for each'; the course in Ethics entails 'the categorical imperative, and six ways to make it work for you', while the prospectus for Astronomy informs that 'The sun, which is made of gas, can explode at any moment, sending our entire planet system hurtling to destruction; students are advised what the average citizen can do in such a case.'

To sum up: the other side of individualization seems to be the corrosion and slow disintegration of citizenship. Joël Roman, co-editor of Ésprit, points out in his recent book (*La Démocratie des individus*, 1998) that 'Vigilance is degraded to the surveillance of goods, while general interest is no more than a syndicate of egoisms, engaging collective emotions and fear of the neighbour.' Roman urges the readers to seek the 'renewed capacity for deciding together' – now salient mostly for its absence.

If the individual is the citizen's worst enemy, and if individual-ization spells trouble for citizenship and citizenship-based politics, it is because the concerns and preoccupations of individuals *qua* individuals fill the public space to the brim, claiming to be its only legitimate occupants, and elbow out from public discourse every-thing else. The 'public' is colonized by the 'private'; 'public inter-est' is reduced to curiosity about the private lives of public figures, and the art of public life is narrowed to the public display of private affairs and public confessions of private sentiments (the more intimate the better). 'Public issues' which resist such reduc-tion become all but incomprehensible.

The prospects of individualized actors being 're-embedded' in the republican body of citizenship are dim. What prompts them to venture onto the public stage is not so much the search for com-mon causes and for the ways to negotiate the meaning of the common good and the principles of life in common, as the desper-ate need for 'networking'. Sharing intimacies, as Richard Sennett keeps pointing out, tends to be the preferred, perhaps the only remaining, method of 'community building'. This building tech-nique can only spawn 'communities' as fragile and short-lived as scattered and wandering emotions, shifting erratically from one target to another and drifting in the forever inconclusive search for a secure haven: communities of shared worries, shared anxieties or shared hatreds – but in each case 'peg' communities, a momentary gathering around a nail on which many solitary individuals hang their solitary individual fears. As Ulrich Beck puts it (in the essay 'On the Mortality of Industrial Society'[11]),

> What emerges from the fading social norms is naked, frightened, aggressive ego in search of love and help. In the search for itself and an affectionate sociality, it easily gets lost in the jungle of the self. . . . Someone who is poking around in the fog of his or her own self is no longer capable of noticing that this isolation, this 'solitary-confinement of the ego' is a mass sentence.

Individualization is here to stay; all thinking about the means of dealing with its impact in the fashion in which we all conduct our lives must start from acknowledging this fact. Individualization brings to the ever-growing number of men and women an unpre-cedented freedom of experimenting – but (*timeo danaos et dona ferentes . . .*) it also brings the unprecedented task of coping with their consequences. The yawning gap between the right of self-assertion and the capacity to control the social settings which render such self-assertion feasible or unrealistic seems to be the main contradiction of fluid modernity – one that, through trial and error, critical reflection and bold experimentation, we would need collectively to learn to tackle collectively.

The plight of critical theory in the society of individuals

The modernizing impulse, in any of its renditions, means the compulsive critique of reality. Privatization of the impulse means compulsive *self*-critique born of perpetual self-disaffection: being an individual *de jure* means having no one to blame for one's own misery, seeking the causes of one's own defeats nowhere except in one's own indolence and sloth, and looking for no remedies other than trying harder and harder still.

Living daily with the risk of self-reprobation and self-contempt is not an easy matter. With the eyes focused on their own performances and thus diverted from the social space where the contradictions of individual existence are collectively produced, men and women are naturally tempted to reduce the complexity of their predicament in order to render the causes of misery intelligible and so tractable and amenable to remedial action. Not that they find 'biographic solutions' onerous and cumbersome: there are, simply, no effective 'biographic solutions to systemic contradictions', and so the dearth of workable solutions at their disposal needs to be compensated for by imaginary ones. Yet – imaginary or genuine – all 'solutions', in order to seem sensible and viable, must be in line with and on a par with the 'individualization' of tasks and responsibilities. There is therefore demand for individual pegs on which frightened individuals could hang collectively, if only for a brief time, their individual fears. Our time is auspicious for scapegoats – be they the politicians making a mess of their private lives, criminals creeping out of the mean streets and rough districts, or 'foreigners in our midst'. Ours is a time of patented locks, burglar alarms, barbed-wire fences, neighbourhood watch and vigilantes; as well as of 'investigative' tabloid journalists fishing for conspiracies to populate with phantoms the public space ominously empty of actors, and for plausible new causes of 'moral panics' ferocious enough to release a good chunk of the pent-up fear and anger.

Let me repeat: there is a wide and growing gap between the condition of individuals *de jure* and their chances to become individuals *de facto* – that is, to gain control over their fate and make the choices they truly desire. It is from that abysmal gap that the most poisonous effluvia contaminating the lives of contemporary individuals emanate. That gap, however, cannot be bridged by individual efforts alone: not by the means and resources available within self-managed life-politics. Bridging that gap is the matter of Politics – with a capital 'P'. It can be supposed that the gap in question has emerged and grown precisely because of the emptying of public space, and particularly the 'agora', that intermediary, public/private site where life-politics meets Politics with the capital 'P', where private problems are translated into the language of public issues and public solutions are sought, negotiated and agreed for private troubles.

The table, so to speak, has been turned: the task of critical theory has been reversed. That task used to be the defence of private autonomy from the advancing troops of the 'public sphere', smarting under the oppressive rule of the omnipotent impersonal state and its many bureaucratic tentacles or their smaller-scale replicas. The task is now to defend the vanishing public realm, or rather to refurnish and repopulate the public space fast emptying owing to the desertion on both sides: the exit of the 'interested citizen', and the escape of real power into the territory which, for all that the extant democratic institutions are able to accomplish, can only be described as an 'outer space'.

It is no more true that the 'public' is set on colonizing the 'private'. The opposite is the case: it is the private that colonizes the public space, squeezing out and chasing away everything which cannot be fully, without residue, expressed in the vernacular of private concerns, worries and pursuits. Told repeatedly that he or she is the master of his or her own fate, the individual has little reason to accord 'topical relevance' (Alfred Schütz's term) to anything which resists being engulfed within the self and dealt with by the self's facilities; but having such reason and acting upon it is precisely the trade mark of the citizen.

For the individual, public space is not much more than a giant screen on which private worries are projected without ceasing to be private or acquiring new collective qualities in the course of magnification: public space is where public confession of private secrets and intimacies is made. From their daily guided tours of the 'public' space individuals return reinforced in their *de jure* individuality and reassured that the solitary fashion in which they go about their life-business is what all other 'individuals like them' do, while – again like them – suffering their own measures of stumblings and (hopefully transient) defeats in the process.

As to the power, it sails away from the street and the market-place, from assembly halls and parliaments, local and national governments, and beyond the reach of citizens' control, into the exterritoriality of electronic networks. The favourite strategic principles of the powers-that-be are nowadays *escape, avoidance* and *disengagement*, and their ideal condition is invisibility. Attempts to anticipate their moves and the unanticipated consequences of their moves (let alone the efforts to avert or arrest the most undesirable among them) have a practical effectivity not unlike that of a League to Prevent Weather Change.

And so public space is increasingly empty of public issues. It fails to perform its past role of a meeting-and-dialogue place for private troubles and public issues. On the receiving end of the individualizing pressures, individuals are being gradually, but consistently, stripped of the protective armour of citizenship and expropriated of their citizen skills and interests. Under the circumstances, the prospect of the individual *de jure* ever turning into the individual *de facto* (that is one which commands the resources indispensable for genuine self-determination) seems ever more remote.

The individual *de jure* cannot turn into the individual *de facto* without first becoming the *citizen*. There are no autonomous individuals without an autonomous society, and the autonomy of society requires deliberate and perpetually deliberated self-constitution, something that may be only a shared accomplishment of its members.

'Society' always stood in an ambiguous relation to individual autonomy: it was, simultaneously, its enemy and its *sine qua non* condition. But the proportions of threats and chances in what is bound to remain an ambivalent relationship have radically changed in the course of modern history. Though the reasons to watch it closely might not have disappeared, society is now primarily the condition which individuals strongly need, yet badly miss – in their vain and frustrating struggle to reforge their *de jure* status into the genuine autonomy and capacity for self-assertion.

This is, in the broadest of outlines, the predicament which sets the present-day tasks of critical theory – and, more generally, social critique. They boil down to tying together once more what the combination of formal individualization and the divorce between power and politics have torn asunder. In other words, to redesign and repopulate the now largely vacant agora – the site of meeting, debate and negotiation between the individual and the common, private and public good. If the old objective of critical theory – human emancipation – means anything today, it means to reconnect the two edges of the abyss which has opened between the reality of the individual *de jure* and the prospects of the individual *de facto*. And individuals who relearned forgotten citizen skills and reappropriated lost citizen tools are the only builders up to the task of this particular bridge building.

Critical theory revisited

The need in thinking is what makes us think, said Adorno.[12] His *Negative Dialectics*, that long and tortuous exploration of the ways of being human in a world inhospitable to humanity, ends with this biting, yet ultimately empty phrase: after hundreds of pages, nothing has been explained, no mystery cracked, no reassurance given. The secret of being human remains as impenetrable as it had been at the beginning of the journey. Thinking makes us human, but it is being human that makes us think. Thinking cannot be explained; but it needs no explanation. Thinking needs no justification; but it would not be justified even if one tried.

This predicament is, Adorno would tell us again and again, neither a sign of the thought's weakness nor the badge of the thinking person's shame. If anything, the opposite is true. Under Adorno's pen, the grim necessity turns into a privilege. The *less* a thought can be explained in terms familiar and making sense to the men and women immersed in their daily pursuit of survival, the nearer it comes to the standards of humanity; the *less* it can be justified in terms of tangible gains and uses or the price-tag attached to it in the superstore or at stock-exchange, the higher is its humanizing worth. It is the active search for market value, and the urge for immediate consumption, that threaten the genuine value of thought. 'No thought is immune', writes Adorno,

> against communication, and to utter it in the wrong place and in wrong agreement is enough to undermine its truth. ... For the intellectual, inviolable isolation is now the only way of showing some measure of solidarity. ... The detached observer is as much entangled as the active participant; the only advantage of the former is insight into his entanglement, and the infinitesimal freedom that lies in knowledge as such.[13]

It will become clear that the insight is the beginning of freedom once we remember that 'to a subject that acts naïvely ... its own conditioning is nontransparent',[14] and that the non-transparency of conditioning is itself the warrant for perpetual naïvety. Just as the thought needs nothing but itself to self-perpetuate, so the naïvety is self-sufficient; as long as it is not disturbed by insight, it will keep its own conditioning intact.

'Not disturbed'; indeed, the entry of insight is hardly ever welcomed by those who have grown used to living without it as the sweet prospect of liberation. The innocence of naïvety makes even the most turbulent and treacherous condition look familiar and therefore secure, and any insight into its precarious scaffolding is the portent of non-confidence, doubt and insecurity, which few people would greet with joyful anticipation. It seems that, for Adorno, that widespread resentment to insight is for the better, though it does not augur an easy ride. The unfreedom of the naïve is the freedom of the thinking person. It makes the 'inviolable isolation' that much easier. 'He who offers for sale something unique that no-one wants to buy, represents, even against his will, freedom from exchange.'[15] There is but one step leading from this thought to another: that of the exile as the archetypal condition to be free from exchange. The products which exile offers are surely such as no one would have the slightest inkling to buy. 'Every intellectual in emigration is, without exception, mutilated', wrote Adorno in his own, American, exile. 'He lives in an environment that must remain incomprehensible to him.' No wonder he is insured against the risk of producing anything of value on the local market. Hence, 'If in Europe the esoteric gesture was often only a pretext for the blindest self-interest, the concept of austerity ...

seems, in emigration, the most acceptable lifeboat.'[16] Exile is to the thinker what home is to the naïve; it is in exile that the thinking person's detachment, his habitual way of life, acquires survival value.

Reading through Deussen's edition of the Upanishads, Adorno and Horkheimer commented bitterly that theoretical and practical systems of the seekers of the union between truth, beauty and justice, those 'outsiders of history', are 'not very rigid and centralized; they differ from the successful systems by an element of anarchy. They set greater store by the idea and the individual than by administration and collective. They therefore arouse anger.'[17] For the ideas to be successful, to reach the imagination of the cave dwellers, the elegant Vedic ritual must take over from the rambling musings of the Upanishads, cool-headed and well-behaved Stoics must replace the impetuous and arrogant Cynics and the utterly practical St Paul must replace the exquisitely impractical St John the Baptist. The big question, though, is whether the emancipatory power of those ideas can survive their earthly success. Adorno's answer to this question drips melancholy: 'The history of the old religions and schools like that of the modern parties and revolutions teaches us that the price for survival is practical involvement, the transformation of ideas into domination.'[18]

In this last sentence the main strategic dilemma which haunted the founder and the most notorious writer of the original 'critical school' found its most vivid expression: whoever thinks and cares is doomed to navigate between the Scylla of clean yet impotent thought and the Charybdis of effective yet polluted bid for domination. *Tertium non datur.* Neither the bid for practice nor the refusal of practice offer a good solution. The first tends, inevitably, to transmogrify into domination – with all its attendant horrors of new constraints bound to be imposed upon freedom, of the utilitarian pragmatics of effects taking precedence over the ethical principles of reasons, and the watering down and subsequent distortion of freedom's ambitions. The second may perhaps satisfy the narcissistic desire for uncompromised purity, but would leave the thought ineffectual and in the end barren: philosophy, as Ludwig Wittgenstein sadly observed, would leave everything as it was; the thought born of revulsion against the inhumanity of the human condition would do little or nothing to make that condition more human. The dilemma of *vita contemplativa* and *vita activa* boils down to a choice between two similarly unappetizing prospects. The better the values preserved in thought are protected against pollution, the less significant they are to the life of those whom they are meant to serve. The greater their effects on that life, the less reminiscent will be the life reformed to the values that prompted and inspired the reform.

Adorno's worry has a long history, reaching back to Plato's problem with the wisdom and feasibility of the 'return to the cave'. That problem sprang from Plato's call to philosophers to leave the dark cave of quotidianity and – in the name of purity of thought – to refuse any truck with the cave-dwellers for the duration of their sojourn in the brightly lit outside world of clear and lucid ideas. The problem was whether philosophers should wish to share their travel trophies with those inside the cave, and – in the case they were willing to do so – whether they would be listened to and believed. True to the idiom of his time, Plato expected the likely breach of communication to result in the messengers of the news being killed. . . .

Adorno's version of Plato's problem took shape in the post-Enlightenment world, where burning heretics at the stake and serving hemlock to the harbingers of a nobler life were definitely out of fashion. In this new world the cave-dwellers, now reincarnated as *Bürger*, were no more credited with the innate enthusiasm for truth and superior values than Plato's originals used to be; they were expected to put up as staunch and rugged resistance to a message bound to disturb the tranquillity of their daily routine. True to the new idiom, however, the outcome of the communication breakdown was envisaged in a different form. The marriage between knowledge and power, a mere fantasy in the times of Plato, has turned into the routine and virtually axiomatic postulate of philosophy and a common and daily deployed claim of politics. From something for which one was likely to be killed, truth became something which offers a good reason to kill. (It was a bit of both all along, but the proportions in the mixture have shifted dramatically.) It was therefore natural and reasonable to expect, in the times of Adorno, that the rejected apostles of good tidings would resort to force whenever they could; they would seek domination to break the resistance and to compel, impel or bribe their opponents to follow the route they were reluctant to enter. To the old quandary – how to find the words telling to the uninitiated ears without compromising the substance of the message, how to express the truth in a form easy to grasp and attractive enough to be wished to be grasped, without twisting or diluting its contents – a new difficulty was added, particularly acute and worrying in the case of a message with emancipatory, liberating ambitions: how to avoid or at least limit the corrupting impact of power and domination, now seen as the principal vehicle conveying the message to the recalcitrant and the lukewarm? The two worries intertwined, sometimes blended – like in the sharp, yet inconclusive dispute between Leo Strauss and Alexandre Kojève.

'Philosophy', Strauss insisted, is the quest for the 'eternal and immutable order within which history takes place, and which remains entirely unaffected by history'. What is eternal and immutable has also the quality of universality; yet universal acceptance of that 'eternal and immutable order' might be reached only on the grounds 'of genuine knowledge or of wisdom' – not through reconciliation and agreement between opinions.

> Agreement based on opinion can never become universal agreement. Every faith that lays claim to universality, i.e., to be universally accepted, of necessity provokes a counter-faith which raises the same claim. The diffusion among the unwise of genuine knowledge that was acquired by the wise would be of no help, for through its diffusion or dilution, knowledge inevitably transforms itself into opinion, prejudice, or mere belief,

For Strauss as much as Kojève, this gap between wisdom and 'mere belief' and the difficulty of communication between them pointed immediately and automatically to the issue of power and politics. The incompatibility between two types of knowledge presented itself to both polemicists as the question of rule, enforcement, and of political engagement of the 'bearers of wisdom', as, to put it bluntly, the problem of relationship between philosophy and the state, considered as the principal site and focus of politics. The problem boils down to a blunt choice between political involvement and the radical distantiation from political practice, and the careful calculation of the potential gains, risks and drawbacks of each.

Given that the eternal order, the true matter of the philosophers' concern, is 'entirely unaffected by history', in what way can commerce with the managers of history, the powers-that-be, help the cause of philosophy? For Strauss, it was a largely rhetorical question, since 'There is no such way' is the only reasonable, and self-evident, answer. The truth of philosophy may indeed be unaffected by history, responded Kojève, but it does not follow that it can steer clear of history: the point of that truth is to enter history in order to re-form it – and so the practical task of commerce with the power-holders, the natural gate-keepers who guard that entry and bar or let through the traffic, remains an integral and vital part of the philosophers' business. History is philosophy's fulfilment; the truth of philosophy finds its ultimate test and confirmation in its acceptance and recognition, in the words of philosophers becoming the flesh of *the polity*. Recognition is the ultimate *telos* and verification of philosophy; and so the object of philosophers' actions is not only the philosophers themselves, their thought, the 'inside business' of philosophizing, but the world as such, and in the end the harmony between the two, or rather the remaking of the world in the likeness of the truth of which the philosophers are the guardians. 'Having no truck' with politics is not, therefore, an answer; it smacks of the betrayal not just of the 'world out there', but of philosophy as well.

There is no avoiding the problem of the 'political bridge' to the world. And since that bridge cannot but be manned by the servants of the state, the question of how, if at all, to use them to smooth the passage of philosophy into the world will not go away and must be confronted. And there is no avoiding either the brutal fact that – at least at the start, as long as the gap between the truth of philosophy and the reality of the world remains unfulfilled – the state takes the form of tyranny. Tyranny (Kojève is adamant that this form of government can be defined in *morally neutral* terms) occurs whenever

> a fraction of the citizens (it matters little whether it be a majority or a minority) imposes on all the other citizens its own ideas and actions, ideas and actions that are guided by an authority which this fraction recognizes spontaneously, but which it has not succeeded in getting the others to recognize; and where this fraction imposes it on those others without 'coming to terms' with them, without trying to reach some 'compromise' with them, and without taking account of their ideas and desires (determined by another authority, which those others recognize spontaneously).

Since it is the disregard for the ideas and the desires of the 'others' that makes the tyranny tyrannical, the task consists in cutting the schismogenetic chain (as Gregory Bateson would say) of lofty neglect on the one side and muted dissent on the other, and find some ground on which both sides may meet and engage in fruitful conversation. That ground (here Kojève and Strauss were of one mind) can only be offered by the truth of philosophy, dealing – as it necessarily does – with things eternal and absolutely as well as universally valid. (All other grounds, offered by 'mere beliefs', may serve as battlegrounds only, not conference halls.) Kojève believed that this can be done, but Strauss did not: 'I do not believe in the possibility of a conversation of Socrates with the *people*.' Whoever engages in such a conversation is not a philosopher but 'a certain kind of rhetorician' concerned not so much with paving the way over which the truth may travel to the people, as with gaining obedience to whatever the powers may need or will to command. Philosophers may do little more than try to advise the rhetoricians, and the likelihood of their success is bound to be minimal. The chances of philosophy and society ever being reconciled and becoming one are dim.[19]

Strauss and Kojève agreed that the link between universal values and the historically shaped reality of social life was politics; writing from inside heavy modernity, they took it for granted that politics overlaps with the actions of the state. And so it followed without further argument that the dilemma confronting philosophers boiled down to the simple choice between 'take it' and 'leave it': either using that link, despite all the risks any attempt to use it must involve, or (for the sake of purity of thought) keeping clear from it and guarding one's distance from power and the power-holders. The choice, in other words, was between truth bound to remain impotent and potency bound to be unfaithful to the truth.

Heavy modernity was, after all, the era of shaping reality after the manner of architecture or gardening; reality compliant with the verdicts of reason was to be 'built' under strict quality control and according to strict procedural rules, and first of all *designed* before the construction works begin. This was an era of drawing-boards and blueprints – not so much for mapping the social territory as for lifting that territory to the level of lucidity and logic that only maps can boast or claim. That was an era which hoped to legislate reason into reality, to reshuffle the stakes in a way that would trigger rational conduct and render all behaviour contrary to reason too costly to contemplate. For the legislative reason, neglecting the legislators and the law-enforcement agencies was, obviously, not an option. The issue of the rapport with the state, whether co-operative or contestant, was its formative dilemma: indeed, a matter of life and death.

The critique of life-politics

With the state no longer hoped, promising or willing to act as the plenipotentiary of reason and the master-builder of the rational society, with drawing-boards in the offices of the good society in the process of being phased out, and with the variegated crowd of counsellors, interpreters and brokers taking over most of the task previously reserved to the legislators, no wonder that critical theorists wishing to be instrumental in the activity of emancipation mourn their bereavement. Not just the assumed vehicle and simultaneously the target of the liberation struggle is falling apart; the central, constitutive dilemma of critical theory, the very axis around which the critical discourse rotated, is unlikely to survive that vehicle's demise. Critical discourse, many may feel, is about to find itself without a subject. And many may – and do – cling desperately to the orthodox strategy of critique only to confirm, inadvertently, that the discourse is indeed devoid of a tangible subject as the diagnoses are increasingly out of touch with current realities and the proposals grow increasingly nebulous; many insist on fighting old battles in which they acquired expertise and prefer this to the change from a familiar and trusty battleground to a new, as yet not fully explored, territory, in many ways a *terra incognita*.

   The prospects of (let alone the demand for) critical theory are not, however, wedded to the now receding forms of life in the same way as the extant self-awareness of critical theorists is to the forms, skills and programmes developed in the course of confronting them. It is only the meaning assigned to emancipation under past but no more present conditions that has become obsolete – not the task of emancipation itself. Something else is now at stake. There is a new public agenda of emancipation still waiting to be occupied by critical theory. This new public agenda, still awaiting its critical public policy, is emerging together with the 'liquefied' version of the modern human condition – and in particular in the wake of the 'individualization' of life tasks arising from that condition.

This new agenda arises in the previously discussed gap between individuality *de jure* and *de facto*, or – if you wish – legally enforced 'negative freedom' and largely absent, or at any rate far from universally available, 'positive freedom' – that is, the genuine potency of self-assertion. The new condition is not unlike the one which, according to the Bible, led to the Israelite rebellion and exodus from Egypt. 'Pharaoh ordered the people's overseers and their foremen not to supply the people with the straw used in making bricks . . . "Let them go and collect their straw, but see that they produce the same tally of bricks as before". ' When the foremen pointed out that one cannot make bricks efficiently unless straw is duly supplied, and charged the pharaoh with demanding the impossible, he reversed the responsibility for failure: 'You are lazy, you are lazy.' Today, there are no pharaohs commanding the foremen to flog the slothful. (Even the flogging has been made a DIY job and replaced with self-flagellation.) But the task of supplying the straw has been discharged all the same by the authorities of the day and the producers of bricks are told that solely their own laziness prevents them from doing the job properly – and above all, doing it to their own satisfaction.

The job with which humans are charged today remains much the same as it has been since the beginning of modern times: the self-constitution of individual life and the weaving as well as the servicing of the networks of bonds with other self-constituting individuals. That job was never put in question by critical theorists. What such theorists were critical of was the sincerity and expedience with which human individuals were set free to accomplish the job they had been assigned to perform. Critical theory accused those who should have provided the right condition for self-assertion with duplicity or inefficiency: there were too many constraints imposed upon freedom of choice, and there was the totalitarian tendency endemic to the way modern society had been structured and run which threatened to abolish freedom altogether, replacing the liberty of choice with imposed or surreptitiously drilled dull homogeneity.

The lot of a free agent is full of antinomies not easy to take stock of, let alone to disentangle. Consider, for instance, the contradiction of self-made identities which must be solid enough to be acknowledged as such and yet flexible enough not to bar freedom of future movements in the constantly changing, volatile circumstances. Or the precariousness of human partnerships, now burdened with expectations greater than ever yet poorly, if at all, institutionalized, and therefore less resistant to the added burden. Or the sorry plight of the repossessed responsibility, sailing dangerously between the rocks of indifference and coercion. Or the fragility of all common action, which has solely the enthusiasm and dedication of the actors to rely on, and yet needs a more lasting adhesive to keep its integrity as long as it takes to reach its purpose. Or the notorious difficulty of generalizing the experiences, lived-through as thoroughly personal and subjective, into problems fit to be inscribed into the public agenda and become matters of public policy. These are but a few off-hand examples, but they offer a fair view of the kind of challenge now facing critical theorists wishing to reconnect their discipline to the public policy agenda.

Not without good reasons the critical theorists suspected that in the 'enlightened despot' version of Enlightenment, as embodied in the political practices of modernity, it is the result – the rationally structured and run society – that counts; they suspected that individual wills, desires and purposes, individual *vis formandi* and *libido formandi*, the poietic propensity to create new significations with no regard to function, use and purpose, are but so many resources, or for that matter obstacles, on the road. Against that practice, or its surmised tendency, critical theorists set the vision of a society that rebels against that perspective, of a society in which precisely those wills, desires and purposes, and their satisfaction, count and need to be honoured, a vision of a society which, for that reason, militates against all schemes of perfection imposed against the wishes, or in disregard of the wishes, of the men and women who are embraced by its generic name. The sole 'totality' recognized and acceptable was for most philosophers of the critical school the one likely to emerge from the actions of creative and freely choosing individuals.

There was an anarchistic streak in all critical theorizing: all power was suspect, the enemy was espied only on the side of power, and the same enemy was blamed for all drawbacks and frustrations suffered by freedom (even for the lack of valour in the troops meant to fight valiantly their wars of liberation, as in the case of the 'mass culture' debate). Dangers were expected to arrive and the blows to fall from the 'public' side, always eager to invade and colonize the 'private', the 'subjective', the 'individual'. Less and altogether little thought was given to the dangers residing in the narrowing or emptying of public space and the possibility of the reversed invasion: the colonization of the public sphere by the private. And yet that underestimated and underdiscussed eventuality has turned today into the principal impediment to emancipation, which in its present stage can only be described as the task of transforming the individual autonomy *de jure* into autonomy *de facto*.

Public power portends *incompleteness* of individual freedom, but its retreat or disappearance augurs the *practical impotence* of legally victorious freedom. The history of modern emancipation veered from a confrontation with the first danger to facing the second. To deploy Isaiah Berlin's terms, one can say that, once the 'negative freedom' had been struggled for and won, the levers needed to transform it into 'positive freedom – that is' the freedom to set the range of choices and the agenda of choice-making – has broken and fallen apart. Public power has lost much of its awesome and resented oppressive potency – but it has also lost a good part of its enabling capacity. The war of emancipation is not over. But to progress any further, it must now resuscitate what for most of its history it did its best to destroy and push out of its way. *Any true liberation calls today for more, not less, of the 'public sphere' and 'public power'*. It is now the public sphere which badly needs defence against the invading private – though, paradoxically, in order to enhance, not cut down, individual liberty.

As always, the job of critical thought is to bring into the light the many obstacles piled on the road to emancipation. Given the nature of today's tasks, the main obstacles which urgently need to be examined relate to the rising difficulties in translating private problems into public issues, in congealing and condensing endemically private troubles into public interests that are larger than the sum of their individual ingredients, in recollectivizing the privatized utopias of 'life-politics' so that they can acquire once more the shape of the visions of the 'good society' and 'just society'. When public politics sheds its functions and life-politics takes over, problems encountered by individuals *de jure* in their efforts to become in-dividuals *de facto* turn out to be notoriously non-additive and non-cumulative, thereby denuding the public sphere of all sub-stance except of the site where private worries are confessed and put on public display. By the same token, not only does the indi-vidualization appear to be a one-way-street, but it seems to destroy as it proceeds all the tools which could conceivably be used in implementing its erstwhile objectives.

This kind of task confronts critical theory with a new addressee. The spectre of Big Brother ceased to hover in the world's attics and dungeons once the enlightened despot made his exit from its sitting and reception rooms. In their new, liquid modern, drastically shrunken versions both found shelter inside the miniature, diminu-tive realm of personal life-politics; it is there that the threats and the chances of individual autonomy – that autonomy which cannot fulfil itself anywhere except in the autonomous society – must be sought and located. The search for an alternative life in common must start from the examination of life-politics alternatives.

2

Individuality

Now, *here*, you see, it takes all the running you can do, to keep in the same place. If you want to get somewhere else, you must run at least twice as fast as that!

Lewis Carroll

It is hard to remember, and harder yet to understand, that no more than fifty years ago the dispute about the substance of popular forebodings, about what there was to be afraid of, and what sort of horrors the future was bound to bring if it wasn't stopped before it was too late, was waged between Aldous Huxley's *Brave New World* and George Orwell's *Nineteen Eighty-four*.

The dispute, to be sure, was quite genuine and earnest, since the worlds so vividly portrayed by the two visionary dystopians were as different as chalk from cheese. Orwell's was a world of shabbiness and destitution, of scarcity and want; Huxley's was a land of opulence and profligacy, of abundance and satiety. Predictably, people inhabiting Orwell's world were sad and frightened; those portrayed by Huxley were carefree and playful. There were many other differences, no less striking; the two worlds opposed each other in virtually every detail.

And yet there was something that united both visions. (Without it, the two dystopias would not talk to each other at all, let alone quarrel.) What they shared was the foreboding of *a tightly controlled world*; of individual freedom not just reduced to a sham or naught, but keenly resented by people drilled to obey commands and to follow set routines; of a small elite holding in their hands all the strings – so that the rest of humanity could move through their lives

the way puppets do; of a world split into managers and the managed, designers and the followers of designs – with the first keeping
the designs close to their chests and the second neither willing to nor
capable of prying into the scripts and grasping the sense of it all; of a
world which made an alternative to itself all but unimaginable.

That the future held in store less freedom, more control, supervision and oppression, was not part of the dispute. Orwell and
Huxley did not disagree on the world's destination; they merely
envisaged differently the road which would take us there were we
to stay ignorant, obtuse, placid or indolent enough to allow things
to go their natural way.

In a letter of 1769 to Sir Horace Mann, Horace Walpole wrote
that 'the world is a comedy to those who think, a tragedy to those
who feel.' But the meanings of the 'comic' and the 'tragic' changes
over time, and on the days when Orwell and Huxley reached for
their pens to sketch the contours of the tragic future, they both felt
that the tragedy of the world was its dogged and uncontrollable
progress towards the split between the increasingly powerful and
remote controllers and the increasingly powerless and controlled
rest. The nightmarish vision which haunted both writers was that
of men and women no longer in charge of their lives. Much like
those thinking men of another time, Aristotle and Plato, who could
not imagine a good or bad society without slaves, Huxley and
Orwell could not conceive of a society, whether a happy or a
miserable one, without managers, designers and supervisors who
jointly wrote the script for others to follow, staged the performance, put the lines in the actors' mouths and fired or locked in
dungeons everyone who would improvise their own texts. They
could not visualize a world without controlling towers and controlling desks. The fears of their time, much as its hopes and
dreams, hovered around Supreme Command Offices.

Capitalism – heavy and light

Nigel Thrift would have perhaps filed Orwell's and Huxley's
stories under the rubric of the 'Joshua discourse', as distinct from
the 'Genesis discourse'.[1] (Discourses, says Thrift, are 'metalanguages
that instruct people how to live as people'.) 'Whereas in the Joshua
discourse order is the rule and disorder is an exception, in the

Genesis discourse disorder is the rule and order the exception.' In the Joshua discourse, the world (here Thrift quotes Kenneth Jowitt) is 'centrally organised, rigidly bounded, and hysterically concerned with impenetrable boundaries'.

'Order', let me explain, means monotony, regularity, repetitiveness and predictability; we call a setting 'orderly' if and only if some events are considerably more likely to happen in it than their alternatives, while some other events are highly unlikely to occur or are altogether out of the question. This means by the same token that someone somewhere (a personal or impersonal Supreme Being) must interfere with the probabilities, manipulate them and load the dice, seeing to it that events do not occur at random.

The orderly world of the Joshua discourse is a tightly controlled one. Everything in that world serves a purpose, even if it is not clear (for the time being for some, but for ever for most) what that purpose is. That world has no room for whatever may lack use or purpose. No use, moreover, would be acknowledged in that world to be a legitimate purpose. To be recognized, it must serve the maintenance and the perpetuation of the orderly whole. It is the order itself, and the order alone, which does not call for legitimation; it is, so to speak, 'its own purpose'. It just *is*, and cannot be wished away: this is all we need or can know about it. Perhaps it is there because this is where God put it in His one-off act of Divine Creation; or because human, but God-like, creatures put it there and keep it there in their ongoing work of designing, building and management. In our modern times, with God on a protracted leave of absence, the task of designing and servicing order has fallen upon human beings.

As Karl Marx discovered, the ideas of the dominant classes tend to be the dominant ideas (a proposition which, with our new understanding of language and its works, we may consider pleonastic). For at least two hundred years it was the managers of capitalist enterprises who dominated the world – that is, set the feasible apart from the implausible, the rational apart from the irrational, the sensible apart from the insane, and otherwise determined and circumscribed the range of alternatives inside which human life trajectories were to be confined. It was therefore their vision of the world, in conjunction with the world itself, shaped and reshaped in the likeness of that vision, that fed into and gave substance to the dominant discourse.

Until recently, this was the Joshua discourse; now, increasingly, it is the Genesis discourse. But, contrary to what Thrift implies, the present-day meeting inside the same discourse of business and academia, the world-makers and the world-interpreters, is no novelty; not a quality unique to the new ('soft', as Thrift calls it) and knowledge-greedy capitalism. For a couple of centuries now academia had no other world to catch in its conceptual nets, to reflect upon, to describe and to interpret, than the one sedimented by the capitalist vision and practice. Throughout that period, business and academia were constantly in meeting, even if – because of their failure to converse with each other – they made an impression of keeping a mutual distance. And the meeting room has been always, as it is now, appointed and furnished by the first partner.

The world sustaining the Joshua discourse and making it credible was the Fordist world. (The term 'Fordism' was first used long ago by Antonio Gramsci and Henri de Man, but, true to the habits of Hegel's Owl of Minerva, has been rediscovered and brought into prominence and common use only when the sun shining on Fordist practices began to set.) In Alain Lipietz's retrospective description, Fordism was in its heyday simultaneously a model of industrialization, of accumulation, and of *regulation*:

> [a] combination of forms of adjustment of the expectations and contradictory behaviour by individual agents to the collective principles of the regime of accumulation . . .
> The industrial paradigm included the Taylorian principle of rationalization, plus constant mechanization. That 'rationalization' was based on separation of the intellectual and manual aspects of labour . . . the social knowledge being systematized from the top and incorporated within machinery by designers. When Taylor and the Taylorian engineers first introduced those principles at the beginning of the twentieth century, their explicit aim was to enforce the control of management on the workers.[2]

But the Fordist model was more than that, an epistemological building site on which the whole world-view was erected and from which it towered majestically over the totality of living experience. The way human beings understand the world tends to be at all times *praxeomorphic*: it is always shaped by the know-how of the day, by what people can do and how they usually go about doing it. The Fordist factory – with its meticulous separation between design and execution, initiative and command-following, freedom and obedience, invention and determination, with its tight inter-locking of the opposites within each of such binary oppositions and the smooth transmission of command from the first element of each pair to the second – was without doubt the highest achievement to date of order-aimed social engineering. No wonder it set the metaphorical frame of reference (even if the reference was not quoted) for everyone trying to comprehend how human reality works on all its levels – the global-societal as well as that of the individual life. Its covert or overt presence is easy to trace in visions apparently as remote as the Parsonian self-reproducing 'social system' ruled by the 'central cluster of values' and the Sartrean 'life project' serving as the guiding design for the self's life-long effort of identity building.

Indeed, there seemed to be no alternative to the Fordist factory and no serious hindrance to stave off the spread of the Fordist model to every nook and cranny of society. The debate between Orwell and Huxley, just as the confrontation between socialism and capitalism, was in this respect not much more than a family squabble. Communism, after all, wished only to clean up the Fordist model of its present pollutions (nay imperfections) – of that malignant market-generated chaos which stood in the way of the ultimate and total defeat of accidents and contingency and made rational planning less than all-embracing. In Lenin's words, the vision of socialism would have been accomplished were the communists to succeed in 'combining the Soviet power and the Soviet organization of management with the latest progress of capitalism',[3] while the 'Soviet organization of management' meant to Lenin the enabling of the 'latest progress of capitalism' (that is, as he kept repeating, the 'scientific organization of labour') to spill out from inside the factory walls in order to penetrate and saturate the whole of social life.

Fordism was the self-consciousness of modern society in its 'heavy', 'bulky', or 'immobile' and 'rooted', 'solid' phase. At that stage in their joint history, capital, management and labour were all, for better or worse, doomed to stay in one another's company for a long time to come, perhaps for ever – tied down by the combination of huge factory buildings, heavy machinery and massive labour forces. To survive, let alone to act efficiently, they had to 'dig in', to draw boundaries and mark them with trenches and barbed wire, while making the fortress large enough to enclose everything necessary to endure a protracted, perhaps prospectless, siege. Heavy capitalism was obsessed with bulk and size, and, for that reason, also with boundaries, with making them tight and impenetrable. The genius of Henry Ford was to discover the way of keeping all the defenders of his industrial fortress inside the walls – to ward off the temptation to defect or change sides. As the Sorbonne economist Daniel Cohen put it:

> Henry Ford decided one day to 'double' the wages of his workers. The (publicly) declared reason, the celebrated phrase 'I want my workers to be paid well enough to buy my cars' was, obviously, a jest. The workers' purchases formed a derisory fraction of his sales, but their wages made a much greater part of his costs ... The genuine reason to raise the wages was the formidable turnover of labour force with which Ford was confronted. He decided to give the workers spectacular rise in order to fix them to the chain ...[4]

The invisible chain riveting the workers to their working places and arresting their mobility was, in Cohen's words, 'the heart of Fordism'. Breaking down that chain was also the decisive, watershed-like change in life experience associated with the decline and accelerated demise of the Fordist model. 'Who starts a career in Microsoft', observes Cohen, 'has no idea where it is going to end. Starting with Ford or Renault, entailed on the contrary the near-certitude that the career would run its course in the same place.'

In its heavy stage, capital was as much fixed to the ground as were the labourers it engaged. Nowadays capital travels light – with cabin luggage only, which includes no more than a briefcase, a cellular telephone and a portable computer. It can stop-over almost anywhere, and nowhere needs to stay longer than the satisfaction lasts. Labour, on the other hand, remains as immobilized as it was in the past – but the place which it once anticipated being fixed to once and for all has lost its past solidity; searching in vain for boulders, anchors fall on friable sands. Some of the world's residents are on the move; for the rest it is the world itself that refuses to stand still. The Joshua discourse sounds hollow when the world, once the legislator, umpire and supreme court of appeal rolled into one, looks more and more like one of the players, keeping its cards close to its chest, setting traps and waiting for its turn to cheat.

The passengers on the 'Heavy Capitalism' ship trusted (not always wisely, to be sure) that the selected members of the crew who were accorded the right to climb onto the captain's deck would navigate the ship to its destination. The passengers could devote their full attention to learning and following the rules set down for them and displayed in bold letters in every passageway. If they grumbled (or sometimes even mutinied), it was against the captain for not taking the ship to harbour fast enough or for being exceptionally neglectful of the passengers' comfort. The passengers of the 'Light Capitalism' aircraft, on the other hand, discover to their horror that the pilot's cabin is empty and that there is no way to extract from the mysterious black box labelled 'automatic pilot' any information about where the plane is flying, where it is going to land, who is to choose the airport, and whether there are any rules which would allow the passengers to contribute to the safety of the arrival.

Have car, can travel

We may say that the turn of events in the world under capitalist rule proved to be the exact opposite of what Max Weber anticipated and confidently predicted when he selected bureaucracy as the prototype of the society to come and portrayed it as the liminal form of rational action. Extrapolating his vision of the future from the contemporary experience of heavy capitalism (the man who coined the phrase 'steely casing' could not possibly be aware that the 'heaviness' was merely a time-bound attribute of capitalism and that other modalities of the capitalist order were conceivable and in the offing), Weber foresaw the impending triumph of 'instrumental rationality': with the destination of human history as good as an open and shut case, and the question of the ends of human actions settled and no longer liable to contest, people would come to preoccupy themselves mostly, perhaps solely, with the issue of means: the future was to be, so to speak, means-obsessed. All further rationalization, in itself a foregone conclusion, would consist in sharpening, adjusting and perfecting the means. Knowing that the rational capacity in human beings tends to be constantly undermined by affective propensities and other equally irrational leanings, one might suspect that the contest about the ends would be unlikely ever to grind to a halt; but that contest would in the future be spat out of the mainstream current moved by relentless rationalization – and left to the prophets and preachers busy on the margins of the paramount (and decisive) business of life.

Weber named also, as it were, another type of goal-oriented action, which he called *value*-rational; but by that he meant pursuit of value 'for its own sake' and 'independently of any prospect of external success'. He also made it clear that the values he had in mind were of the ethical, aesthetic or religious kind – that is, belonging to the category which modern capitalism degraded and declared all but redundant and irrelevant, if not downright damaging, to the calculating, rational conduct it promoted.[5] We can only guess that the need to add value-rationality to his inventory of action-types occurred to Weber as an afterthought, under the fresh impact of the Bolshevik revolution, which seemed to refute the conclusion that the question of goals has been settled once and for all, but implied on the contrary, that a situation might still arise when certain people would hold onto their ideals, however meagre the chances of ever reaching them and however exorbitant the cost of trying – and so would be diverted from the sole legitimate concerns with the calculation of means appropriate to set ends.

Whatever the applications of the value-rationality concept in Weber's scheme of history, that concept is of no use if one wants to grasp the substance of the current historical turn. Present-day light capitalism is not 'value-rational' in the Weberian sense, even if it departs from the ideal type of the instrumental-rational order. From value-rationality Weberian style, light capitalism seems to be light-years away: if ever in history values were embraced 'absolutely', it is most certainly not the case today. What has actually happened in the course of the passage from heavy to light capitalism is the dissipation of invisible 'politburos' capable of 'absolutizing' the values of the supreme courts meant to pass no-appeal-allowed verdicts concerning the goals worth pursuing (the institutions indispensable and central to the Joshua discourse).

In the absence of a Supreme Office (or, rather, in the presence of many offices vying for supremacy, none of which boasts more than a sporting chance of winning the contest), the question of objectives is once more thrown wide open and bound to become the cause of endless agony and much hesitation, to sap confidence and

generate the unnerving feeling of unmitigated uncertainty and therefore also the state of perpetual anxiety. In the words of Gerhard
Schulze, this is a new type of uncertainty: 'not knowing the ends
instead of the traditional uncertainty of not knowing the means'.[6]
It is no longer the question of trying, under conditions of incomplete knowledge, to measure the means (those already had and
those thought to be needed and zealously sought) against the given
end. It is, rather, the question of considering and deciding, in the
face of all the risks known or merely guessed, which of the many
floating, seductive ends 'within reach' (that is, such as can be
reasonably pursued) offer priority – given the quantity of means in
possession and taking into account the meagre chances of their
lasting usefulness.

Under the new circumstances, the odds are that most of human
life and most of human lives will be spent agonizing about the
choice of goals, rather than finding the means to the ends which do
not call for reflection. Contrary to its predecessor, light capitalism
is bound to be *value-obsessed*. The apocryphal small ad in the
'Jobs sought' column – 'Have car, can travel' – may serve as the
epitome of the new problematics of life, alongside the query attrib-
uted to the heads of the present-day scientific and technological
institutes and laboratories: 'We have found the solution. Now let
us find a problem.' The question 'What can I do?' has come to
dominate action, dwarfing and elbowing out the question 'How to
do best what I must or ought to do anyway?'

With the Supreme Offices seeing to the regularity of the world
and guarding the boundary between right and wrong no longer in
sight, the world becomes an infinite collection of possibilities: a
container filled to the brim with a countless multitude of opportunities yet to be chased or already missed. There are more – painfully more – possibilities than any individual life, however long,
adventurous and industrious, can attempt to explore, let alone to
adopt. It is the infinity of chances that has filled the place left empty
in the wake of the disappearing act of the Supreme Office.

No wonder that dystopias are no longer written these days: the
post-Fordist, 'fluid modern' world of freely choosing individuals
does not worry about the sinister *Big* Brother who would punish
those who stepped out of line. In such a world, though, there is not
much room either for the benign and caring *Elder* Brother who
could be trusted and relied upon when it came to decide which

things were worth doing or having and who could be counted on to protect his kid brother against the bullies who stood in the way of getting them; and so the utopias of the good society have stopped being written as well. Everything, so to speak, is now down to the individual. It is up to the individual to find out what she or he is capable of doing, to stretch that capacity to the utmost, and to pick the ends to which that capacity could be applied best – that is, to the greatest conceivable satisfaction. It is up to the individual to 'tame the unexpected to become an entertainment'.[7]

Living in a world full of opportunities – each one more appetizing and alluring than the previous one, each 'compensating for the last, and providing grounds for shifting towards the next'[8] – is an exhilarating experience. In such a world, little is predetermined, even less irrevocable. Few defeats are final, few if any mishaps irreversible; yet no victory is ultimate either. For the possibilities to remain infinite, none may be allowed to petrify into everlasting reality. They had better stay liquid and fluid and have a 'use-by' date attached, lest they render the remaining opportunities off-limits and nip the future adventure in the bud. As Zbyszko Melosik and Tomasz Szkudlarek point out in their insightful study of identity problems,[9] living amidst apparently infinite chances (or at least among more chances than one can reasonably hope to try) offers the sweet taste of 'freedom to become anybody'. This sweetness has a bitter after-taste, though, since while the 'becoming' bit suggests that nothing is over yet and everything lies ahead, the condition of 'being somebody' which that becoming is meant to secure, portends the umpire's final, end-of-game whistle: 'you are no more free when the end has been reached; you are not yourself when you have become somebody.' The state of unfinishedness, incompleteness and underdetermination is full of risk and anxiety; but its opposite brings no unadultered pleasure either, since it forecloses what freedom needs to stay open.

The awareness that the game goes on, that much is still going to happen and the inventory of wonders which life may offer is far from closed, is richly safisfying and pleasurable. The suspicion that nothing which has been already tested and appropriated is insured against decay and guaranteed to last is, though, the proverbial fly in the barrelful of tasty ointment. The losses balance the gains. Life is bound to navigate between the two, and no sailor can boast of having found a safe, let alone risk-free, itinerary.

The world full of possibilities is like a buffet table set with mouth-watering dishes, too numerous for the keenest of eaters to hope to taste them all. The diners are *consumers*, and the most taxing and irritating of the challenges consumers confront is the need to establish priorities: the necessity to forsake some unexplored options and to leave them unexplored. The consumers' misery derives from the surfeit, not the dearth of choices. 'Have I used my means to the best advantage?' is the consumer's most haunting, insomnia-causing question. As Marina Bianchi put it in a collective study produced by economists with the sellers of consumer goods in mind,

> in the case of the consumer, the objective function . . . is empty . . .
> Ends coherently match the means, but ends themselves are not rationally chosen . . .
> Hypothetically consumers, but not firms, may never – or never be found to – err.[10]

But if you may never err, you can never be sure of being in the right either. If there are no wrong moves, there is nothing to distinguish a move as a better one, and so nothing to recognize the right move among its many alternatives – neither before nor after the move has been made. That the danger of error is not on the cards is a mixed blessing – a doubtful joy, to be sure, since the price it commands is one of perpetual uncertainty and of a desire never likely to be satiated. This is good news, a promise of staying in business, for the sellers, but for the buyers an assurance of staying in agony.

Stop telling me; show me!

Heavy, Fordist-style capitalism was the world of law-givers, routine-designers and supervisors, the world of other-directed men and women pursuing fixed-by-others ends in a fixed-by-others fashion. For this reason it was also the world of authorities: of leaders who know better and of teachers who tell you how to proceed better than you do.

Light, consumer-friendly capitalism did not abolish the law-proffering authorities, nor did it make them redundant. It has merely brought into being and allowed to coexist authorities too numerous for any one of them to stay in authority for long, let alone to carry the 'exclusive' label. Unlike error, the truth is one, and may be acknowledged as the truth (that is, given the right to declare all alternatives to itself erroneous) only in so far as it is unique. 'Numerous authorities' is, come to think of it, a contradiction in terms. When the authorities are many, they tend to cancel each other out, and the sole effective authority in the field is one who must choose between them. It is by courtesy of the chooser that a would-be authority becomes an authority. Authorities no longer command; they ingratiate themselves with the chooser; they tempt and seduce.

The 'leader' was a by-product, and a necessary supplement, of the world which aimed at the 'good society', or the 'right and proper' society however defined, and tried hard to hold its bad or improper alternatives at a distance. The 'liquid modern' world does neither. Margaret Thatcher's infamous catchphrase 'There is no such thing as society' was simultaneously a shrewd reflection on the changing nature of capitalism, a declaration of intent and a self-fulfilling prophecy: in its wake, there followed the dismantling of normative and protective networks, which greatly helped the word on its road to turning into flesh. 'No society' means no utopia and no dystopia: as Peter Drucker, the guru of light capitalism, put it, 'No more salvation by society' – suggesting (albeit by omission rather than commission) that, by implication, the responsibility for damnation cannot be laid at society's door either: redemption and doom alike are of your making and solely your concern – the outcome of what you, the free agent, have been freely doing with your life.

There is, of course, no shortage of those who claim to be in the know, and quite a few of them have numerous followers ready to agree. Such people 'in the know', even those whose knowledgeability has not been publicly doubted, are not, however, *leaders*; they are, at the most, *counsellors* – and one crucial difference between leaders and counsellors is that the first are to be followed while the latter need to be hired and can be fired. Leaders demand and expect discipline; counsellors may at best count on the willingness to listen and pay heed. That willingness they must first earn by currying favour with the would-be listeners. Another crucial difference between leaders and counsellors is that the first act as two-way translators between individual good and the 'good of us all', or (as

Wright C. Mills would have put it) between private worries and public issues. Counsellors, on the contrary, are wary of ever stepping beyond the closed area of the private. Illnesses are individual, and so is the therapy; worries are private, and so are the means to fight them off. The counsels which the counsellors supply refer to *life-politics*, not to Politics with a capital P; they refer to what the counselled persons might do by themselves and for themselves, each one for himself or herself – not to what they all together might achieve for each one of them, once they join forces.

In one of the most successful among the exceedingly popular 'teach-yourself' books (it has sold more than 5 million copies since its publication in 1987), Melody Beattie warns/advises her readers: 'The surest way to make ourselves crazy is to get involved with other people's businesses, and the quickest way to become sane and happy is to tend to our own affairs.' The book owed its instant success to the catchy title (*Codependent No More*), which encapsulated the message of the book: trying to straighten out other people's crooked problems makes you dependent, and being dependent means giving hostages to fate – or, more precisely, the things you cannot master or people you cannot control; so mind your own business, and your business only, with a clear conscience. There is little to be gained from doing the job for others, and it would divert your attention from the job no one can do but you. Such a message sounds sweet – as a much-needed reassurance, absolution and green light – to all those loners who are forced to follow, with or against their better judgement and not without pangs of conscience, Samuel Butler's exhortation that 'Pleasure after all is a safer guide than either right or duty.'

'We' is the personal pronoun most frequently used by leaders. As to the counsellors, they have little use for it: 'we' is nothing more than an aggregate of I's, and the aggregate, unlike Émile Durkheim's 'group', is not greater than the sum of its parts. At the end of the counselling session the counselled persons are as alone as before the session started. If anything, they are reinforced in their loneliness: their hunch that they would be abandoned to their own devices has been corroborated and turned into near-certainty. Whatever the content of the advice, it referred to things which the counselled persons must do themselves, accepting full responsibility for doing them properly and blaming no one for the unpleasant consequences which could be ascribed only to their own error or neglect.

The most successful counsellor is one aware of the fact that what the prospective recipients of counselling wish to obtain is an object-lesson. Providing that the nature of troubles is such as can be tackled only by individuals on their own and coped with by individual efforts, what the advice-seeking people need (or believe they need) is an *example* of how other men or women, facing a similar trouble, go about the task. And they need the example of others for yet more essential reasons: many more people feel 'unhappy' than are able to pinpoint and name the causes of their unhappiness. The sentiment of 'being unhappy' is all too often diffuse and unanchored; its contours are blurred, its roots scattered; it still needs to be made 'tangible' – hammered into shape and named, in order to reforge the equally vague longing for happiness into a specific task. Looking at other people's experience – getting a glimpse of other people's trials and tribulations – one hopes to discover and locate the troubles which caused one's own unhappiness, attach to them a name, and so come to know where to look for ways of resisting or conquering them.

Explaining the phenomenal popularity of *Jane Fonda's Workout Book* (1981) and the technique of self-drill which that book put at the disposal of millions of American women, Hilary Radner points out that

> The instructor offers herself as an example . . . rather than as an authority . . .
>
> [T]he exerciser possesses her body through the identification with an image that is not her own but that of the exemplary bod(ies) offered her.

Jane Fonda is quite outspoken about the substance of her offer and straightforward about what sort of example her readers and watchers ought to follow: 'I like to think a lot of my body is my own doing and my own blood and guts. It's my responsibility.'[11] Fonda's message for every woman is to treat her body as her own possession (*my* blood, *my* guts) her own product (*my* own doing) and, above all, her own *responsibility*. To sustain and reinforce the postmodern *amour de soi*, she invokes (alongside the consumer tendency to self-identify through possessions) the memory of a very pre-postmodern – in fact more pre-modern than modern – instinct of workmanship: the product of my work is as good as (and no better than) the skills, attention and care which I invest in its production. Whatever the results, I have no one else to praise (or to blame, as the case may be). The obverse side of the message is also unambiguous, even if not spelled out with similar clarity: you *owe* your body thought and care, and if you neglect that duty you should feel guilty and ashamed. Imperfections of *your* body are *your* guilt and *your* shame. But the redemption of sins is in the hands of the sinner, and in his or her hands alone.

Let me repeat after Hilary Redner: saying all this, Fonda does not act as authority (law-giver, norm-setter, preacher or teacher). What she is doing is 'offering herself as an example'. I am famous and loved; I am an object of desire and admiration. For what reason? Whatever that reason might be, it is there because I put it there. Look at my body: it is lean, flexible, shapely – and perpetually youthful. You would surely like to have – to be – a body like mine. My body is my work; if you work as I do, you may have it. If 'being like Jane Fonda' is something you dream of, remember that it was I, Jane Fonda, who made myself into the Jane Fonda of these dreams.

Being rich and famous helps, of course; it adds weight to the message. Though Jane Fonda goes out of her way to set herself up as an example, not an authority, it would be foolish to deny that, since she is who she is, her example carries 'naturally' an authority which other people's examples would need hard work to obtain. Jane Fonda is in a way an exceptional case: she inherited the state of 'being in the limelight' and drew yet more limelight upon herself through her various widely publicized activities long before she took it upon herself to make an example of her body. In general, however, one cannot be sure of the direction in which the causal link between the willingness to follow the example and the authority of the exemplary person works. As Daniel J. Boorstin wittily, though not at all jokingly, observed (in *The Image*, 1961), the celebrity is a person who is known for his well-knownness, while a best-seller is a book which sold well because it was selling well. Authority expands the ranks of the followers, but in the world of uncertain and chronically underdetermined ends it is the number of the followers that makes – that *is* – the authority.

Whatever may be the case, in the example–authority couple it is the example part that matters most and is most in demand. Celebrities with enough capital of authority to make what they say

worthy of attention even before they say it are far too few to
furnish the innumerable TV chat-shows (and they seldom appear
on the most popular among them, like Oprah's or Trisha's), but
this does not stop the chat-shows from being daily compulsive
viewing for millions of guidance-hungry men and women. The
authority of the person sharing her or his life-story may help viewers watch the example attentively and add a few thousand to the
ratings. But the absence of the story-teller's authority, her not-being-
a-celebrity, his anonymity, may make the example easier to follow
and so may have a value-adding potential of its own. The
non-celebrities, the 'ordinary' men and women 'like you and me',
who appear on the screen only for a fleeting moment (no longer
than it takes to tell the story and to get their share of applause for
telling it, as well as the usual measure of rebuke for withholding
tasty bits or dwelling on the uninteresting pieces for too long) are
people as helpless and as hapless as their watchers, smarting under
the same kind of blows and seeking desperately an honourable exit
from trouble and a promising road to a happier life. And so what
they could have done, I can do as well; perhaps even better. I may
learn something *useful* from their victories and their defeats alike.

It would be demeaning, and in addition wrong and misleading,
to condemn or ridicule the chat-show addiction as an effect of
unleashing the eternal human greed for gossip and pandering to
the 'base kind of curiosity'. In a world tightly packed with means
yet notoriously unclear about ends, the lessons drawn from chat-
shows answer a genuine demand and have undeniable pragmatic
value, since I know already that it is up to me and me alone to
make (and go on making) the best of my life; and since I also know
that whatever resources such an undertaking may require can be
sought and found only in my own skills, courage and nerve, it is
vital to know how other people, faced with similar challenges,
cope. They might have come across a wondrous stratagem which I
have missed; they might have explored the parts of the 'inside'
which I passed by without paying attention to or did not dig deep
enough to discover.

This is not, though, the only benefit. As mentioned before, naming the trouble is itself a daunting task, while without attaching a
name to the feeling of unease or unhappiness there is no hope for
cure. Yet, while suffering is personal and private, a 'private language' is an incongruity. Whatever is to be named, including the

most secret, personal and intimate sentiments, is properly named only if the names chosen have public currency, only if they belong to language which can be interpersonally shared and public and are understood by people who communicate in that language. Chat-shows are public lessons in an as-yet-unborn-but-about-to-be-born language. They offer the words which may be used to 'name the problem' – to express, in publicly legible ways, what has been so far ineffable and would remain so if not for that offer.

This is, by itself, a gain of the utmost importance – but there are yet more gains. In chat-shows words and phrases referring to the experience deemed intimate and so unfit to be talked about are uttered in public – and to universal approval, amusement and applause. By the same token, chat-shows *legitimize* public discourse about private affairs. They render the unspeakable speakable, the shameful decent, and transform the ugly secret into a matter of pride. To an important degree, they are rites of exorcism – and very effective ones. Thanks to chat-shows, I may speak from now on openly about things which I thought (mistakenly, as I see it now) were disgraceful and disgracing and so bound to be kept secret and suffered in silence. Since my confession is no more secret, I gain more than just the comfort of the absolution: I need no longer feel ashamed or wary of being frowned upon, rebuked for impudence and ostracized. These are, after all, the kinds of things which people talk about without compunction in the presence of millions of viewers. Their private problems, and so also my own problems so similar to theirs, are *fit for public discussion*. Not that they turn in effect into *public issues*; they enter the discussion precisely in their capacity of *private issues* and, however long you discuss them, like leopards, they will not change their spots. On the contrary, they are reconfirmed as private and will emerge from their public exposure reinforced in their privacy. After all, every speaker agreed that, as much as they are experienced and lived through privately, so privately these things must be confronted, handled and coped with.

Many influential thinkers (Jürgen Habermas most prominent among them) warn about the prospect of the 'private sphere' being invaded, conquered and colonized by 'the public'. Harking back as they do to the fresh memory of the era which inspired Orwell- or Huxley-style dystopias, voicing such fears may be understood. The premonitions seem, however, to arise from reading the process taking place before our eyes through the wrong pair of spectacles. In fact, a tendency opposite to the warnings seems to be currently in operation – the colonization of the public sphere by issues previously classified as private and unsuitable for public venting.

What is currently happening is not just another renegotiation of the notoriously mobile boundary between the private and the public. What seems to be at stake is a redefinition of the public sphere, as a scene on which private dramas are staged, put on public display and publicly watched. The current definition of 'public interest', promoted by the media yet widely accepted by all or almost all sections of society, is the duty to play out such dramas in public and the right of the public to watch the performance. The social conditions which make such a development unsurprising and even seem 'natural' ought to be evident in the light of the preceding argument; but the consequences of the development are far from having been explored in full. They might be further-reaching than generally understood or accepted.

The consequence arguably most seminal is the demise of 'politics as we know it' – Politics with a capital P, the activity charged with the task of translating private problems into public issues (and vice versa). It is the effort of such translation which is nowadays grinding to a halt. Private problems do not turn into public issues by dint of being vented in public; even under public gaze they do not cease to be private, and what they seem to be accomplishing by being transferred to the public stage is pushing all other, 'non-private' problems out of the public agenda. What are commonly and ever more often perceived as 'public issues' are *private problems of public figures*. The time-honoured question of democratic politics – how useful or detrimental is the way public figures exercise their public duties to the welfare and well-being of their subjects/electors? – has fallen by the board, beckoning to public interests in good society, public justice, or collective responsibility for individual welfare to follow them into oblivion.

Buffetted by a series of 'public scandals' (that is, public disclosures of moral laxities in the private lives of public figures), Tony Blair (as reported by the *Guardian* of 11 January 1999) complained of 'politics diminished to a gossip column' and called the audience to face the alternative: 'We either have the news agenda dominated by scandal and gossip and trivia or by the things that really matter.'[12] Such words cannot but baffle, coming as they do from a politician who daily consults 'focus groups' in the hope of being regularly informed about the grass-root feelings and the 'things that really matter' in the *opinion* of his electors, and whose way of handling the things that really matter to the *conditions* in which his electors live is itself an important factor in the kind of life responsible for that 'diminishing of politics to a gossip column' which he bewails.

The life conditions in question prompt men and women to seek examples, not leaders. They prompt them to expect people in the limelight – all of them and any one of them – to show how 'things that matter' (now confined to their own four walls and locked there) are done. After all, they are told daily that what is wrong with their own lives comes from their own mistakes, has been their own fault and ought to be repaired with their own tools and by their own efforts. No wonder, therefore, if they assume that showing them how to handle the tools and make the efforts is the major – perhaps the only – use of people who pretend to be 'in the know'. They have been told repeatedly by those 'people in the know' that no one else will do the job which could be done only by themselves, by each one of them separately. Why should someone be puzzled, therefore, if for so many men and women it is what the politicians (or other celebrities) do privately that attracts attention and arouses interest? No one among the 'great and mighty', let alone the offended 'public opinion', proposed the impeachment of Bill Clinton for abolishing welfare as a 'federal issue' and so, for all practical purposes, making null and void the collective promise and duty to insure individuals against vagaries of fate notorious for their nasty habit of targeting their blows individually.

In the colourful pageant of broadcast and headlined celebrities, statesmen and stateswomen do not occupy a position of privilege. It does not matter much what are the reasons for that 'knownness' which, according to Boorstin is the cause of celebrity being a celebrity. A place in the limelight is a modality of being in its own right, in which film stars, football high-scorers and ministers of government share in equal measure. One of the requirements that apply to them all is that they are expected – 'have a public duty' – to confess for public consumption and put their private lives on public display, and not to grumble if others do it for them. Once disclosed, such private lives may prove to be unilluminating or downright unattractive: not all private secrets contain lessons which

other people may find useful. Disappointments, however numerous, are unlikely to change confessional habits or dispel the appetite for confessions: after all – let me repeat – the way individual
people define individually their individual problems and try to
tackle them deploying individual skills and resources is the sole
remaining 'public issue' and the sole object of 'public interest'. And
as long as this remains the case, spectators and listeners trained to
rely on their own judgement and effort when seeking enlightenment and guidance will go on looking into the private lives of
others 'like them' with the same zeal and hope with which they
might have looked toward the lessons, homilies and sermons of
visionaries and preachers when they believed that only through
'getting heads together', 'closing ranks' and 'walking in step' could
private miseries be alleviated or cured.

Compulsion turned into addiction

Looking for examples, for counsel and guidance is an addiction:
the more you do it, the more you need to do it and the unhappier
you feel when deprived of fresh supplies of the sought-after drugs.
As a means of quenching thirst, all addictions are self-destructive;
they destroy the possibility of being ever satisfied.

Examples and recipes remain attractive as long as they remain
untested. But hardly any of them delivers on its promise – virtually
every one stops short of the fulfilment it pledged to bring. Even if
any of them proved to be working in just the way which was
expected, the satisfaction would not last long, since in the world of
the consumers possibilities are infinite, and the volume of seductive
goals on offer can never be exhausted. The recipes for the good life
and the gadgets that serve them carry a 'use by' date, but most of
them will fall out of use well before that date, dwarfed, devalued
and stripped of their allurements by the competition of 'new and
improved' offers. In the consumer race the finishing line always
moves faster than the fastest of runners; but most runners forced
onto the track have muscles too flabby and lungs too small to run
fast. And so, as in the annual London Marathon, one may admire
and praise the winners, but what truly counts is staying in the race
to the end. At least the London Marathon has an end, but that
other race – to reach the elusive and ever receding promise of a

trouble-free life – never ends once it is started: I've started, but I may *not* finish.

And so it is the continuation of the running, the gratifying aware-ness of staying in the race, that becomes the true addiction – not any particular prize waiting for those few who may cross the finishing line. None of the prizes is sufficiently satisfying to strip other prizes of their power of attraction, and there are so many other prizes beckoning and alluring because (as yet, always as yet, hopelessly as yet) they are untried. Desire becomes its own purpose, and the sole uncontested and unquestionable purpose. The role of all other purposes, followed up only to be abandoned at the next round and forgotten the round after, is to keep the runner running – after the pattern of 'pace-setters', runners hired by the race managers to run a few rounds only but at the greatest speed they can manage, and then to retire having pulled the other runners to the record-breaking pace, or in the likeness of the auxiliary rockets which, once they have brought the space-ship to the needed velocity, are ejected into space and allowed to disintegrate. In a world in which the range of ends is too wide for comfort and always wider than that of available means, it is to the volume and effectiveness of means that one needs to attend with the greatest care. Staying in the race is the most important of means, indeed the meta-means: the means to keep alive the trust in other means and the demand for other means.

The archetype of that particular race in which every member of a consumer society is running (everything in a consumer society is a matter of choice, except the compulsion to choose – the compul-sion which grows into addiction and so is no longer perceived as compulsion) is the activity of shopping. We stay in the race as long as we shop around, and it is not just the shops or supermarkets or department stores or George Ritzer's 'Temples of Consumption' where we do our shopping. If 'shopping' means scanning the as-sortment of possibilities, examining, touching, feeling, handling the goods on display, comparing their costs with the contents of the wallet or the remaining credit limit of credit cards, putting some of them in the trolley and others back on the shelf – then we shop outside shops as much as inside; we shop in the street and at home, at work and at leisure, awake and in dreams. Whatever we do and whatever name we attach to our activity is a kind of shopping, an activity shaped in the likeness of shopping. The code in which our 'life policy' is scripted is derived from the pragmatics of shopping.

Shopping is not just about food, shoes, cars or furniture items. The avid, never-ending search for new and improved examples and recipes for life is also a variety of shopping, and a most important variety, to be sure, in the light of the twin lessons that our happiness depends on personal competence but that we are (as Michael Parenti put it[13]) personally incompetent, or not as competent as we should and could be if only we tried harder. There are so many areas in which we need to be more competent, and each calls for 'shopping around'. We 'shop' for the skills needed to earn our living and for the means to convince would-be employers that we have them; for the kind of image it would be nice to wear and ways to make others believe that we are what we wear; for ways of making the new friends we want and the ways of getting rid of past friends no longer wanted; for ways of drawing attention and ways to hide from scrutiny; for the means to squeeze most satisfaction out of love and the means to avoid becoming 'dependent' on the loved or loving partner; for ways to earn the love of the beloved and the least costly way of finishing off the union once love has faded and the relationship has ceased to please; for the best expedients of saving money for a rainy day and the most convenient way to spend money before we earn it; for the resources for doing faster the things that are to be done and for things to do in order to fill the time thus vacated; for the most mouth-watering foods and the most effective diet to dispose of the consequences of eating them; for the most powerful hi-fi amplifiers and the most effective headache pills. There is no end to the shopping list. Yet however long the list, the way to opt out of shopping is not on it. And the competence most needed in our world of ostensibly infinite ends is that of skilful and indefatigable shopper.

Present-day consumerism, though, is no longer about satisfying the needs – not even the more sublime, detached (some would say, not quite correctly, 'artificial', 'contrived', 'derivative') needs of identification or the self-assurance as to the degree of 'adequacy'. It has been said that the *spiritus movens* of consumer activity is no longer the measurable set of articulated needs, but *desire* – a much more volatile and ephemeral, evasive and capricious, and essentially non-referential entity than 'needs', a self-begotten and self-propelled motive that needs no other justification or 'cause'.

Despite its successive and always short-lived reifications, desire has itself for its constant object, and for that reason is bound to remain insatiable however high the pile of other (physical or psychical) objects marking its past course may rise.

And yet, whatever its obvious advantages over much less pliable and slower-moving needs, desire would place more constraints on the consumer's readiness to shop than the suppliers of consumer goods found palatable or indeed bearable. After all, it takes time, effort and considerable financial outlay to arouse desire, bring it to the required temperature and channel it in the right direction. Consumers guided by desire must be 'produced', ever anew, and at high cost. Indeed, the production of consumers itself devours an intolerably large fraction of the total costs of production – a fraction which the competition tends to enlarge further, rather than cut down.

But (fortunately for the producers and the merchandisers of consumer commodities) consumerism in its present-day form is not, as Harvie Ferguson suggests, 'founded upon the regulation (stimulation) of desire, but upon the liberation of wishful fantasies'. The notion of desire, Ferguson observes,

> links consumption to self-expression, and to notions of taste and discrimination. The individual expresses himself or herself through their possessions. But for advanced capitalist society, committed to the continuing expansion of production, this is a very limiting psychological framework which ultimately gives way to a quite different psychic 'economy'. The wish replaces desire as the motivating force of consumption.[14]

The history of consumerism is the story of breaking down and discarding the successive 'solid' obstacles which limit the free flight of fantasy and shave the 'pleasure principle' down to the size dictated by the 'reality principle'. The 'need', deemed by nineteenth-century economists to be the very epitome of 'solidity' – inflexible, permanently circumscribed and finite – was discarded and replaced for a time by desire, which was much more 'fluid' and expandable than need because of its half-illicit liaisons with fickle and plastic dreams of the authenticity of an 'inner self' waiting to be expressed. Now it is desire's turn to be discarded. It has outlived its usefulness: having brought consumer addiction to its present state, it can no more set the pace. A more powerful, and above all more versatile stimulant is needed to keep consumer demand on a level with the consumer offer. The 'wish' is that much needed replacement: it completes the liberation of the pleasure principle, purging and disposing of the last residues of the 'reality principle' impediments: the naturally gaseous substance has finally been released from the container. To quote Ferguson once more:

> where the facilitation of desire was founded upon comparison, vanity, envy and the 'need' for self-approbation, nothing underlies the immediacy of the wish. The purchase is casual, unexpected and spontaneous. It has a dream quality of both expressing and fulfilling a wish, and like all wishes, is insincere and childish.[15]

The consumer's body

As I argued in *Life in Fragments* (Polity Press,1996), postmodern society engages its members primarily in their capacity as consumers rather than producers. That difference is seminal.

Life organized around the producer's role tends to be normatively regulated. There is a bottom line to what one needs in order to stay alive and be capable of doing whatever the producer's role may require, but also an upper limit to what one may dream of, desire and pursue while counting on social approval for one's ambitions – that is, without fear of being frowned upon, rebuked and brought into line. Whatever rises above that limit is a luxury, and desiring luxury is a sin. The main concern is therefore that of *conformity*: of settling securely between the bottom line and the upper limit – to 'keep up' (or down, as the case may be) 'with the Joneses'.

Life organized around consumption, on the other hand, must do without norms: it is guided by seduction, ever rising desires and volatile wishes – no longer by normative regulation. No particular 'Joneses' offer a reference point for one's own successful life; a society of consumers is one of universal comparison – and the sky is the only limit. The idea of 'luxury' makes little sense, as the point is to make today's luxuries into tomorrow's necessities, and to reduce the distance between 'today' and 'tomorrow' to the minimum – to 'take the waiting out of wanting'. As there is no norm to transform some desires into needs and to delegitimize other desires as 'false needs', there is no benchmark against which one could measure the standard of 'conformity'. The main concern is therefore that of *adequacy* – of being 'ever ready', of having the ability to rise to the opportunity as it comes, to develop new desires made to the measure of new, previously unheard-of and unexpected allurements, to 'get in' more than before, not to allow the established needs to render new sensations redundant or to restrain the capacity to absorb and experience them.

If the society of producers sets health as the standard which its members ought to meet, the society of consumers brandishes before its members the ideal of *fitness*. The two terms – health and fitness – are often taken to be coterminous and are used synonymously; after all, they both refer to the care of the body, to the state which one wishes one's body to achieve and the regime which the owner of the body should follow to fulfil that wish. To treat the two terms synonymously is, though, a mistake – and not merely for the well-known fact that not all fitness regimes 'are good for one's health' and that what helps one to stay healthy does not necessarily make one fit. Health and fitness belong to two quite different discourses and appeal to very different concerns.

Health, like all other normative concepts of the society of producers, draws and guards the boundary between 'norm' and 'abnormality'. 'Health' is the proper and desirable state of the human body and spirit – a state which (at least in principle) can be more or less exactly described and once described also precisely measured. It refers to a bodily and psychical condition which allows the satisfaction of the demands of the socially designed and assigned role – and those demands tend to be constant and steady. 'To be healthy' means in most cases to be 'employable': to be able to perform properly on the factory floor, to 'carry the load' with which the work may routinely burden the employee's physical and psychical endurance.

The state of 'fitness', on the contrary, is anything but 'solid'; it cannot by its nature be pinned down and circumscribed with any precision. Though it is often taken to be an answer to the question 'How do you feel today?' (if I am 'fit', I will probably answer 'I feel great'), its real test lies for ever in the future: 'being fit' means to have a flexible, absorptive and adjustable body, ready to live through sensations not yet tried and impossible to specify in advance. If health is a 'no more and no less' type of condition, fitness stays permanently open on the side of 'more': it does not refer to any particular standard of bodily capacity, but to its (preferably unlimited) potential of expansion. 'Fitness' means being ready to take in the unusual, the non-routine, the extraordinary – and above all the novel and the surprising. One may almost say that if health is about 'sticking to the norm', fitness is about the capacity to break all norms and leave every already achieved standard behind.

Arriving at an interpersonal norm would be a tall order anyway, since no objective comparison between individual degrees of fitness is feasible. Fitness, unlike health, is about *subjective experience* (in the sense of 'lived' experience, 'felt' experience – not a state or an event that may be observed from outside, verbalized and communicated). Like all subjective states, the experience of 'being fit' is notoriously difficult to articulate in a fashion suitable for interpersonal communication, let alone interpersonal comparison. Satisfaction and pleasure are feelings which cannot be grasped in abstract terms: to be grasped, they need to be 'subjectively experienced' – lived through. You will never know for sure whether your sensations are as deep and exciting, or indeed 'pleasurable', as those of the next person. The pursuit of fitness is a chase after a quarry which one cannot describe until it is reached; however, one has no means to decide that the quarry has indeed been reached, but every reason to suspect that it has not. Life organized around the pursuit of fitness promises a lot of victorious skirmishes, but never the final triumph.

Unlike the care for health, the pursuit of fitness has therefore no natural end. Targets may be set only for the current stage of the never-ending effort – and the satisfaction brought by hitting a set target is but momentary. In the life-long pursuit of fitness there is no time to rest, and all celebration of the success-thus-far is but a short break before another round of hard work. One thing the fitness-seekers know for sure is that they are not fit enough, yet, and that they must keep trying. The pursuit of fitness is the state of perpetual self-scrutiny, self-reproach and self-deprecation, and so also of continuous anxiety.

Health, circumscribed by its standards (quantifiable and measurable, like bodily temperature or blood pressure) and armed with a clear distinction between 'norm' and 'abnormality', should in principle be free from such insatiable anxiety. Again, in principle, it should be clear what is to be done in order to reach the state of health and protect it, under what condition one may declare a person to be 'in good health', or at what point of therapy one is allowed to decide that the state of health has been restored and nothing more needs to be done. Yes – in principle . . .

As a matter of fact, however, the status of all norms, the norm of health included, has, under the aegis of 'liquid' modernity, in a society of infinite and indefinite possibilities, been severely shaken and become fragile. What yesterday was considered normal and thus satisfactory may today be found worrying, or even pathological and calling for remedy. First, ever-new states of the body become legitimate reasons for medical intervention – and the medical therapies on offer do not stay put either. Second, the idea of 'disease', once clearly circumscribed, becomes ever more blurred and misty. Rather than perceived as an exceptional one-off event with a beginning and an end, it tends to be seen as a permanent accompaniment of health, its 'other side' and always present threat: it calls for never-lapsing vigilance and needs to be fought and repelled day and night, seven days a week. Care for health turns into a permanent war against disease. And finally, the meaning of 'a healthy regime of life' does not stand still. The concepts of 'healthy diet' change more quickly than it takes for any of the successively or simultaneously recommended diets to run its course. Nourishment thought to be health-serving or innocuous is announced to have damaging long-term effects before its benign influence can be fully savoured. Therapies and preventive regimes focused on one kind of jeopardy are discovered to be pathogenic in other respects; ever larger proportions of medical intervention are called for by the 'iatrogenic' diseases – the ailments caused by past therapy courses. Almost every cure is strewn with risks, and more cures are needed to heal the consequences of past risk-taking.

All in all, health-care, contrary to its nature, becomes uncannily similar to the pursuit of fitness: continual, never likely to bring full satisfaction, uncertain as to the propriety of its current direction and generating on its way a lot of anxiety.

While health-care becomes more and more like the pursuit of fitness, the latter tries to imitate, usually in vain, what used once to be the basis of health-care's self-confidence: the measurability of the standard of health, and consequently also of the therapeutic progress. This ambition explains for instance the remarkable popularity of weight-watching among the many 'fitness regimes' on offer: the vanishing inches and disappearing ounces are two of the few ostensible gains in fitness which can actually be measured and defined with some degree of precision – just like body temperature in the case of the diagnosis of health. The similarity is, of course, an illusion: just imagine a thermometer with no bottom end to its scale or body temperature that gets better the further it falls.

In the wake of the recent adjustments to the ruling 'fitness' model, the lid tends to be taken off the expansion of health care (including self-care), so that, as Ivan Illich has recently suggested, 'pursuit of health has itself become the prevailing pathogenic factor'. No longer does diagnostics take the individual as its object: its true object in a rising number of cases is the spread of probabilities, an estimate of what may follow the condition in which the diagnosed patient has been found.

Health is increasingly identified with the optimalization of risks. This is, at any rate, what the denizens of the consumer society drilled to work for their bodily fitness expect and wish their doctors to do – and what makes them angry with, and hostile to the doctors who fail to oblige. In a precedent-setting case a doctor in Tübingen was convicted for telling the expectant mother that the probability of the child being born malformed was 'not too great', instead of quoting the probability statistics.[16]

Shopping as a rite of exorcism

One might surmise that the fears haunting the 'body owner' obsessed with unattainable heights of fitness and ever less clearly defined, ever more 'fitness-like' health, would prompt caution and circumspection, moderation and austerity – attitudes utterly out of tune with, and potentially disastrous for, the logic of consumer society. This would be, however, an erroneous conclusion. Exorcizing the inner demons requires a positive attitude and a good deal of action – not a withdrawal or quiescence. Like almost all action undertaken in a consumer society, this one is a costly affair; it requires a lot of special gear and tools which only the consumer market can supply. The 'my body a besieged fortress' attitude does not lead to asceticism, abstinence or renunciation; if anything, it means consuming more – but consuming special 'healthy' foods, commercially supplied. Before it came to be shunned for its damaging side-effects and eventually withdrawn from the market, the most popular among the weight watchers was a drug called Xenilin, advertised under the slogan 'Eat more – weigh less'. According to Barry Glassner's calculations, in one year – 1987 – the body-conscious Americans spent $74 billion on diet foods, $5 billion on health clubs, $2.7 billion on vitamins and $738 million on exercise equipment.[17]

There are, in short, more than enough reasons to 'shop around'. Any reductive explanation of the shopping obsession narrowed down to a single cause risks missing the point. The common interpretations of compulsive shopping as a manifestation of the post-modern value revolution, the tendency to represent the shopping addiction as an overt manifestation of dormant materialistic and hedonistic instincts, or as a product of 'commercial conspiracy' that is an artificial (and artful) incitement to pursue pleasure as the foremost purpose of life, capture at best only part of the truth. Another part, and the necessary complement of all such explanations, is that the shopping compulsion-turned-into-addiction is an uphill struggle against acute, nerve-breaking uncertainty and the annoying, stultifying feeling of insecurity.

As T. H. Marshall remarked on another occasion, when many people simultaneously run in the same direction, two questions need to be asked: what are they running *after* and what are they running *from*. Consumers may be running after pleasurable – tactile, visual or olfactory – sensations, or after the delights of the palate, promised by colourful and glittering objects displayed on the supermarket shelves or department-store hangers, or after the deeper, even more comforting sensations promised by a session with a counselling expert. But they are also trying to find an escape from the agony called insecurity. They want to be, for once, free from the fears of mistake, neglect or sloppiness. They want to be, for once, sure, confident, self-assured and trusting; and the awesome virtue of the objects they find when shopping around is that they come (or so it seems for a time) complete with the promise of certainty.

Whatever else compulsive/addictive shopping may be, it is also a daytime ritual to exorcize the gruesome apparitions of uncertainty and insecurity which keep haunting the nights. It is, indeed, a *daily* ritual: exorcisms need to be repeated daily, since hardly anything is put on the supermarket shelves without being stamped with a 'best before' date, and since the kind of certainty available for sale in the shops does little to cut the roots of the insecurity which prompted the shopper to visit the shops in the first place. What matters, though, and allows the game to go on – its evident inconclusiveness and lack of prospects notwithstanding – is the wondrous quality of exorcisms: they are effective and gratifying not so much for chasing the ghosts away (which they seldom do) as for the very fact of being performed. As long as the art of exorcism is alive, the spectres cannot claim invincibility. And in the society of individualized consumers, everything that needs to be done is to be done in a DIY fashion. What else besides shopping meets so well the prerequisites of DIY exorcism?

Free to shop – or so it seems

People of our times, Albert Camus noted, suffer from not being able to possess the world completely enough:

> Except for vivid moments of fulfilment, all reality for them is incomplete. Their actions escape them in the form of other actions, return, in unexpected guises, to judge them and disappear like the water Tantalus longed to drink, into some still undiscovered orifice.

This is what each of us knows from introspective insight: this is what our own biographies, when scrutinized in retrospect, teach us about the world we inhabit. Not so, however, when we look around: as to the other people we know, and particularly such people as we know of – 'seen from a distance, [their] existence seems to possess a coherence and a unity which they cannot have, in reality, but which seems evident to the spectator'. This, of course, is an optical illusion. The distance (that is, the paucity of our knowledge) blurs the details and effaces everything that fits ill into the *Gestalt*. Illusion or not, we tend to see other people's lives as works of art. And having seen them this way, we struggle to do the same: 'Everyone tries to make his life a work of art.'[18]

That work of art which we want to mould out of the friable stuff of life is called 'identity'. Whenever we speak of identity, there is at the back of our minds a faint image of harmony, logic, consistency: all those things which the flow of our experience seems – to our perpetual despair – so grossly and abominably to lack. The search for identity is the ongoing struggle to arrest or slow down the flow, to solidify the fluid, to give form to the formless. We struggle to deny or at least to cover up the awesome fluidity just below the thin wrapping of the form; we try to avert our eyes from sights which they cannot pierce or take in. Yet far from slowing the flow, let alone stopping it, identities are more like the spots of crust hardening time and again on the top of volcanic lava which melt and dissolve again before they have time to cool and set. So there is need for another trial, and another – and they can be attempted only by clinging desperately to things solid and tangible and thus promising duration, whether or not they fit or belong together and whether or not they give ground for expecting that they will stay together once put together. In the words of Deleuze and Guattari, 'Desire constantly couples continuous flow and partial objects that are by nature fragmentary and fragmented.'[19]

Identities seem fixed and solid only when seen, in a flash, from outside. Whatever solidity they might have when contemplated from the inside of one's own biographical experience appears fragile, vulnerable, and constantly torn apart by shearing forces which lay bare its fluidity and by cross-currents which threaten to rend in pieces and carry away any form they might have acquired.

The experienced, lived identity could only be held together with the adhesive of fantasy, perhaps day-dreaming. Yet, given the stubborn evidence of biographical experience, any stronger glue – a substance with more fixing power than easy-to-dissolve-and-wipe-out fantasy – would seem as repugnant a prospect as the absence of day-dreams. This is precisely why fashion, as Efrat Tseëlon observed, fits the bill so well: just the right stuff, no weaker, yet no stronger either, than the fantasies are. It provides 'ways of exploring limits without commitment to action, and . . . without suffering the consequences'. 'In fairy tales', Tseëlon reminds us, 'the dream attire is the key to bringing out the true identity of the princess, as the fairy godmother knows only too well when she dresses Cinderella for the ball.'[20]

Given the intrinsic volatility and unfixity of all or most identities, it is the ability to 'shop around' in the supermarket of identities, the degree of genuine or putative consumer freedom to select one's identity and to hold to it as long as desired, that becomes the royal road to the fulfilment of identity fantasies. Having that ability, one is free to make and unmake identities at will. Or so it seems.

In a consumer society, sharing in consumer dependency – in the *universal* dependency on shopping – is the condition *sine qua non* of all *individual* freedom; above all, of the freedom to be different, to 'have identity'. In a flash of brash sincerity (though at the same time winking at the sophisticated clients who know what the game is about and how it is run), a TV commercial shows a crowd of women with a variety of hair-styles and hair colours, while the captions comment: 'All unique; all individual; all choose X' (X being the advertised brand of hair conditioner). The mass-produced appliance is the tool of individual variety. Identity – 'unique' and 'individual' – can be carved only in the substance everyone buys and can get hold of only through shopping. You gain independence by surrender. When in the film *Elizabeth* the Queen of England decides to 'change her personality', become 'her father's daughter' and force the courtiers to respect her commands, she does so by changing her hair-style, covering her face with a thick layer of craftsman-made paints and donning craftsman-made head jewellery.

The extent to which freedom grounded in consumer choice, notably consumers' freedom of self-identification through the use of mass-produced and merchandized commodities, is genuine or putative is a notoriously moot question. Such freedom cannot do without market-supplied gadgets and substances. But given that, how broad is the happy purchasers' range of fantasy and experimentation?

Their dependency, to be sure, is not confined to the act of purchase. Remember, for instance, the formidable power which the mass media exercise over popular – collective and individual – imagination. Powerful, 'more real than reality' images on ubiquitous screens set the standards for reality and for its evaluation, as well as for the urge to make the 'lived' reality more palatable. The desired life tends to be life 'as seen on TV'. Life on screen dwarfs and strips of its charm the life lived: it is the lived life which seems unreal, and will go on looking and feeling unreal as long as it is not refashioned in its own turn into screenable images. (To complete the reality of one's own life, one needs to 'camcord' it first, using for that purpose, of course, the videotape – that comfortingly erasable stuff, forever ready for the effacement of old recordings and inscribing new ones.) As Christopher Lasch puts it: 'Modern life is so thoroughly mediated by electronic images that we cannot help responding to others as if their actions – and our own – were being recorded and simultaneously transmitted to an unseen audience or stored up for close scrutiny at some later time.'[21]

In a later book[22] Lasch reminds his readers that 'the older meaning of identity refers both to persons and to things. Both have lost their solidity in modern society, their definiteness and continuity.' Lasch implies that in this universal 'melting of all solids' the initiative belonged to the things; and, because things are the symbolic trappings of identities and the tools of identification efforts, people soon followed suit. Referring to Emma Rothschild's famous study of the automobile industry, Lasch suggests that

> Alfred Sloan's innovations in marketing – the annual model change, constant upgrading of the product, efforts to associate it with social status, the deliberate inculcation of a boundless appetite for change – constituted the necessary counterpart of Henry Ford's innovation in production ... Both tended to discourage enterprise and independent thinking and to make the individual distrust his own judgment, even in matters of taste. His own untutored preferences, it appeared, might lag behind current fashion, they too needed to be periodically upgraded.

Alfred Sloane was a pioneer of what was later to become a universal trend. Commodity production as a whole today replaces 'the world of durable objects' 'with disposable products designed for immediate obsolescence'. The consequences of that replacement have been perceptively described by Jeremy Seabrook:

> It is not so much that capitalism has delivered the goods to the people, as that the people have been increasingly delivered to the goods; that is to say, that the very character and sensibility of the people have been re-worked, re-fashioned, in such a way that they assort approximately ... with the commodities, experiences and sensations. ... the selling of which alone gives shape and significance to our lives.[23]

In a world in which deliberately unstable things are the raw building material of identities that are by necessity unstable, one needs to be constantly on the alert; but above all one needs to guard one's own flexibility and speed of readjustment to follow swiftly the changing patterns of the world 'out there'. As Thomas Mathiesen recently observed, Bentham's and Foucault's powerful metaphor of Panopticon no longer grasps the ways power is working. We have moved now, so Mathiesen suggests, from a Panopticon-style to a *Synopticon*-style society: the tables have been reversed, and it is now the many who watch the few.[24] Spectacles take the place of surveillance without losing any of the disciplining power of their predecessor. Obedience to standards (a pliable and exquisitely adjustable obedience to eminently flexible standards, let me add) tends to be achieved nowadays through enticement and seduction rather than by coercion – and it appears in the disguise of the exercise of free will, rather than revealing itself as an external force.

These truths need to be restated again and again, since the corpse of the 'romantic concept of the self', guessing a deep inner essence hiding beneath all the external and superficial appearances, tends today to be artificially reanimated by the joint efforts of what Paul Atkinson and David Silverman have aptly dubbed 'the interview society' ('relying pervasively on face-to-face interviews to reveal the personal, the private self of the subject') and of a large part of present-day social research (which aims at 'getting down to the subjective truth of the self' through provoking and then dissecting personal narratives in the hope of finding in them a revelation of the inner truth). Atkinson and Silverman object to that practice:

> we do not in the social sciences reveal selves by collecting narratives, we create selfhood through narrative of biographical work . . .
> The desire for revelation and revelations of desire furnish the appearance of authenticity even when the very possibility of authenticity is under question.[25]

The possibility in question is, indeed, highly questionable. Numerous studies show that personal narratives are merely rehearsals of public rhetoric designed by the public media to 'represent subjective truths'. But the inauthenticity of the allegedly authentic self is thoroughly covered up by the spectacles of sincerity – the public rituals of in-depth interviews and public confessions of which chat-shows are the most prominent, though by no means the only examples. Ostensibly, the spectacles are meant to give vent to the stirrings of the 'inner selves' striving to be let out; in fact, they are the vehicles of the consumer society version of a sentimental education': they display and stamp with public acceptability the yarn of emotive states and their expressions from which the 'thoroughly personal identities' are to be woven.

As Harvie Ferguson put it recently in his inimitable way,

in the postmodern world all distinctions become fluid, boundaries dissolve, and everything can just as well appear to be its opposite; irony becomes the perpetual sense that things could be somewhat different, though never fundamentally or radically different.

In such a world concerns with identity tend to acquire an entirely new gloss:

> the 'age of irony' passed to be replaced by an 'age of glamour' in which appearance is consecrated as the only reality . . .
> Modernity thus moves through a period of 'authentic' selfhood to one of 'ironic' selfhood to a contemporary culture of what might be termed 'associative' selfhood – a continuous 'loosening' of the tie between 'inner' soul and the 'outer' form of social relation . . . Identities, thus, are continuous oscillations . . .[26]

This is what the present condition looks like when put under the microscope of cultural analysts. The picture of publicly produced inauthenticity may be true; the arguments supporting its truth are indeed overwhelming. But it is not the truth of that picture that determines the impact of the 'spectacles of sincerity'. It is how the contrived necessity of identity building and rebuilding feels, how it is perceived from 'inside', how it is 'lived through', that matters. Whether genuine or putative to the eye of the analyst, the loose, 'associative' status of identity, the opportunity to 'shop around', to pick and shed one's 'true self', to 'be on the move', has come in present-day consumer society to signify freedom. Consumer choice is now a value in its own right; the activity of choosing matters more than what is being chosen, and the situations are praised or censured, enjoyed or resented depending on the range of choices on display.

The life of a chooser will always be a mixed blessing, though, even if (or rather because) the range of choices is wide and the volume of possible new experience seems infinite. That life is fraught with risks: uncertainty is bound to remain for ever a rather nasty fly in the otherwise tasty ointment of free choice. In addition (and this is an important addition) the balance between shopping addicts' joy and misery depends on factors other than merely the range of choices on display. Not all choices on display are realistic; and the proportion of realistic choices is not the function of the number of items to choose from, but of the volume of resources at the disposal of the chooser.

When resources are plentiful one can always hope, rightly or wrongly, to stay 'on top of' or 'ahead of' things, to be able to catch up with the fast-moving targets; one might then be inclined to play down the risks and insecurity and assume that the profusion of choices compensates many times over for the discomforts of living in the dark, of never being sure when and where the struggle ends or whether it has an end at all. It is the running itself which is exhilarating, and, however tiring it may be, the track is a more enjoyable place than the finishing line. It is to this situation that the old proverb 'It is better to travel hopefully than to arrive' applies. The arrival, the definite end to all choice, seems much more dull and considerably more frightening than the prospect of tomorrow's choices cancelling the choices of today. Solely the desiring is desirable – hardly ever its satisfaction.

One would expect that the enthusiasm for the running would wilt together with the strength of the muscles – that the love of risk and adventure would fade as the volume of resources shrinks and the chance to choose a truly desirable option appears increasingly nebulous. Such an expectation is bound to be refuted, though, since the runners are many and different, but the track is one for them all. As Jeremy Seabrook points out,

> The poor do not inhabit a separate culture from the rich. They must live in the same world that has been contrived to the benefit of those with money. And their poverty is aggravated by economic growth, just as it is intensified by recession and non-growth.[27]

In a synoptical society of shopping/watching addicts, the poor cannot avert their eyes; there is nowhere they could avert their eyes to. The greater the freedom on the screen and the more seductive the temptations beckoning from the shopping-mall displays, the deeper the sense of impoverished reality, the more overwhelming becomes the desire to taste, if only for a fleeting moment, the bliss of choosing. The more choices the rich seem to have, the less bearable to all is a life without choosing.

Divided, we shop

Paradoxically, though by no means unexpectedly, the kind of freedom which the society of shopping addicts has elevated to the uppermost rank of value – freedom translated above all as the plenitude of consumer choice and as the ability to treat any life-decision as a consumer choice – has a much more devastating effect on the unwilling bystanders than on those for whom it is ostensibly meant. The life-style of the resourceful elite, of the masters of the choosing art, undergoes a fateful change in the course of its electronic processing. It trickles down the social hierarchy, filtered through the channels of electronic Synopticon and shrinking volumes of resources, as a caricature or a monstrous mutant. The ultimate product of the 'trickling' is stripped of most of the pleasures which the original promised to deliver – instead laying bare its destructive potential.

The freedom to treat the whole of life as one protracted shopping spree means casting the world as a warehouse overflowing with consumer commodities. Given the profusion of tempting offers, the pleasure-generating potential of any commodity tends to be rapidly exhausted. Fortunately for *resourceful* customers, their resourcefulness insures them against such unpalatable consequences of commodification. They may as easily discard the possessions which they no longer want as they could obtain those which they once desired. They are insured against rapid ageing and the in-built obsolescence of desires and their transient satisfactions.

Resourcefulness means the freedom to pick and choose, but also – and perhaps most importantly – the freedom from bearing the consequences of wrong choices, and so freedom from the least appetizing attributes of the life of choosing. For instance, 'plastic sex', 'confluent love' and 'pure relationships', the aspects of commodification or consumerization of human partnerships, were portrayed by Anthony Giddens as the vehicles of emancipation and a warrant of a new happiness that comes in its wake – the new, unprecedented scale of individual autonomy and freedom to choose. Whether this is indeed true, and nothing but true, for the mobile elite of the rich and mighty is debatable. Even in their case one can support Giddens's assertion whole-heartedly only if one focuses on the stronger and more resourceful members of partnerships, which necessarily include also the weaker, not so lavishly endowed with the resources needed to follow freely their desires (not to mention the children – these involuntary, though lasting consequences of partnerships, who hardly ever view the breakdown of marriage as a manifestation of their own freedom). Changing identity may be a private affair, but it always includes cutting off certain bonds and cancelling certain obligations; those on the receiving side are seldom consulted, let alone given the chance to exercise free choice.

And yet, even if one takes into account such 'secondary effects' of 'pure relationships', one can still argue that in the case of the high and mighty the customary divorce settlements and financial provisions for children go some way towards alleviating the insecurity endemic to until-further-notice partnerships, and that whatever insecurity remains is not an excessive price to pay for the right to 'cut one's losses' and avoid the need for an eternal repentance for once-committed sins or errors. But there is little doubt that when 'trickled down' to the poor and powerless, the new-style partnership with its fragility of marital contract and the 'purification' of the union of all but the 'mutual satisfaction' function spawns much misery, agony and human suffering and an ever-growing volume of broken, loveless and prospectless lives.

To sum up: the mobility and the flexibility of identification which characterize the 'shopping around' type of life are not so much vehicles of *emancipation* as the instruments of the *redistribution of freedoms*. They are for that reason mixed blessings – enticing and desired as much as repelling and feared, and arousing most contradictory sentiments. They are highly ambivalent values which tend to generate incoherent and quasi-neurotic reactions. As Yves Michaud, a philosopher at the Sorbonne, puts it, 'With the excess of opportunity, grow the threats of destructuration, fragmentation and disarticulation.'[28] The task of self-identification has sharply disruptive side-effects. It becomes the focus of conflicts and triggers mutually incompatible drives. Since the task shared by all has to be performed by each under sharply different conditions, it divides human situations and prompts cut-throat competition rather than unifying a human condition inclined to generate co-operation and solidarity.

3

Time/Space

George Hazeldon, a British-born architect settled in South Africa, has a dream: a city unlike ordinary cities, full of ominous-looking strangers oozing from dark corners, creeping out of mean streets and leaking from notoriously rough districts. The city of Hazeldon's dream is more like an updated, high-tech version of the medieval town sheltering behind its thick walls, turrets, moats and draw-bridges, a town fenced off securely from the world's risks and dangers. A city made to the measure of the individuals who wish to manage and monitor their togetherness. Something, as he said himself, not unlike Mont-Saint-Michel, simultaneously a cloister and an inaccessible, closely guarded fortress.

As anyone looking at Hazeldon's blueprints would agree, the 'cloister' part has been imagined by their draftsman after the like-ness of Rabelais's Thélème, that city of compulsory joy and amuse-ment, where happiness is the sole commandment, rather than the hideaway of other-worldly, self-immolating, pious, praying and fasting ascetics. The 'fortress' part, for a change, is quite genuine. Heritage Park, the city Hazeldon is about to build from scratch on 500 acres of empty land not far from Cape Town, is to stand out from other towns for its self-enclosure: high-voltage electric fen-cing, the electronic surveillance of access roads, barriers all along the way and heavily armed guards.

If you can afford to buy yourself into a Heritage Park residence, you may spend a good deal of your life away from the risks and dangers of the turbulent, inhospitable and frightening wilderness that begins just on the other side of the township's gates. Everything that gracious living needs in order to be complete and wholly satisfying will be provided for: Heritage Park will have its own shops, churches, restaurants, theatres, recreation grounds, forests, central park, salmon-filled lakes, playgrounds, jogging tracks, sports fields and tennis courts – and enough spare sites to add whatever the changing fashion of a decent life may demand in the future. Hazeldon is quite outspoken when it comes to explaining the advantages of Heritage Park over the places where most people nowadays live:

> Today the first question is security. Like it or not, it's what makes the difference . . . When I grew up in London you had a community. You wouldn't do anything wrong because everyone knew you and they'd tell your mum and dad . . . We want to re-create that here, a community which doesn't have to worry.[1]

So this is what it is all about: for the price of a house in Heritage Park you will buy your entry to a *community*. 'Community' is these days the last relic of the old-time utopias of the good society; it stands for whatever has been left of the dreams of a better life shared with better neighbours all following better rules of cohabitation. For the utopia of harmony slimmed down, realistically, to the size of the immediate neighbourhood. No wonder 'community' is a good selling point. No wonder either that in the prospectus distributed by George Hazeldon, the land developer, community has been brought into focus as an indispensable, yet elsewhere missing, supplement to the good restaurants and picturesque jogging courses that other towns also offer.

Please note, however, what the sense of that sense-giving communal togetherness is. The community Hazeldon remembers from his London childhood years and wants to re-create in the virgin land of South Africa is first and foremost, if not solely, a territory closely surveilled, where those who do what the others may dislike and are for that reason resented are promptly punished and brought into line – while loiterers, vagabonds and other intruders who 'do not belong here' are either refused entry or rounded up and chased away. The one difference between the fondly remembered past and its updated replica is that what the community of Hazeldon's childhood memories achieved by using their own eyes, tongues and hands, matter-of-factly and without much thinking, in Heritage Park is to be entrusted to hidden TV cameras and dozens of hired gun-carrying guards checking passes at the security gates and discreetly (or ostentatiously, if need be) patrolling the streets.

A group of psychiatrists from the Victorian Institute of Forensic Mental Health in Australia have warned recently that 'more and more people are falsely claiming to be the victims of stalkers, using up credibility and public money', money which, as the authors of the report postulate, 'should go to genuine sufferers'.[2] Some of the 'false sufferers' investigated were diagnosed as victims of 'severe mental disorders', 'thinking they were being stalked in their delusion that everybody was conspiring against them'.

We may comment on the psychiatrists' observations that belief in other people's conspiracy against ourselves is by no means novel; surely it has tormented selected humans in all times and at all corners of the globe. Never and nowhere was there a shortage of people eager to find a logic to their unhappiness, humiliating defeats and life frustrations by pinning the blame on someone's malevolent intentions and fiendish plots. What is truly novel is that it is the *stalkers* (in company with prowlers and other loiterers, characters from outside the place through which they move) who carry the blame now, deputizing for the devil, incubi, evil spirits, hobgoblins, the evil eye, mischievous gnomes, witches or reds under the beds. If 'false sufferers' may 'use up public credibility', it is because 'stalker' has already become a common and popular name for the ambient fears that haunt our contemporaries; and so the ubiquitous presence of stalkers has become credible and the fear of being stalked widely shared. And if people *falsely* obsessed with the threat of being stalked can 'use up public money', it is because public money has already been set aside in quantities that rise year by year for the purpose of tracing and chasing the stalkers, the prowlers and other updated editions of that modern scare, the *mobile vulgus* – the inferior kind of people on the move, dribbling or gushing into places where only the right kind of people should have the right to be – and because the defence of stalked streets, like the exorcizing of haunted houses once was, has been recognized as a worthy goal and the proper way to protect the protection-needing people against the fears and the dangers which make them jumpy, nervous, diffident and frightened.

Quoting Mike Davis's *City of Quartz* (1990), Sharon Zukin

describes the new look of Los Angeles public spaces reshaped by the security concerns of the residents and their elected or appointed custodians: 'Helicopters buzz the skies over ghetto neighbourhords, police hassle teenagers as putative gang members, homeowners buy into the type of armed defense they can afford . . . or have nerve enough to use.' The 1960s and early 1970s were, Zukin says, 'a watershed in the institutionalization of urban fear'.

> Voters and elites – a broadly conceived middle class in the United States – could have faced the choice of approving government policies to eliminate poverty, manage ethnic competition, and integrate everyone into common public institutions. Instead, they chose to buy protection, fuelling the growth of the private security industry.

The most tangible danger to what she calls 'public culture' Zukin finds in 'the politics of everyday fear'. The blood-curdling and nerve-breaking spectre of 'unsafe streets' keeps people away from public spaces and turns them away from seeking the art and the skills needed to share public life.

> 'Getting tough' on crime by building more prisons and imposing the death penalty are all too common answers to the politics of fear. 'Lock up the whole population,' I heard a man say on the bus, at a stroke reducing the solution to its ridiculous extreme. Another answer is to privatize and militarize public space – making streets, parks, and even shops more secure but less free . . . [3]

Community defined by its closely watched borders rather than its contents; 'defence of the community' translated as the hiring of armed gatekeepers to control the entry; stalker and prowler promoted to the rank of public enemy number one; paring public areas down to 'defensible' enclaves with selective access; separation in lieu of the negotiation of life in common, rounded up by the criminalization of residual difference – these are the principal dimensions of the current evolution of urban life.

When strangers meet strangers

In Richard Sennett's classic definition, a city is 'a human settlement in which strangers are likely to meet'.[4] This means, let me add, that strangers are likely to meet in their capacity of strangers, and likely to emerge as strangers from the chance encounter which ends as abruptly as it started. Strangers meet in a fashion that befits strangers; a meeting of strangers is unlike the meetings of kin, friends, or acquaintances – it is, by comparison, a *mis*-meeting. In the meeting of strangers there is no picking up at the point where the last encounter stopped, no filling in on the interim trials and tribulations or joys and delights, no shared recollections: nothing to fall back on and to go by in the course of the present encounter. The meeting of strangers is *an event without a past*. More often than not, it is also *an event without a future* (it is expected to be, hoped to be, free of a future), a story most certainly '*not* to be continued', a one-off chance, to be consummated in full while it lasts and on the spot, without delay and without putting the unfinished business off to another occasion. Like the spider whose entire world is enclosed in the web it spins out of its own abdomen, the sole support which strangers-in-meeting may count on must be woven from the thin and loose yarn of their looks, words and gestures. At the time of the meeting, there is no room for trial and error, no learning from mistakes and no hope of another go.

What follows is that urban living calls for a rather special and quite sophisticated type of skill, a whole family of skills which Sennett listed under the rubric of 'civility', that is

> the activity which protects people from each other and yet allows them to enjoy each other's company. Wearing a mask is the essence of civility. Masks permit pure sociability, detached from the circumstances of power, malaise, and private feelings of those who wear them. Civility has as its aim the shielding of others from being burdened with oneself.[5]

This aim is, of course, pursued in the hope of reciprocation. Shielding others from being unduly burdened by refraining from interfering with their ways makes sense as long as one may expect similar generosity of self-restraint from the others. Civility, like language, cannot be 'private'. Before it becomes the individually learned and privately practised art, civility must first be a feature of the social setting. It is the urban environment which must be 'civil', if its inhabitants are to learn the difficult skills of civility.

What does it mean, though, for the urban environment to be 'civil', and so to be a site hospitable to the individual practice of civility? It means, first and foremost, the provision of spaces which people may share as *public personae* – without being nudged, pressed or cajoled to take off their masks and 'let themselves go', 'express themselves', confess their inner feelings and put on display their intimate thoughts, dreams and worries. But it also means a city presenting itself to its residents as a common good which cannot be reduced to the aggregate of individual purposes and as a shared task which cannot be exhausted by a multitude of individual pursuits, as a form of life with a vocabulary and logic all its own and its own agenda, which is (and is bound to remain) longer and richer than the fullest list of individual concerns and cravings – so that 'wearing a public mask' is an act of engagement and participation rather than one of noncommitment, and withdrawal of the 'true self', opting out from intercourse and mutual involvement, manifesting the wish for being let alone and going it alone.

There are numerous sites in contemporary cities which pass under the name of 'public spaces'. They come in many kinds and sizes, but most of them fall into one of two broad categories. Each category departs from the ideal model of *civil* space in two opposite, yet complementary directions.

The place called La Défense, a huge square on the right bank of the Seine, conceived, commissioned and built by François Mitterand (as a lasting monument of his presidency, in which the splendour and grandeur of the office was carefully disconnected from the personal weaknesses and failings of its incumbent), embodies all the traits of the first of the two categories of the public, yet emphatically not 'civil' urban space. What strikes the visitor to La Défense is first and foremost the inhospitality of the place: everything within sight inspires awe yet discourages staying. Fantastically shaped buildings which encircle the huge and empty square are meant to be looked *at*, not *in*: wrapped from top to bottom in reflective glass, they seem to have neither windows nor entry doors opening towards the square; ingeniously, they manage to turn their backs to the square they face. They are imperious and impervious to the eye – imperious *because* impervious, these two qualities complementing and reinforcing each other. These hermetically sealed fortresses/hermitages are in the place but not of it – and they prompt everyone lost in the flat vastness of the square to follow their example and feel likewise. Nothing mitigates, let alone interrupts the uniform and monotonous emptiness of the square. There are no benches on which to rest, no trees beneath which to hide from the scorching sun and to cool off in the shade. (There is, to be sure, a group of geometrically arranged benches on the far side of the expanse; they are set on a flat platform raised a few feet above the flatness of the square – a stage-like platform, whose staginess would make the act of sitting down and resting into a spectacle for all the others who, unlike the sitters, *have some business* to be here.) Time and again, with the dull regularity of the Metro time-table, those others – ant-like files of pedestrians in a hurry – emerge from beneath the ground, stretch over the stony pavement separating the Metro exit from one of the shining monsters encircling (besieging) the square and fast disappear from view. And then the place is empty again – until the next train arrives.

The second category of public yet non-civil space is meant to serve the consumers or, rather, to transubstantiate the city resident into a consumer. In the words of Liisa Uusitalo, 'Consumers often share physical spaces of consumption such as concert or exhibition halls, tourist resorts, sport activity sites, shopping malls and cafeterias, without having any actual social interaction.'[6] Such spaces encourage action, not *inter*-action. Sharing physical space with other actors engaged in a similar activity adds importance to the action, stamps it with the 'approval of numbers' and so corroborates its sense, justifies it without the need to argue. Any inter-action between the actors would, however, keep them away from the actions in which they are individually engaged and would be a liability to each, not an asset. It would add nothing to the pleasures of shopping while distracting mind and body from the task in hand.

The task is consumption, and consumption is an utterly, irre-deemably *individual* pastime, a string of sensations which can be experienced – lived through – only subjectively. The crowds filling the interiors of George Ritzer's 'temples of consumption' are gatherings, not congregations; clusters, not squads; aggregates, not totalities. However crowded they may be, there is nothing 'collective' in the places of collective consumption. To deploy Althusser's memorable phrase, whoever enters such spaces is 'interpellated' qua individual, called to suspend or tear up the bonds and shed loyalties or put them on a side burner.

Encounters, unavoidable in a crowded space, interfere with the purpose. They need to be brief and shallow: no longer and not

deeper than the actor wishes them to be. The place is well protected against those likely to break this rule – all sorts of intruders,
meddlers, spoilsports and other busybodies who would interfere
with the consumer's or shopper's splendid isolation. The well supervised, properly surveilled and guarded temple of consumption
is an island of order, free from beggars, loiterers, stalkers and
prowlers – or at least expected and assumed to be so. People do not
flock to these temples in order to talk and sociate. Whatever company they may wish to enjoy (or are willing to tolerate) they carry
with them, like snails carry their homes.

Emic places, phagic places, non-places, empty spaces

Whatever may happen inside the temple of consumption has little
or no bearing on the rhythm and tenor of daily life flowing 'outside
the gate'. Being in a shopping mall feels like 'being elsewhere'.[7]
Trips to the consumption places differ from Bakhtin's carnivals,
which also entailed the experience of 'being transported': shopping
trips are primarily voyages in space, and travels in time only sec-
ondarily.

Carnival was the same city transformed, more exactly a time
interlude during which the city was transformed before falling
back into its routine quotidianity. For a strictly defined stretch of
time, but a time cyclically returning, the carnival uncovered the
'other side' of daily reality, a side which stayed constantly within
reach but was normally concealed from view and barred from
touching. The memory of discovery and the anticipation of other
sightings yet to come did not allow the awareness of that 'other
side' to be completely suppressed.

A trip to the temple of consumption is quite another matter. To
go for such a trip is like being transported to another world, rather
than witnessing the wondrous transubstantiation of the familiar
one. The temple of consumption (in sharp distinction from the
'corner grocery shop' of yore) may be in the city (if not erected,
symbolically, outside the city limits, off a motorway), but is not a
part of it; not the ordinary world temporarily transmogrified, but a
'completely other' world. What makes it 'other' is not the reversal,
denial or suspension of the rules that govern quotidianity, as in the

case of the carnival, but the display of the mode of being which quotidianity either precludes or strives to achieve but in vain – and which few people ever hope to experience in places they daily inhabit.

Ritzer's metaphor of the 'temple' is apt; the shopping/consuming spaces are indeed temples for the pilgrims – definitely not meant to accommodate the black masses held annually by carnival revellers in their local parishes. Carnival showed that reality is not as hard as it seems and that the city may be transformed; temples of consumption reveal nothing of the nature of daily reality except its dull sturdiness and impregnability. The temple of consumption, like Michel Foucault's 'boat', 'is a floating piece of space, a place without a place, that exists by itself, that is closed in on itself and at the same time is given over to the infinity of the sea';[8] it can accomplish that 'giving itself to infinity' thanks to sailing away from the home port and keeping its distance.

That self-enclosed 'place without a place', unlike all the places occupied or traversed daily, is also a *purified* space. Not that it has been cleansed of variety and difference, which constantly threatens other places with pollution and muddle and casts cleanliness and transparency outside the reach of those who use them; on the contrary, shopping/consuming places owe a great part of their magnetic power of attraction to the colourful, kaleidoscopic variety of sensory sensations on offer. But the differences inside, unlike the differences outside, are tamed, sanitized, guaranteed to come free of dangerous ingredients – and so be unthreatening. They can be enjoyed without fear: once the risk has been taken out of the adventure, what is left is pure, unalloyed and uncontaminated amusement. Shopping/consuming places offer what no 'real reality' outside may deliver: the near-perfect balance between freedom and security.

Inside their temples the shoppers/consumers may find, moreover, what they zealously, yet in vain, seek outside: the comforting feeling of belonging – the reassuring impression of being part of a community. As Sennett suggests, the absence of difference, the 'We are all alike' feeling, the 'No need to negotiate since we are all of the same mind' assumption, are the deepest meanings of the 'community' idea and the ultimate cause of its attraction, known to rise in proportion to the plurality and multi-vocality of the life-setting. We may say that 'community' is a short-cut to togetherness, and to a kind of togetherness which hardly ever occurs in 'real life': a togetherness of sheer likeness, of the 'us who are all the same' kind; a togetherness which for this reason is unproblematic, calling for no effort and no vigilance, truly pre-ordained; a kind of togetherness which is not a task but 'the given', and *given* well before any effort to *make it be* has started. In Sennett's words,

> Images of communal solidarity are forged in order that men can avoid dealing with each other . . . . By an act of will, a lie if you like, the myth of community solidarity gave these modern people the chance to be cowards and hide from each other . . . The image of the community is purified of all that may convey a feeling of difference, let alone conflict, in who 'we' are. In this way the myth of community solidarity is a purification ritual.[9]

The snag, though, is that 'the feeling of a common identity . . . is a counterfeit of experience'. If this is so, then whoever has designed and whoever supervises and runs the temples of consumption are indeed masterforgers or artful confidence tricksters. In their hands, impression is all: further questions need not be asked and will remain unanswered if asked nevertheless.

Inside the temple the image becomes the reality. The crowds filling the corridors of shopping malls come as close as conceivable to the imagined ideal 'community' that knows no difference (more exactly, no difference that counts, a difference that requires confrontation, facing up to the otherness of the other, negotiation, clarification and agreement on *modus vivendi*). For that reason that community demands no bargaining, no deals, no effort to empathize, understand and compromise. Everyone within the walls can safely assume that everyone else likely to be bumped into or passed by has come there for the same purpose, has been lured by the same attractions (thereby acknowledging them as attractions), is moved and guided by the same motives. 'Being inside' makes a true community of believers, unified by the ends and means alike, by the values they cherish and the logic of conduct they follow. All in all, a trip to 'consumer spaces' is a voyage to the badly missed community which, like the shopping experience itself, is now permanently 'elsewhere'. For the few minutes or the few hours it lasts, one can rub one's shoulders with 'others like him (or her)', co-religionists, fellow church-goers; others whose otherness may be, in this place at least, here and now, safely left out of sight, out of mind and out of account. To all intents and purposes, that place is pure, as pure as only the sites of religious cult and the imagined (or postulated) community may be.

Claude Lévi-Strauss, the greatest cultural anthropologist of our time, suggested in *Tristes tropiques* that just two strategies were deployed in human history whenever the need arose to cope with the otherness of others: one was the *anthropoemic*, the other was the *anthropophagic* strategy.

The first strategy consisted in 'vomiting', spitting out the others seen as incurably strange and alien: barring physical contact, dialogue, social intercourse and all varieties of *commercium*, commensality or *connubium*. The extreme variants of the 'emic' strategy are now, as always, incarceration, deportation and murder. The upgraded, 'refined' (modernized) forms of the 'emic' strategy are spatial separation, urban ghettos, selective access to spaces and selective barring from using them.

The second strategy consists in a soi-disant 'disalienation' of alien substances: 'ingesting', 'devouring' foreign bodies and spirits so that they may be made, through metabolism, identical with, and no longer distinguishable from, the 'ingesting' body. This strategy took an equally wide range of forms: from cannibalism to enforced assimilation – cultural crusades, wars of attrition declared on local customs, calendars, cults, dialects and other 'prejudices' and 'superstitions'. If the first strategy was aimed at the exile or annihilation of *the others*, the second was aimed at the suspension or annihilation of their *otherness*.

The resonance between the dichotomy of Lévi-Strauss's strategies and the two categories of contemporary 'public but non-civil' spaces is amazing, though not at all surprising. La Défense in Paris (alongside the numerous varieties of 'interdictory spaces', which, according to Steven Flusty, occupy pride of place among current urbanist innovations)[10] is an architectural rendition of the 'emic' strategy, while the 'consumer spaces' deploy the 'phagic' one. Both – each in its own way – respond to the same challenge: the task of coping with the likelihood of meeting strangers, that constitutive feature of urban life. Coping with that likelihood is a problem calling for 'power-assisted' measures if the habits of civility are missing or insufficiently developed and not deeply enough entrenched. The two kinds of 'public but not civil' urban spaces are derivatives of the glaring absence of skills of civility; they both deal with the potentially damaging consequences of that absence not through promoting the study and acquisition of the missing skills, but through making their possession irrelevant, indeed unnecessary, in practising the art of urban living.

To the two responses described so far a third and increasingly common one needs to be added. This is represented by what Georges Benko, following Marc Augé, dubs 'non-places' (or alternatively, after Garreau, 'nowherevilles').[11] 'Non-places' share some characteristics with our first category of ostensibly public but emphatically non-civil sites: they discourage the thought of 'settling in', making colonization or domestication of the space all but impossible. Unlike La Défense, however, that space whose sole destiny is to be passed through and left behind as quickly as possible, or 'interdictory spaces' whose main function consists in barring access and which are meant to be passed around rather than through, the non-places accept the inevitability of a protracted, sometimes very long sojourn of strangers, and so do all they can to make their presence 'merely physical' while socially little different, preferably indistinguishable altogether, from absence, to cancel, level up or make null and void the idiosyncratic subjectivities of their 'passengers'. The temporary residents of non-places are likely to vary, each variety having its own habits and expectations; the trick is to make all that irrelevant for the duration of their stay. Whatever their other differences, they should follow the same patterns of behaviour hints: and clues triggering the uniform pattern of conduct should be legible to them all, regardless of the languages they prefer or are used to deploy in their daily endeavours. Whatever needs to be done and is done in 'non-places', everyone there should *feel* as if *chez soi*, while no one should *behave* as if truly at home. Non-place 'is a space devoid of the symbolic expressions of identity, relations and history: examples include airports, motorways, anonymous hotel rooms, public transport . . . Never before in the history of the world have non-places occupied so much space.'

Non-places do not require a mastery of the sophisticated and hard-to-study art of civility, since they reduce behaviour in public to a few simple and easy-to-grasp precepts. Because of that simplification, they are not schools of civility either. And since these days they 'occupy so much space', since they colonize ever larger chunks of public space and refashion them in their own likeness, the occasions to learn the art of civility are ever fewer and further between.

Differences may be spat away, eaten away, kept away, and there are places which specialize in each eventuality. But differences may also be made invisible or, rather, prevented from being seen. This is the achievement of 'empty spaces'. As Jerzy Kociatkiewicz and Monika Kostera, who coined that term, propose, empty spaces are

> places to which no meaning is ascribed. They do not have to be physically cut off by fences or barriers. They are not prohibited places, but empty spaces, inaccessible because of their invisibility.
>
> If . . . sensemaking is an act of patterning, comprehending, re-dressing surprise, and creating meaning, our experience of empty spaces does not include sensemaking.[12]

Empty spaces are first and foremost empty of *meaning*. Not that they are meaningless because of being empty: it is because they carry no meaning, nor are believed to be able to carry one, that they are seen as empty (more precisely, unseen). In such meaning-resistant places the issue of negotiating differences never arises: there is no one to negotiate with. The way in which empty spaces deal with differences is radical to a degree which other kinds of places designed to repel or mollify the impact of strangers cannot match.

The empty spaces Kociatkiewicz and Kostera list are non-colonized places and places which neither the designers nor the managers of perfunctory users wish to, or feel the need to, earmark for colonization. They are, we may say, the 'leftover' places which remain after the job of structuration has been performed on such spaces as really matter: they owe their ghostly presence to the lack of overlap between the elegance of structure and the messiness of the world (any world, also the purposefully designed world) noto-rious for its defiance of neat classifications. But the family of empty spaces is not confined to the waste-products of architectural blueprinting and the neglected fringes of urbanist visions. Many empty spaces are, in fact, not just unavoidable waste, but necessary ingredients of another process: that of the mapping of space shared by many different users.

On one of my lecturing trips (to a populous, sprawling and lively South-European city) I was met at the airport by a young lecturer, the daughter of a local couple of highly educated and wealthy professionals. She apologized that driving to the hotel would not be an easy ride and would take rather a long time, since there was no avoiding the busy avenues leading through the centre of the city which were constantly clogged by heavy traffic. Indeed, it took us almost two hours to arrive at the place. My guide offered to drive me back to the airport on the day of departure. Knowing how tiresome and exhausting driving in that city was, I thanked her for her kindness and goodwill, but I said I would take a taxi. And I did. This time the drive to the airport took less than ten minutes. But the taxi-driver went along winding rows of shabby, drab, God-forsaken slums, full of rather uncouth and evidently idle people and unwashed children in rags. My guide's assurance that there was no way to avoid the centre's traffic was no pretence. It was sincere and faithful to her mental map of the city in which she was born and had lived ever since. That map did not record the un-sightly streets of the 'rough districts' through which the taxi took me. In the mental map of my guide, in the place where those streets should have been plotted, there was, purely and simply, an empty space.

That city, just as other cities, has many inhabitants, each carry-ing a map of the city in her or his head. Each map has its empty spaces, though on different maps they are located in different places. The maps that guide the movements of various categories of inhabitants do not overlap, but for any map to 'make sense', some areas of the city must be left out as senseless, and – as far as the sense-making is concerned – unpromising. Cutting out such places allows the rest to shine and bristle with meaning.

The emptiness of place is in the eye of the beholder and in the legs or the car-wheels of the city-goer. Empty are places one does not enter and where one would feel lost and vulnerable, surprised, taken aback and a little frightened by the sight of humans.

Don't talk to strangers

The main point about civility is – let me repeat – the ability to interact with strangers without holding their strangeness against them and without pressing them to surrender it or to renounce some or all the traits that have made them strangers in the first place. The main feature of the 'public, but not civil' places – all four categories of such places listed above – is *the redundancy of interaction*. If physical proximity – sharing a space – cannot be completely avoided, it can be perhaps stripped of the challenge of 'togetherness' it contains, with its standing invitation to meaningful encounter, dialogue and interaction. If meeting strangers cannot be averted, one can at least try to avoid the dealings. Let strangers, like the children of the Victorian era, be seen but not heard or if hearing them cannot be escaped, then, at least, not listened to. The point is to make whatever they may say irrelevant and of no consequence to what can be done, is to be done, and is desired to be done.

All such expedients are, to be sure, merely half-measures: the second-best solutions or the least damaging and detestable of evils. 'Public but non-civil places' allow one to wash one's hands of any truck with the strangers around and avoid the risk-fraught commerce, the mind-taxing communication, the nerve-breaking bargaining and the irritating compromises. They do not, however, prevent the meeting of strangers; on the contrary, they assume that meeting cannot be avoided – they have been designed and deployed because of that assumption. They are, so to speak, cures for a disease already contracted – not a preventive medicine which would make the therapy unnecessary. And all therapies, as we all know, may or may not defeat the disease. There are few, if any, foolproof therapeutic regimes. How nice it would be, therefore, to make therapy unnecessary by immunizing the organism against the disease. Hence getting rid of the company of strangers seems a more attractive, safer prospect than the most sophisticated expedients to neutralize their presence.

This may seem a better solution, but it is certainly not free of its own dangers. Tampering with the immune system is a risky business and may prove pathogenic in its own right. Besides, making organisms resistant to certain threats is virtually bound to render them vulnerable to other threats. Hardly any interference is free of gruesome side-effects: quite a few medical interventions are known to generate iatrogenic ailments – diseases that result from medical intervention itself, which are no less (if not more) dangerous than the ones it heals.

As Richard Sennett points out,

cries for law and order are greatest when the communities are most isolated from the other people in the city . . .

Cities in America during the past two decades have grown in such a way that ethnic areas have become relatively homogeneous; it appears no accident that the fear of the outsider has also grown to the extent that these ethnic communities have been cut off.[13]

The ability to live with differences, let alone to enjoy such living and to benefit from it, does not come easily and certainly not under its own impetus. This ability is an art which, like all arts, requires study and exercise. The inability to face up to the vexing plurality of human beings and the ambivalence of all classifying/filing decisions are, on the contrary, self-perpetuating and self-reinforcing: the more effective the drive to homogeneity and the efforts to eliminate the difference, the more difficult it is to feel at home in the face of strangers, the more threatening the difference appears and the deeper and more intense is the anxiety it breeds. The project to hide from the unnerving impact of urban multi-vocality in the shelters of communal uniformity, monotony and repetitiveness is as self-defeating as it is self-propelling. This could be a trivial truth, if not for the fact that the resentment of difference happens also to be self-corroborating: as the drive to uniformity grows more intense, so does the perceived horror of the dangers presented by the 'strangers at the gate'. The danger presented by the company of strangers is a classic self-fulfilling prophecy. It becomes ever easier to blend the sight of the strangers with the diffuse fears of insecurity; what has been merely surmised in the beginning turns into a truth proved many times over, and in the end self-evident.

The quandary becomes a vicious circle. With the art of negotiating common interests and shared destiny falling into disuse, seldom if ever practised, half-forgotten or never properly mastered, with the idea of 'the common good' (let alone 'the good society') branded suspect, threatening, nebulous or addle-brained, seeking security in a common identity rather than in an agreement on shared interests emerges as the the most sensible, nay most effective and profitable, way to proceed; but concerns with identity and its defence against pollution make the idea of common interests, and most notably *negotiated* common interests, all the more incredible and fanciful, and the ability and will to pursue them all the less likely to appear. As Sharon Zukin sums up the resulting predicament: 'No one knows how to talk to anyone else'.

Zukin suggests that 'The exhaustion of the ideal of a common destiny has strengthened the appeal of culture'; but 'In common American usage, culture is, first of all, "ethnicity" ' – the ethnicity being, in its turn, a 'legitimate way of carving a niche in society.'[14] Carving a niche, let there be no doubt, means above all *territorial* separation, the right to a separate 'defensible space' which needs defence and is worth defending precisely because of its being separate – that is because it has been surrounded by guarded border posts which let in only people of 'the same' identity and bar access to anyone else. The purpose of territorial separation being aimed at the homogeneity of neighbourhood, 'ethnicity' suits it better than any other imagined 'identity'.

Unlike other varieties of postulated identities, the idea of ethnicity is semantically loaded. It assumes axiomatically a marriage made in heaven that no human effort can tear asunder, a kind of preordained bond of unity which precedes all bargaining and eventual agreements on rights and obligations. In other words, homogeneity which allegedly marks ethnic entities is *heteronomous*: not a human artefact, and most certainly not the product of the generation of humans currently alive. No wonder then that ethnicity more than any other kind of postulated identity is the first choice when it comes to the withdrawal from the frightening, polyphonic space where 'No one knows how to talk to anyone else' into a 'secure niche' where 'Everyone is like anyone else' and so there is little to talk about and the talking is easy. No wonder either that, without much regard for logic, other postulated communities, while clamouring for their own 'niches in society', are eager to steal feathers from ethnicity's cap and busily invent their own roots, traditions, shared history and common future – but first and foremost their separate and unique culture, which because of its genuine or putative uniqueness they claim to be 'a value in its own right'.

It would be wrong to explain away the born-again communitarianism of our times as a hiccup of not yet fully eradicated instincts or proclivities which further progress of modernization is bound sooner or later to neuter or defuse; it would be equally wrong to dismiss it as a momentary failure of reason – a regrettable, but not really avoidable case of irrationality, blatantly at odds with what rationally pursued 'public choice' would imply. Each social setting promotes its own kind of rationality, invests its own meaning into the idea of rational life strategy – and much can be said in support of the hypothesis that the current avatar of communitarianism is a *rational* response to the genuine crisis of 'public space' – and so of politics, that human activity for which public space is the natural home ground.

With the realm of politics narrowing down to public confessions, public displays of intimacy and public examination and censure of private virtues and vices; with the issue of the credibility of people in public view replacing the consideration of what the business of politics is and ought to be; with the vision of a good and just society all but absent from political discourse – no wonder that (as Sennett observed already twenty years ago)[15] people 'become the passive spectators to a political personage who offers them his intentions, his sentiments, rather than his acts, for their consumption'. The point is, though, that the spectators do not expect much else from the politicians, just as they do not expect from other personages currently in the limelight anything but a good spectacle. And so the spectacle of politics, like other publicly staged spectacles, turns into a relentlessly and monotonously hammered message of the priority of identity over interests, or into a continuing public lesson that it is identity, not the interests, that truly matters, and that it is who you are, rather than what are you doing, that truly counts. From the top to the bottom, it is the revelation of the true self that becomes increasingly the substance of the relations in public and of public life as such; and it is self-identity that becomes the straw at which the shipwrecked seeking rescue are most likely to clutch once the interest-navigated boats have foundered. And then, as Sennett suggests, 'maintaining community becomes an end in itself; the purge of those who don't really belong becomes the community's business'. No 'rationale of refusing to negotiate, of continual purge of outsiders' is needed any more.

Efforts to keep the 'other', the different, the strange and the foreign at a distance, the decision to preclude the need for communication, negotiation and mutual commitment, is not the only conceivable, but the expectable response to the existential uncertainty rooted in the new fragility or fluidity of social bonds. That decision, to be sure, fits well with our contemporary obsessive concern with pollution and purification, with our tendency to identify danger to personal safety with the invasion of 'foreign bodies' and to identify safety unthreatened and secure with purity. The acutely apprehensive attention to the substances entering the body through mouth or nostrils, and to the foreigners leaking surreptitiously into the neighbourhood of the body, is accommodated side by side in the same cognitive frame. Both prompt a similar wish to 'get it (them) out of my (our) system'.

Such wishes converge, coalesce and condense in the politics of ethnic separation, and particularly of the defence against the influx of the 'foreigners'. As Georges Benko put it,[16]

> There are Others who are still more Other than the Others, the foreigners. To exclude people as foreigners because we are no longer able to conceive of the Other attests to a social pathology.

Pathology it may well be, but this is not a pathology of the mind trying in vain to force sense upon a world devoid of stable and trustworthy meaning, but a pathology of public space resulting in a pathology of politics: the wilting and waning of the art of dialogue and negotiation, the substitution of the techniques of escape and elision for engagement and mutual commitment.

'Do not talk to strangers' – once a warning given by worrying parents to their hapless children – has now become the strategic precept of adult normality. This precept recasts as a prudent rule the reality of a life in which strangers are such people with whom one refuses to talk. Governments impotent to strike at the roots of the existential insecurity and anxiety of their subjects are only too eager and happy to oblige. A united front among the 'immigrants', that fullest and most tangible embodiment of 'otherness', promises to come as near as conceivable to patching the diffuse assortment of fearful and disoriented individuals together into something vaguely reminiscent of a 'national community'; and this is one of the few jobs the governments of our times can do and be seen doing.

George Hazeldon Heritage Park would be a place where, at long last, all passers-by could talk freely to each other. They would be free to talk since they would have little to talk about – except exchanging the routine and familiar phrases entailing no controversy, but no commitment either. The dreamt-of purity of the Heritage Park community could be gained only at the price of disengagement and broken bonds.

Modernity as history of time

When I was a child (and that happened in another time and another space) it was not uncommon to hear the question 'How far is it from here to there?' answered by 'About an hour, or a bit less, if you walk briskly.' In a time more ancient yet than my childhood years the more usual answer, I suppose, would have been 'If you start now, you will be there around noon' or 'Better start now, if you want to be there before dusk.' Nowadays, you may hear on occasion similar answers. But it will normally be preceded by a request to be more specific: 'Do you have a car? Or do you mean on foot?'

'Far' and 'long', just like 'near' and 'soon', used to mean nearly the same: just how much or how little effort it would take for a human being to span a certain distance – be it by walking, by ploughing, or harvesting. If people were pressed hard to explain what they meant by 'space' and 'time', they could have said that 'space' is what you can pass in a given time, while 'time' is what you need to pass it. Unless pressed hard, though, they would not play the game of definition at all. And why should they? Most things immersed in daily life one understands fairly enough until asked to define them; and unless asked, one would hardly need to define them in the first place. The way one understood those things which we tend now to call 'space' and 'time' was not just satisfactory, but as precise as needed, as long as it was but the 'wetware' – the humans, the oxen or the horses – who made the effort and set its limits. One pair of human legs may be different from another, but the replacement of one pair with another would not make a large enough difference to call for measures other than the capacity of human muscles.

In the times of the Greek Olympics no one thought of track or Olympic records, let alone of breaking them. The invention and deployment of something other than the power of human or animal muscles was needed for such ideas and for the decision to assign importance to the differences between the capacities of human individuals to move, to be conceived and to stimulate practice – and so for the *prehistory* of time, that long era of wetware-bound practice, to end, and the *history* of time to start. The history of time began with modernity. Indeed, modernity is, apart from anything else, perhaps even more than anything else, *the history of time*: modernity is the time when time has a history.

If one searches history books for the reason why space and time, once blended in human life-labours, have fallen apart and drifted away from each other in human thought and practice, one will often find uplifting stories of discoveries made by the valiant knights of reason – intrepid philosophers and courageous scientists. One learns of astronomers measuring distances and the velocity of celestial bodies, of Newton calculating the exact relations between acceleration and the distance passed by the 'physical body' and their painstaking efforts to express all that in numbers – those most abstract and objective of imaginable measures; or of Kant being sufficiently impressed by their achievements to cast space and time as two transcendentally separate and mutually independent categories of human cognition. And yet, however justified the claim of philosophers to think *sub specie aeternitatis*, it is always a section of infinity and eternity, its finite part currently within the reach of human practice, that supplies the 'epistemological ground' for philosophical and scientific reflection and the empirical stuff that can be kneaded into timeless truths; this limitation, as a matter of fact, sets the great thinkers apart from those who have gone down in history as addle-brained fantasists, mythmakers, poets and other dreamers of dreams. And so something must have happened to the scope and carrying capacity of human practice for the sovereignties of space and time to stare suddenly in the philosophers' eyes.

That 'something' was, one is entitled to guess, the construction of vehicles which could move faster than the legs of humans or horses could ever do; and vehicles which, in sharp opposition to the humans and the horses, could be made quicker and quicker, so that traversing ever-larger distances could take less and less time. When such non-human and non-animal means of transportation appeared, the time needed to travel ceased to be the feature of distance and inflexible 'wetware'; it became instead the attribute of the technique of travelling. Time has become the problem of the 'hardware' humans could invent, build, appropriate, use and control, not of the hopelessly unstretchable 'wetware' nor the notoriously capricious and whimsical powers of wind or water indifferent to human manipulation; by the same token, time has become a factor independent of inert and immutable dimensions of land-masses or seas. Time was different from space because, unlike space, it could be changed and manipulated; it has become a factor of disruption: the dynamic partner in the time–space wedlock.

Benjamin Franklin famously proclaimed time to be money; he could make that declaration with confidence since he had already defined man as the 'tool-making animal'. Summing up the experience of a further two centuries, John Fitzgerald Kennedy could advise his fellow Americans in 1961 that 'We must use time as a tool, not as a couch.' Time became money once it had become a tool (or a weapon?) deployed primarily in the ongoing effort of overcoming resistance of space: shortening distances, stripping the 'remoteness' of the meaning of an obstacle, let alone of a limit, to human ambition. Armed with that weapon, one could set oneself the task of conquering space and in all earnestness set about its implementation.

Kings could perhaps travel more comfortably than their bailiffs, and barons more conveniently than their serfs; but, in principle, none of them could travel at much greater speed than the others could. Wetware made humans similar; hardware made them different. These differences (unlike those deriving from the dissimilarity of human muscles) were the *outcomes* of human actions before they could become conditions of their effectiveness, and before they could be deployed to make yet more differences, and the differences more profound and less contestable than before. Come the steam and the internal combustion engines, and the wetware-based equality came to an end. Some people could now arrive where they wished to arrive well before anyone else; they could also escape the chase and effectively resist being caught up with, slowed down or stopped. Whoever travelled faster, could claim more territory – and, having done that, could control it, map it and supervise it – keeping the competitors at arm's length and the intruders out of bounds.

One can associate the beginning of the modern era with various facets of changing human practices, but the emancipation of time from space, its subordination to human inventiveness and technical capacity, and so setting it against the space as a tool of the space conquest and land appropriation is no worse a moment to start reckoning from than any other departure. Modernity was born under the stars of acceleration and land conquest, and these stars form a constellation which contains all the information about its character, conduct and fate. It needs but a trained sociologist, not an imaginative astrologer, to read it out.

The relation between time and space was to be from now on

processual, mutable and dynamic, not preordained and stagnant. The 'conquest of space' came to mean faster machines. Accelerated movement meant larger space, and accelerating the moves was the sole means of enlarging the space. In this chase, spatial expansion was the name of the game and space was the stake; space was value, time was the tool. To maximize the value, it was necessary to sharpen the instruments: much of the 'instrumental rationality' which, as Max Weber suggested, was the operative principle of modern civilization, focused on designing ways to perform tasks faster, while eliminating 'unproductive', idle, empty and so wasted time; or, to tell the same story in terms of effects rather than means of action, it focused on filling space with objects more densely and enlarging the space which could be so filled in a given time. At the threshold of the modern conquest of space Descartes, looking forward, identified existence with spatiality, defining whatever exists materially as *res extensa*. (As Rob Shields wittily put it, one could rephrase Descartes' famous *cogito*, without distorting its meaning, as 'I occupy space therefore I exist.')[17] At a time when that conquest ran out of steam and drew to a close, Michel de Certeau – looking backward – declared that power was about territory and boundaries. (As Tim Cresswell summarized de Certeau's view recently, 'the weapons of the strong are ... classification, delineation, division. The strong depend on the certainty of mapping';[18] note that all weapons listed are operations performed on space). One could say that the difference between the strong and the weak is the difference between a territory shaped in the image of the map – closely guarded and tightly controlled – and a territory open to intrusion, to redrawing of boundaries and recharting the maps. At least it has become so and has stayed so for a good part of modern history.

From heavy to light modernity

That part of history, now coming to its close, could be dubbed, for the lack of a better name, the era of *hardware*, or *heavy* modernity – the bulk-obsessed modernity, 'the larger the better' kind of modernity, of 'the size is power, the volume is success' sort. That was the *hardware* era; the epoch of weighty and ever more cumbersome machines, of the ever longer factory walls enclosing ever

wider factory floors and ingesting ever more populous factory
crews, of ponderous rail engines and gigantic ocean liners. To
conquer space was the supreme goal – to grasp as much of it as one
could hold, and to hold to it, marking it all over with the tangible
tokens of possession and 'No trespassing' boards. Territory was
among the most acute of modern obsessions, its acquisition among
the most compulsive of modern urges – while guarding the boundaries figured high among the most ubiquitous, resilient and relentlessly growing modern addictions.

Heavy modernity was the era of territorial conquest. Wealth
and power was firmly rooted or deposited deep inside the land –
bulky, ponderous and immovable like the beds of iron ore and
deposits of coal. Empires spread to fill every nook and cranny of
the globe: only other empires of equal or superior strength set
limits to their expansion. Anything lying between the outposts of
competing imperial realms was seen as masterless, a no man's
land, and so *an empty space* – and empty space was a challenge to
action and reproach to idlers. (The popular science of the time
grasped the mood of the era perfectly when informing laymen
that 'Nature suffers no void.') Even more off-putting and less
bearable was the thought of the globe's 'blank spots': islands and
archipelagos as yet unheard of and unadumbrated, land-masses
waiting to be discovered and colonized, the untrodden and un-
claimed interiors of continents, the uncounted 'hearts of darkness' clamouring for light. Intrepid explorers were the heroes of
the new, modern versions of Walter Benjamin's 'sailor stories', of
childhood dreams and adult nostalgia; enthusiastically cheered
on their departure and showered with honours on their return,
expedition after expedition wandered through the jungle, bush or
permafrost in search of as yet uncharted mountain range, lake or
plateau. Also the modern paradise, like James Hilton's Shangri-
La, was 'out there', in a still 'undiscovered' place, hidden and
inaccessible, somewhere beyond the unpassed and impassable
mountain masses or deadly deserts, at the end of a trail yet to be
blazed. Adventure and happiness, wealth and might were geo-
graphical concepts or 'land estates' – tied to their place, immovable and untransferable. All that called for impenetrable walls,
dense and tight checkpoints, unsleeping borderguards, and se-
crecy of the locations. (One of the most closely guarded secrets of
World War II, the American air base from which the murderous

raid on Tokyo was to be launched in 1942, was nicknamed 'Shangri-La'.)

Wealth and might which depend on the size and the quality of hardware tend to be sluggish, unwieldy and awkward to move. Both are 'embodied' and fixed, tied in steel and concrete and measured by their volume and weight. They grow by expanding the place they occupy and are protected by protecting that place: the place is, simultaneously, their hotbed, their fortress and their prison. Daniel Bell described one of the most powerful and most envied and emulated of such hotbeds/fortresses/prisons: the General Motors 'Willow Run' plant in Michigan.[19] The site occupied by the plant was two-thirds by a quarter of a mile. All the materials needed to produce cars were gathered under one gigantic roof, in a single monstrous cage. The logic of power and the logic of control were both grounded in the strict separation of the 'inside' from the 'outside' and a vigilant defence of the boundary between the two. Both logics, blended in one, were embodied in the logic of size, organized around one precept: bigger means more efficient. In the heavy version of modernity, progress meant growing size and spatial expansion.

It was the routinization of time that held the place whole, compact and subject to homogeneous logic. (Bell invoked the principal tool of routinization when calling such time 'metric'.)

In the conquest of space, time had to be pliant and malleable, and above all shrinkable through the increased 'space-devouring' capacity of each unit: to go around the world in eighty days was an alluring dream, but to do it in eight days was infinitely more attractive. Flying over the English Channel and then over the Atlantic were the milestones by which progress was measured. When, however, it came to the fortification of the conquered space, to its taming, colonization and domestication, a tough, uniform and inflexible time was needed: the kind of time that could be cut in slices of similar thickness fit to be arranged in monotonous and unalterable sequences. Space was truly 'possessed' when controlled – and control meant first and foremost the 'taming of time', neutralizing its inner dynamism: in short, the uniformity and coordination of time. It was wonderful and exciting to reach the sources of the Nile before other explorers managed to find it, but a train running ahead of schedule or automobile parts arriving on the assembly line ahead of other parts were heavy modernity's most gruesome nightmares.

Routinized time joined forces with high brick walls crowned with barbed wire or broken glass and closely guarded gates in protecting the place against intruders; it also prevented all those inside the place from leaving it at will. The 'Fordist factory', that most coveted and avidly pursued model of engineered rationality in times of heavy modernity, was the site of face-to-face meeting, but also a 'till death us do part' type of marriage vow between capital and labour. The wedding was of convenience or necessity, hardly ever a marriage of love – but it was meant to last 'for ever' (whatever that might have meant in terms of individual life), and more often than not it did. The marriage was, essentially, mono-gamic – and for both partners. Divorce was out of the question. For better or worse, the partners in marriage were bound to stay in each other's company; neither could survive without the other.

Routinized time tied labour to the ground, while the massiveness of the factory buildings, the heaviness of the machinery and, last but not least, the permanently tied labour 'bonded' the capital. Neither capital nor labour was eager, or able, to move. Like any other marriage that lacked the safety valve of painless divorce, the story of cohabitation was full of sound and fury, fraught with violent eruptions of enmity and marked by somewhat less dra-matic, but more relentless and persistent, day in, day out, trench war. At no time, however, did the plebeians think of leaving the city; the patricians were no more free to do so. Menenius Agrippa's oratory was not needed to keep either in place. The very intensity and perpetuity of conflict was a vivid evidence of commonality of fate. The frozen time of factory routine, together with the bricks and mortar of factory walls, immobilized capital as effectively as it bound the labour it employed. It all changed, though, with the advent of software capitalism and 'light' modernity. The Sorbonne economist Daniel Cohen put it in a nutshell: 'Whoever begins a career at Microsoft has not the slightest idea where it will end. Whoever started it at Ford or Renault, could be well-nigh certain that it will finish in the same place.'[20]

I am not sure whether in both of the cases described by Cohen the use of the term 'career' is legitimate. 'Career' brings to mind a set trajectory, not unlike the American universities' 'tenure tracks', with a sequence of stages marked in advance and accompanied by moderately clear conditions of entry and rules of admission. The 'career paths' tend to be shaped by co-ordinated pressures of space and time. Whatever happens to the employees of Microsoft or its countless watchers and imitators, where all concern of the managers is 'with looser organizational forms which are more able to go with the flow', and where business organization is increasingly seen as a never conclusive, ongoing attempt 'to form an island of superior adaptability' in a world perceived as 'multiple, complex and fast moving, and therefore as "ambiguous", "fuzzy" or "plastic"',[21] militates against durable structures, and notably against structures with a built-in life-expectation commensurable with the customary length of a working life. Under such conditions the idea of a 'career' seems nebulous and utterly out of place.

This is, though, merely a terminological quibble. Whether the terms are correctly or wrongly used, the main point is that Cohen's comparison grasps unerringly the watershed-like change in the modern history of time and hints at the impact it is beginning to make on the human existential condition. The change in question is the new irrelevance of space, masquerading as the annihilation of time. In the software universe of light-speed travel, space may be traversed, literally, in 'no time'; the difference between 'far away' and 'down here' is cancelled. Space no more sets limits to action and its effects, and counts little, or does not count at all. It has lost its 'strategic value', the military experts would say.

All values, as Georg Simmel observed, are 'valuable' in so far as they are to be gained 'only by forgoing other values'; it is the 'detour to the attainment of certain things' which is the cause to 'regard them as valuable'. Without using these words, Simmel tells the story of a 'value fetishism': things, wrote Simmel, 'are worth just what they cost'; and this circumstance appears, perversely, 'to mean that they cost what they are worth'. It is the obstacles which need to be negotiated on the way that lead to their appropriation, 'the tension of the struggle for it' which makes values valuable.[22] If no time needs to be lost and forgone – 'sacrificed' – to reach even the remotest of places, places are stripped of value in the Simmelian sense. Once distances can be spanned (and so the materially distant parts of space acted upon and affected) with the velocity of electronic signals, all references to time appear, as Jacques Derrida would put it, *'sous rature'*. 'Instantaneity' apparently refers to a very quick movement and very short time, but in fact it denotes the absence of time as a factor of the event and by the same token as an element in the calculation of value. Time is no longer the 'detour to the attainment', and thus no longer bestows value on space. The near-instantaneity of software time augurs the devaluation of space.

In the era of hardware, of heavy modernity, which in Max Weber's terms was also the era of instrumental rationality, time was the means which needed to be husbanded and managed prudently so that the returns of value, which were space, could be maximized; in the era of software, of light modernity, the effectiveness of time as a means of value-attainment tends to approach infinity, with the paradoxical effect of levelling up (or rather down) the value of all units in the field of potential objectives. The question mark has moved from the side of the means to that of the ends. If applied to the time–space relation, this means that since all parts of space can be reached in the same time-span (that is in 'no-time'), no part of space is privileged, none has 'special value'. If all parts of space can be reached at any moment, there is no reason to reach any of them at any particular moment and no reason to worry about securing the right of access to any. If you know that you can visit a place at any time you wish, there is no urge to visit it often or to spend money on a valid-for-life ticket. There is even less reason to bear the expenditure of perpetual supervision and management, of laborious and risk-fraught husbandry and cultivation of lands which can be easily reached and as easily abandoned following the shifting interests and 'topical relevances'.

The seductive lightness of being

The insubstantial, instantaneous time of the software world is also an inconsequential time. 'Instantaneity' means immediate, 'on-the-spot' fulfilment – but also immediate exhaustion and fading of interest. Time-distance separating the end from the beginning is shrinking or vanishing altogether; the two notions, which were once used to plot the passing, and so to calculate the 'forfeited value', of time, have lost much of their meaning, which – as all meanings – arose from the starkness of their opposition. There are only 'moments' – points without dimensions. But is such a time, time with the morphology of an aggregate of moments, still time 'as we know it'? The expression 'moment of time' seems, at least in certain vital respects, an oxymoron. Perhaps, having killed space as value, time has committed suicide? Was not space merely the first casualty in time's frenzied rush to self-annihilation?

What has been described here is, of course, a *liminal* condition in the history of time – what seems to be, at its present stage, that history's ultimate *tendency*. However close to zero is the time needed to reach a spatial destination, it has not yet quite arrived. Even the most advanced technology armed with ever more powerful processors has still some way to go to attain genuine 'instantaneity'. Nor has the logically following irrelevance of space truly and fully happened, nor has the weightlessness, the infinite volatility and flexibility of human agency, been achieved. But the condition described is indeed the developmental horizon of light modernity. More importantly yet, it is the ever-to-be-pursued though (or is it because?) never-to-be-reached-in-full ideal of its major operators, one that in the avatar of a new norm pervades and saturates every organ, tissue and cell of the social body. Milan Kundera portrayed 'the unbearable lightness of being' as the hub of modern life's tragedy. Lightness and speed (together!) have been offered by Italo Calvino, the inventor of those totally free characters (free completely, owing to their being uncatchable, unensnarable, elusive, impossible to lay hold of) – the tree-jumping baron and the bodyless knight – as the fullest, ultimate incarnations of the eternal emancipatory function of literary art.

More than thirty years ago (in his classic *Bureaucratic Phenomenon*) Michel Crozier identified domination (in all its varieties) with the closeness to the sources of uncertainty. His verdict still holds: people who manage to keep their own actions unbound, norm-free and so unpredictable, while normatively regulating (routinizing, and thereby rendering monotonous, repetitive and predictable) the actions of their protagonists, rule. People whose hands are untied rule over people with tied hands; the freedom of the first is the main cause of the unfreedom of the second – while the unfreedom of the second is the ultimate meaning of the freedom of the first.

Nothing has changed in this respect with the passage from heavy to light modernity. But the frame has filled with a new content; more precisely, the pursuit of the 'closeness to the source of uncertainty' has narrowed down to, and focused on, one objective – instantaneity. People who move and act faster, who come nearest to the momentariness of movement, are now the people who rule.

And it is the people who cannot move as quickly, and more conspicuously yet the category of people who cannot at will leave their place at all, who are ruled. Domination consists in one's own capacity to escape, to disengage, to 'be elsewhere', and the right to decide the speed with which all that is done – while simultaneously stripping the people on the dominated side of their ability to arrest or constrain their moves or slow them down. The contemporary battle of domination is waged between forces armed, respectively, with the weapons of acceleration and procrastination.

Differential access to instantaneity is crucial among the present-day versions of the everlasting and indestructible foundation of social division in all its historically changing forms: the differential access to unpredictability, and hence to freedom. In a world populated by ground-plodding serfs, tree-jumping was for the barons a foolproof recipe for freedom. It is the facility of the present-day barons to behave in a fashion akin to jumping the trees which keeps the successors of the serfs in place, and it is these successors' enforced immobility, boundedness to the ground, that allows the barons to go on jumping. However deep and depressing the serfs' misery, there is no one in sight to rebel against, and had the serfs rebelled they would not have caught up with the fast-moving targets of their rebellion. Heavy modernity kept capital and labour in an iron cage which none of them could escape.

Light modernity let one partner out of the cage. 'Solid' modernity was an era of mutual engagement. 'Fluid' modernity is the epoch of disengagement, elusiveness, facile escape and hopeless chase. In 'liquid' modernity, it is the most elusive, those free to move without notice, who rule.

Karl Polanyi (in *The Great Transformation: The Political and Economic Origin of our Time*, published in 1944) proclaimed the treatment of labour as 'commodity' to be a fiction and unwrapped the consequences of the social arrangement based on that fiction. Labour, Polanyi pointed out, cannot be a commodity (at least not a commodity like other commodities), since it cannot be sold or bought separately from its carriers. The labour which Polanyi wrote about was indeed *embodied* labour: labour which could not be moved around without moving the labourers in the flesh. One could hire and employ human labour only together with the rest of the labourers' bodies, and the inertia of the hired bodies set limits to the freedom of the employers. To supervise labour and to channel it according to the design, one had to manage and supervise the labourers; to control the work process, one had to control the workers. That requirement brought capital and labour face to face and kept them, for better or worse, in each other's company. The result was much conflict, but also a lot of mutual accommodation: acrimonious charges, bitter struggle and altogether little love lost, but also tremendous ingenuity in designing the moderately satisfying or just bearable rules of cohabitation. Revolutions and welfare state were both the unanticipated but unavoidable outcome of the condition which precluded the disengagement from being a feasible and viable option.

We now live through another 'great transformation', and one of its most prominent aspects is a phenomenon exactly opposite to the condition which Polanyi took for granted: the 'disembodiment' of that type of human labour which serves as the principal source of nourishment, or the grazing ground, of contemporary capital. Panopticon-like, bulky, clumsy and awkward installations of surveillance and drill are no longer necessary. Labour has been let out of the Panopticon, but, most importantly, capital has shed the vexing burden and exorbitant costs of running it; capital got rid of the task which tied it to the ground and forced it into direct engagement with the agents exploited for the sake of its self-reproduction and self-aggrandizement.

The disembodied labour of the software era no longer ties down capital: it allows capital to be exterritorial, volatile and fickle. Disembodiment of labour augurs weightlessness of capital. Their mutual dependency has been broken unilaterally; while the capacity to labour is as before incomplete and unfulfillable if left alone, and dependent on the presence of capital for its fulfilment, the reverse does not apply any more. Capital travels hopefully, counting on brief profitable adventures and confident that there will be no shortage of them or of partners to share them with. Capital can travel fast and travel light and its lightness and motility have turned into the paramount source of uncertainty for all the rest. This has become the present-day basis of domination and the principal factor of social divisions.

Bulkiness and size are turning from assets into liabilities. For capitalists who would rather exchange massive office buildings for hot-air balloon cabins, buoyancy is the most profitable and the most cherished of assets; and buoyancy can be best enhanced by throwing overboard every bit of non-vital load and leaving the non-indispensable members of the crew on the ground. One of the most cumbersome items of ballast which needs to be disposed of is the onerous task of management and supervision of a large staff – a task which has an irritating tendency to swell incessantly and to put on weight through the addition of ever new layers of commitments and obligations. If the 'managerial science' of heavy capitalism focused on keeping the 'manpower' in and forcing or bribing it to stay put and to work on schedule, the art of management in the era of light capitalism is concerned with letting 'humanpower' out and better still forcing it to go. Brief encounters replace lasting engagements. One does not plant a citrus-tree grove to squeeze a lemon.

The managerial equivalent of liposuction has become the paramount stratagem of managerial art: slimming, downsizing, phasing out, closing down or selling out some units because they are not effective enough and some others because it is cheaper to let them fight for survival on their own than to undertake the burdensome, time-taxing managerial supervision, are this new art's principal applications.

Some observers have hastened to conclude that 'bigger' is no longer considered to be 'more efficient'. In such generalized rendition, though, this conclusion is not correct. The downsizing obsession is, as it happens, an undetachable complement of the merger mania. The best players in the field are known to negotiate or enforce mergers in order to acquire more scope for downsizing operations, while the radical, 'right to the bare bone' 'stripping of assets' is widely accepted as the vital precondition for the success of the merger plans. Merger and downsizing are not at cross-purposes: on the contrary, they condition each other, support and reinforce. This only appears to be a paradox; the apparent contradiction dissolves once the 'new and improved' rendition of Michel Crozier's principle is considered. It is the blend of merger and downsizing strategies that offers capital and financial power the space to move and move quickly, making the scope of its travel ever more global, while at the same time depriving labour of its bargaining and nuisance-making power, immobilizing it and tying its hands ever more firmly.

Merger augurs a longer rope for the lean, buoyant, Houdini-style capital which has made the major vehicles of its domination out of evasion and escape, the substitution of short-term deals and fleeting encounters for lasting commitments, and keeping the option of the 'disappearing act' permanently open. Capital acquires more room for manoeuvre – more shelters to hide in, a larger matrix of possible permutations, a wider assortment of available avatars, and so more strength to keep the labour it deploys in check together with the cost-saving ability to wash its hands of the devastating consequences of successive rounds of downsizing; this is the contemporary face of domination – over those who have been already hit and those who fear they are in line for future blows. As the American Management Association learned from a study it commissioned, 'The morale and motivation of workers dropped sharply in the various squeeze plays of downsizing. Surviving workers waited for the next blow of the ax rather than exulting in competitive victory over those who were fired.'[23]

Competition for survival, to be sure, is not just the fate of the workers – or, more generally, of those on the receiving side of the changed time and space relationship. It penetrates the obsessively dieting and slimming company of light modernity from top to bottom. Managers must downsize worker-employing outfits to stay alive; top managers must downsize their managerial offices in order to earn the recognition of the stock-exchange, gain shareholders' votes and secure the right to the golden handshake when the current round of hatchet jobs has been completed. Once embarked upon, the 'slimming' trend develops its own momentum. The tendency becomes self-propelling and self-accelerating, and (like Max Weber's perfectionist businessmen who no longer needed Calvin's exhortations to repent in order to keep going) the original motive – increased efficiency – becomes increasingly irrelevant; the fear of losing in the competition game, of being overtaken, left behind or put out of business altogether are quite sufficient to keep the merging/downsizing game going. This game becomes, increasingly, its own purpose and its own reward; or, rather, the game no longer needs a purpose if staying in the game is its only reward.

Instant living

Richard Sennett was for a number of years a regular observer of the world-wide gathering of the high and mighty, held annually in

Davos. Money and time spent on Davos trips paid handsomely; Sennett brought from his escapades quite a few striking and shocking insights into the motives and character traits which keep the present-day top players of the global game on the move. Judging from his report,[24] Sennett was particularly impressed by the personality, performance, and publicly articulated life-creed of Bill Gates. Gates, says Sennett, 'seems free of the obsession to hold on to things. His products are furious in coming forth and as rapid in disappearing, whereas Rockefeller wanted to own oil rigs, buildings, machinery, or railroads for the long term.' Gates repeatedly announced that he preferred 'positioning oneself in a network of possibilities rather than paralyzing oneself in one particular job'. What seems to have struck Sennett most was Gates's unashamed, outspoken, even boastful willingness to 'destroy what he has made, given the demands of the immediate moment'. Gates appeared to be a player who 'flourishes in the midst of dislocation'. He was cautious not to develop attachment (and particularly a sentimental attachment) or lasting commitment to anything, including his own creations. He was not afraid of taking a wrong turn since no turn would keep him going in one direction for long, and since turning back or aside remained constantly and immediately available options. We may say that, except for the widening range of accessible opportunities, nothing else was accumulating or accruing along Gates's life-track; the rails kept being dismantled as soon as the engine moved a few yards further, footprints were blown away, things were dumped as quickly as they were put together – and forgotten soon after.

Anthony Flew quotes one of the characters impersonated by Woody Allen: 'I don't want to achieve immortality through my work, I want to achieve immortality by not dying.'[25] But the meaning of immortality is derivative of the sense attached to the admittedly mortal life; the preference for 'not dying' is not so much a choice of another form of immortality (an alternative to 'immortality through one's works'), as a declaration of unconcern with eternal duration in favour of *carpe diem*. Indifference to duration transforms immortality from an idea into an experience and makes of it an object of immediate consumption: it is the way you live-through-the-moment that makes that moment into an 'immortal experience'. If 'infinity' survives the trasmutation, it is only as a measure of the depth or intensity of the *Erlebnis*. The boundlessness of possible sensations slips into the place vacated in dreams by infinite duration. Instantaneity (nullifying the resistance of space and liquefying the materiality of objects) makes every moment seem infinitely capacious; and infinite capacity means that there are no limits to what could be squeezed out of any moment – however brief and 'fleeting'.

The 'long term', though still referred to by habit, is a hollow shell carrying no meaning; if infinity, like time, is instantaneous, meant to be used on the spot and disposed of immediately, then 'more time' can add little to what the moment has already offered. Not much can be gained from the 'long-term' considerations. If 'solid' modernity posited eternal duration as the main motive and principle of action, 'fluid' modernity has no function for the eternal duration to play. The 'short term' has replaced the 'long term' and made of instantaneity its ultimate ideal. While promoting time to the rank of an infinitely capacious container, fluid modernity dissolves – denigrates and devalues – its duration.

Twenty years ago Michael Thompson published a pioneering study of the convoluted historical fate of the durable/transient distinction.[26] 'Durable' objects are meant to be preserved for a long, long time; they come as close as possible to embody and tokenize the otherwise abstract and ethereal notion of eternity; in fact, it is from the postulated or projected antiquity of the 'durables' that the image of eternity is extrapolated. Durable objects are assigned special value and are cherished and coveted thanks to their association with immortality – that ultimate value, 'naturally' desired and requiring no argument or persuasion to be embraced. The opposite of the 'durable' objects is 'transient' ones, meant to be used up – consumed – and to disappear in the process of their consumption. Thompson points out that 'those people near the top . . . can ensure that their own objects are always durable and those of others are always transient . . . [T]hey cannot lose.' Thompson takes it for granted that the desire to 'make their own objects durable' is the constant wish of 'those people near the top'; perhaps even that ability to make objects durable, to amass them, keep them, insure against their theft and spoliation, best of all monopolize them, is what puts people 'near the top'.

Such thoughts rang true (or at least credible) amidst the realities of solid modernity. I suggest, though, that the advent of fluid modernity has radically undermined their credibility. It is Bill Gates-style capacity to shorten the timespan of durability, to forget about the 'long term', to focus on the manipulation of transience rather than durability, to dispose of things lightly in order to clear the site for other things similarly transient and similarly meant to be instantly used up, that is nowadays the privilege of the top people and which makes them the top people they are. Being stuck with things for a long time, beyond their 'use up and abandon' date and beyond the moment when their 'new and improved' replacements and 'upgrades' are on offer, is, on the contrary, the symptom of deprivation. Once the infinity of possibilities empties the infinity of time of its seductive power, durability loses its attraction and turns from an asset into a liability. Perhaps more to the point is to observe that the very borderline dividing the 'durable' from the 'transient', once a focus of intense contention and engineering bustle, has been by now all but deserted by the border police and building battalions.

The devaluation of immortality cannot but augur a cultural upheaval, arguably the most decisive turning point in human cultural history. The passage from heavy to light capitalism, from solid to fluid modernity, may yet prove to be a departure more radical and seminal than the advent of capitalism and modernity themselves, previously seen as by far the most crucial milestones of human history at least since the neolithic revolution. Indeed, throughout human history the work of culture consisted in sifting and sedimenting hard kernels of perpetuity out of transient human lives and fleeting human actions, in conjuring up duration out of transience, continuity out of discontinuity, and in transcending thereby the limits imposed by human mortality by deploying mortal men and women in the service of the immortal human species. Demand for this kind of work is nowadays shrinking. The consequences of falling demand remain to be seen and are difficult to visualize in advance, since there are no precedents to recall and to lean on.

The novel instantaneity of time radically changes the modality of human cohabitation – and most conspicuously the way in which humans attend to (or do not attend to, as the case may be) their collective affairs, or rather the way in which they make (or do not make, as the case may be) certain affairs into collective ones.

The 'public choice theory' currently making truly phenomenal advances in political science aptly grasped the new departure (though – as often happens when new human practices set a new stage for the human imagination – it hurried to generalize relatively recent developments into the eternal truth of the human condition, allegedly overlooked, neglected or belied by 'all past scholarship'). According to Gordon Tullock, one of the most distinguished promoters of the new theoretical fashion, 'The new approach begins by assuming that voters are much like customers and that politicians are much like businesspeople.' Sceptical about the value of the 'public choice' approach, Leif Lewin caustically retorted that the thinkers of the 'public choice' school of thought 'depict political man as . . . a myopic cave man'. Lewin thinks this is utterly wrong. It might have been true in the troglodyte's era, 'before man "discovered tomorrow" and learned to make long-term calculations', but not now, in our modern times, when everyone knows, or most of us, electors and politicians alike, know, that 'tomorrow we meet again' and so credibility is 'the politician's most valuable asset'[27] (while the allocation of trust, we may add, is the elector's most eagerly used weapon). To support his critique of 'public choice' theory, Lewin refers to numerous empirical studies, showing that few electors own up to voting with their wallets, while most of them declare that what guides their voting behaviour is the state of the country as a whole. This is, Lewin says, what could have been expected; this is, as I would rather suggest, what the interviewed voters thought they were expected to say and what would be *comme il faut* for them to say. If one makes the necessary allowances for the notorious disparity between what we do and how we narrate our actions, one would not reject off-hand the claims of 'public choice' theorists (as distinct from the universal and extemporal validity of those claims). In this case, their theory might have actually gained in insight by cutting itself loose from what has been taken, uncritically, for 'empirical data'.

It is true that once upon a time the cavemen 'discovered tomorrow'. But history is a process of forgetting as much as it is a process of learning, and memory is famous for its selectivity. Perhaps we will 'meet tomorrow again'. But then again, perhaps we will not, or rather the 'we' who will meet tomorrow won't be the 'we' who met a moment ago. If this is the case, are the credibility and the allocation of trust assets, or liabilities?

Lewin recalls Jean-Jacques Rousseau's parable of stag hunters. Before men 'discovered tomorrow' – so the story goes – it could happen that a hunter, instead of waiting patiently for the stag to emerge from the woods, might have been distracted by his appetite for a rabbit running by, despite the fact that his share of meat in the jointly hunted stag would have been greater. Indeed so. But it so happens that today few hunting teams stay together for as long as it takes for the stag to appear, so whoever puts her or his trust in the benefits of the joint enterprise may be bitterly disappointed. And it so happens that, unlike the stags which, to be trapped and caught, require hunters who close ranks, stand arm to arm and act in solidarity, the rabbits fit for individual consumption are many and different and need little time to be shot, skinned and cooked. These are also discoveries – *new* discoveries, perhaps as pregnant with consequences as the 'discovery of tomorrow' once was.

'Rational choice' in the era of instantaneity means *to pursue gratification while avoiding the consequences*, and particularly the responsibilities which such consequences may imply. Durable traces of today's gratification mortgage the chances of tomorrow's gratifications. Duration changes from an asset into a liability; the same may be said about everything bulky, solid and heavy – everything that hinders and restricts the move. Giant industrial plants and corpulent bodies have had their day: once they bore witness to their owners' power and might; now they presage defeat in the next round of acceleration and so signal impotence. Lean body and fitness to move, light dress and sneakers, cellular telephones (invented for the use of the nomad who needs to be 'constantly in touch'), portable or disposable belongings – are the prime cultural tokens of the era of instantaneity. Weight and size, and above all the fat (literal or metaphorical) blamed for the expansion of both, share the fate of durability. They are the dangers one should beware of and fight against, and best of all steer clear of.

It is difficult to conceive of culture indifferent to eternity and shunning durability. It is similarly difficult to conceive of morality indifferent to the consequences of human actions and shunning responsibility for the effects these actions may have on others. The advent of instantaneity ushers human culture and ethics into unmapped and unexplored territory, where most of the learned habits of coping with the business of life have lost their utility and sense. As Guy Debord famously put it, 'Men resemble their times more than their fathers.' And present-day men and women differ from their fathers and mothers by living in a present 'which wants to forget the past and no longer seems to believe in the future'.[28]

But the memory of the past and trust in the future have been thus far the two pillars on which the cultural and moral bridges between transience and durability, human mortality and the immortality of human accomplishments, as well as taking responsibility and living by the moment, all rested.

4

Work

_____

The Town Hall of Leeds, the city in which I have spent the last
thirty years, is a majestic monument to the swaggering ambitions
and matching self-confidence of the captains of the Industrial Revolution. Built in the middle of the nineteenth century, grandiose and
opulent, heavy and cast in stone meant to last for ever, like the
Parthenon and Egyptian temples which it architecturally imitates.
It contains as its centre-piece a huge assembly hall where the towns-
people were to meet regularly to discuss and decide the further
steps on the road to the city's and the British Empire's greater
glory. Under the ceiling of the assembly hall were spelled out in
gold and purple letters the rules meant to guide anyone joining that
road. Among the sacrosanct principles of the self-assured and
self-assertive bourgeois ethics, like 'Honesty is the best policy',
'Auspicium melioris aevi' or 'Law and Order', one precept strikes
by its self-assured and uncompromising brevity: 'Forward'. Unlike
the contemporary visitor to the Town Hall, the city elders who
composed the code must have had no doubts about its meaning.
Surely they felt no need to ask what was meant by the idea of
'moving forward', called 'progress'. They knew the difference between 'forward' and 'backward'. And they could claim to know it
because they _practised_ the action that made this difference: next to
'Forward' another precept had been painted in gold and purple –
'Labor omnia vincit'. 'Forward' was the destination, labour was
the vehicle bound to take them there, and the town elders who

commissioned the Town Hall felt strong enough to stay on the track as long as it took to reach the destination.

On 25 May 1916 Henry Ford told the correspondent of the *Chicago Tribune*:

> History is more or less bunk. We don't want tradition. We want to live in the present and the only history that is worth a tinker's damn is the history we make today.

Ford was famous for saying loud and clear what others would think twice about before admitting. Progress? Do not think of it as 'the work of history'. It is *our* work, the work of *us*, who live in *the present*. The sole history that counts is one not-yet-made-but-being-made at the moment and bound-to-be-made: that is *the future*, of which another pragmatic and down-to-earth American, Ambrose Bierce, had written ten years earlier in his *Devil's Dictionary*, that it is 'that period of time in which our affairs prosper, our friends are true and our happiness is assured'.

Modern self-confidence gave an entirely new gloss to the eternal human curiosity about the future. Modern utopias were never mere prophecies, let alone idle dreams: openly or covertly, they were both declarations of intent and expressions of faith that what was desired could be done and will be done. The future was seen like the rest of the products in that society of producers: something to be thought through, designed, and then seen through the process of its production. The future was the creation of work, and work was the source of all creation. Still in 1967, Daniel Bell wrote that

> every society today is consciously committed to economic growth, to raising the standard of living of its people, and *therefore* [my emphasis – Z.B.] to the planning, direction, and control of social change. What makes the present studies, therefore, so completely different from those in the past is that they are oriented to specific social-policy purposes; and along with this new dimension, they are fashioned, self-consciously, by a new methodology which gives the promise of providing a more reliable foundation for realistic alternatives and choices . . .[1]

Ford would have proclaimed triumphantly what Pierre Bourdieu has recently wistfully noted: to master the future, one needs a hold on the present.[2] Those who keep the present in their grip can be confident of being able to force the future to make their affairs prosper, and for this very reason may ignore the past: they, and only they, can treat past history as 'bunk', which translates into more elegant English as 'nonsense', 'idle boast' or 'humbug'. Or, at least, give the past no more attention than things of such a kind deserve. Progress does not elevate or enoble history. 'Progress' is a declaration of belief that history is of no account and of the resolve to leave it out of account.

Progress and trust in history

This is the point: 'Progress' stands not for any quality of history, but for *the self-confidence of the present*. The deepest, perhaps the sole meaning of progress is made up of two closely interrelated beliefs – that 'time is on our side', and that we are the ones who 'make things happen'. The two beliefs live together and die together – and they go on living as long as the power to make things happen finds its daily corroboration in the deeds of people who hold them. As Alain Peyrefitte put it, 'the only resource capable of transforming a desert in the land of Canaan is the confidence of the society members in each other, and the trust of all in the future they are going to share'.[3] All the rest which we may like to say or hear about the 'essence' of the idea of progress is an understandable, yet misleading and futile effort to 'ontologize' that feeling of trust and self-confidence.

Indeed, is history a march towards better living and more happiness? Were that true, how would we know? We, who say that, did not live in the past; those who lived in the past do not live today. So who is to make the comparison? Whether (as the Bejamin/Klee Angel of History) we run away into the future repelled and pushed by the horrors of the past, or whether (as the sanguine rather than dramatic Whig version of history would wish us to believe) we hurry into the future attracted and pulled by the hope of 'our affairs to prosper', the sole 'evidence' to go by is the play of memory and imagination, and what links them or separates them is our self-confidence or its absence. To people confident of their power to change things, 'progress' is an axiom. To people who feel that things fall out of their hands, the idea of progress would not occur and would be laughable if heard. Between the two polar conditions there is little room for a *sine ira et studio* debate, let alone a consensus. Henry Ford would perhaps apply to progress an opinion similar to that he expressed on exercise: 'Exercise is bunk. If you are healthy, you don't need it; if you are sick, you won't do it.'

But if self-confidence – the reassuring feeling of 'keeping hold on the present' – is the sole foundation on which the trust in progress rests, no wonder that in our times trust must be unsteady and rickety. And the reasons why it should be the case are not difficult to locate.

First, the conspicuous absence of an *agency* able to 'move the world forward'. The most poignant yet the least answerable question of our times of liquid modernity is not 'What is to be done?' (in order to make the world better or happier), but 'Who is going to do it?' Kenneth Jowitt[4] announced the collapse of the 'Joshua discourse', which until recently used to shape our thoughts about the world and its prospects and which held the world to be 'centrally organized, rigidly bounded, and hysterically concerned with impenetrable boundaries'. In such a world the doubts about agency could hardly arise: after all, the world of the 'Joshua discourse' was little else than a conjunction of a powerful agency and the residues/effects of its actions That image had a solid epistemological foundation which comprised entities as solid, unshakeable and indomitable as the Fordist factory or the order-designing-and-administering sovereign states (sovereign if not in reality, then at least in their ambition and determination).

That foundation of trust in progress is nowadays prominent mostly for its cracks, fissures and chronic fissiparousness. The most solid and least questionable of its elements are fast losing their compactness together with their sovereignty, credibility and trustworthiness. The jading of the modern state is perhaps felt most acutely, since it means that the power to goad people to work – the power to do things – is taken away from politics, which used to decide what sort of things ought to be done and who was to do them. While all the agencies of political life stay where 'liquid modernity' times found them, tied as before to their respective localities, power flows well beyond their reach. Ours is an experience akin to that of the airline passengers who discover, high in the sky, that the pilot's cabin is empty. To quote Guy Debord, 'The controlling centre has now become occult: never to be occupied by a known leader, or clear ideology.'[5]

Secondly, it gets less and less clear what the agency – any agency – should do to improve the shape of the world in the unlikely case that it is powerful enough to do it. The images of a happy society painted in many colours and by many brushes in the course of the past two centuries all proved to be either unattainable pipe-dreams or (in those cases where their arrival was announced) unliveable. Each form of social design has been proved to produce as much misery as happiness, if not more. This applies in equal measure to both principal antagonists – the now bankrupt Marxism and the presently buoyant economic liberalism. (As Peter Drucker, admittedly a most outspoken advocate of the liberal state, pointed out in 1989, '*laissez-faire* too promised "salvation by society": to remove all obstacles to the pursuit of individual gain would in the end produce a perfect – or at least the best possible – society' – and for that reason its bravado can no longer be taken seriously.) As to other once serious competitors, the question put by François Lyotard, 'What kind of thought is able to sublate Auschwitz in a general . . . process towards a universal emancipation', stays as before unanswered and will remain so. The heyday of the Joshua discourse is over: all already painted visions of a made-to-measure world feel unpalatable, and those not yet painted are *a priori* suspect. We now travel without an idea of destination to guide us, neither looking for a good society nor quite sure what in the society we inhabit makes us listless and eager to run. Peter Drucker's verdict 'no more salvation by society . . . [A]nyone who now proclaims the "Great Society" as Lyndon Baines Johnson did only twenty years ago, would be laughed out of court'[6] has flawlessly captured the mood of the time.

The modern romance with progress – with life that can be 'worked out', to be more satisfactory than it is and bound to be so improved – is not over, though, and is unlikely to end soon. Modernity knows of no other life but 'made': the life of modern men and women is a task, not a given, and a task as yet uncompleted and relentlessly calling for more care and new effort. If anything, the human condition in the stage of 'fluid' modernity or 'light' capitalism has made that modality of life yet more salient: progress is no longer a temporary measure, an interim matter, leading eventually (and soon) to a state of perfection (that is a state in which whatever had to be done would have been done and no other change would be called for), but a perpetual and perhaps never-ending challenge and necessity, the very meaning of 'staying alive and well'.

If, however, the idea of progress in its present incarnation looks so unfamiliar that one wonders whether it is still with us, it is because progress, like so many other parameters of modern life, has now been 'individualized'; more to the point – *deregulated* and *privatized*. It is now deregulated – since the offers to 'upgrade' present realities are many and diverse and since the question whether a particular novelty indeed means an improvement has been left to free contest before and after its introduction and bound to remain contentious even after the choice has been made. And it is privatized since the matter of improvement is no longer a collective but an individual enterprise: it is individual men and women on their own who are expected to use, individually, their own wits, resources and industry to lift themselves to a more satisfactory condition and leave behind whatever aspect of their present condition they may resent. As Ulrich Beck put it in his eye-opening study of contemporary *Risikogesellschaft*,

> the tendency is towards the emergence of individualized forms and conditions of existence, which compel people – for the sake of their own material survival – to make themselves the centre of their own planning and conduct of life ... In fact, one has to choose and change one's social identity as well as take the risks of doing so ... *The individual himself or herself becomes the reproduction unit of the social in the lifeworld.*[7]

The issue of the *feasibility* of progress, whether seen as the species' destiny or the individual's task, remains however very much as it was before deregulation and privatization set in – and exactly as Pierre Bourdieu articulated it: to design the future, a hold on the present is needed. The sole novelty here is that it is now the individual's hold on her or his own present which matters. And for many, perhaps most, contemporary people their individual hold on the present is at best shaky and more often than not blatantly absent. We live in a world of universal flexibility, under conditions of acute and prospectless *Unsicherheit*, penetrating all aspects of individual life – the sources of livelihood as much as the partnerships of love or common interests, parameters of professional as much as cultural identity, modes of presentation of self in public as much as patterns of health and fitness, values worth pursuing as much as the ways to pursue them. Safe ports for trust are few and far between, and most of the time trust floats

unanchored vainly seeking storm-protected havens. We have all
learned the hard way that even the most carefully and laboriously
made plans have a nasty tendency to go amiss and bring results far
removed from the expected, that our earnest efforts to 'put things
in order' often result in more chaos, formlessness and confusion,
and that our labour to eliminate contingency and accident is little
more than a game of chance.

True to its habits, science promptly took the hint from the new
historical experience and reflected the emerging mood in the prolif-
eration of scientific theories of chaos and catastrophe. Once moved
by the belief that 'God does not play dice', that the universe is
essentially deterministic and that the human task consists in making a full inventory of its laws so that there will be no more groping
in the dark and human action will be unerring and always on
target, contemporary science took a turn towards the recognition
of the endemically indeterministic nature of the world, of the enormous role played by chance, and of the exceptionality, rather than
the normality, of order and equilibrium. Also true to their habits,
the scientists bring the scientifically processed news back to the
realm in which they were first intuited, to wit to the world of
human affairs and human actions. And so we read, for instance, in
David Ruelle's popular and influential rendition of contemporary
science-inspired philosophy, that 'the deterministic order creates a
disorder of chance':

> Economic treatises ... make an impression that the role of the
> legislators and the responsible government officials is to find out
> and implement an equilibrium particularly favourable to the com-
> munity. Examples of chaos in physics teach us, however, that in-
> stead of leading to an equilibrium, certain dynamic situations trigger
> temporarily chaotic and unpredictable developments. The legisla-
> tors and responsible officials should therefore face the possibility
> that their decisions, meant to produce a better equilibrium, will
> instead produce violent and unanticipated oscillations, with poss-
> ibly disastrous effects.[8]

For whichever of its many virtues work had been elevated to the
rank of the foremost value of modern times, its wondrous, nay
magical, ability to give shape to the formless and duration to the
transient figured prominently among them. Thanks to that ability,
work could be justly assigned a major role, even the decisive one,

in the modern ambition to subdue, harness and colonize the future in order to replace chaos with order and contingency with a predictable (and so controllable) sequence of events. Work was assigned many virtues and beneficial effects, like, for instance, the increase of wealth and the elimination of misery; but underlying every merit assigned it was its assumed contribution to that ordermaking, to the historic act of putting the human species in charge of its own destiny.

'Work' so understood was the activity in which humanity as a whole was supposed to be engaged by its fate and nature, rather than by choice, when making its history. And 'work' so defined was a collective effort of which every single member of humankind had to partake. All the rest was but a consequence: casting work as the 'natural condition' of human beings, and being out of work as an abnormality; blaming departure from that natural condition for extant poverty and misery, deprivation and depravity; ranking men and women according to the assumed value of the contribution their work made to the species-wide endeavour; and assigning to work the prime place among human activities, leading to moral self-improvement and to the rise of the overall ethical standards of society.

When *Unsicherheit* becomes permament and is seen as such, being-in-the-world feels less like a law-bound and law-abiding, logical, consistent and cumulative chain of actions, and more like a game, in which the 'world out there' is one of the players and behaves as all players do, keeps its cards close to its chest. As in any other game, plans for the future tend to become transient, protean and fickle, reaching no further than the next few moves.

With no state of ultimate perfection looming on the horizon of human efforts, with no trust in the foolproof effectiveness of any effort, the idea of 'total' order to be erected floor by floor in a protracted, consistent, purpose-guided effort of labour makes little sense. The less hold one has on the present, the less of the 'future' can be embraced in the design. Stretches of time labelled 'future' get shorter, and the time-span of life as a whole is sliced into episodes dealt with 'one at a time'. Continuity is no longer the mark of improvement. The once cumulative and long-term nature of progress is giving way to demands addressed to every successive episode separately: the merit of each episode must be revealed and consumed in full before it is finished and a next episode starts. In a life ruled by the precept of flexibility, life strategies and plans can be but short-term.

Jacques Attali has recently suggested that it is the image of the labyrinth which nowadays comes to dominate, even if surreptitiously, our thinking about the future and our own part in it; that image becomes the principal mirror in which our civilization in its present stage contemplates its own likeness. The labyrinth as an allegory of the human condition was a message transmitted by the nomads to the settlers. Millennia have passed, and the settlers have finally acquired the self-confidence and courage to rise to the challenge of the labyrinthine fate. 'In all European languages', Attali points out, 'the word *labyrinth* became a synonym of artificial complexity, useless darkness, tortuous system, impenetrable thicket. "Clarity" became a synonym of logic.'

The settlers set about making the walls transparent, the devious passages straight and well signed, the corridors well lit. They also produced guide-books and clear-cut, unambiguous instructions for the use of all future wanderers about which turns to take and which to avoid. They did all this only to discover in the end that the labyrinth is firmly in place; if anything, the labyrinth has become yet more treacherous and confusing owing to the illegible tangle of criss-crossing footprints, the cacophony of commands and the continuous addition of new twisting passages to the ones already left behind and new dead ends to the ones already blundered into. The settlers have become 'involuntary nomads', belatedly recalling the message they received at the beginning of their historical travels and trying desperately to recover its forgotten contents which – as they suspect – may well carry the 'wisdom necessary for their future'. Once more, the labyrinth becomes the master image of the human condition – and it means 'the opaque place where the layout of the roads may not obey any law. Chance and surprise rule in the labyrinth, which signals the defeat of Pure Reason.'[9]

In the uncompromisingly labyrinthine world human labours split into self-enclosed episodes just like the rest of human life. And as in the case of all other actions humans may undertake, the goal of holding their course close to the actors' designs is elusive, perhaps unattainable. Work has drifted from the universe of order-building and future-control to the realm of a game; acts of work become more like the strategy of a player who sets himself modestly short-term objectives reaching no further than one or two moves ahead. What counts is the immediate effects of every move; the effects must be fit to be consumed on the spot. The world is suspected of being full of bridges too far, the kind of bridges one would rather not think of crossing before one comes to them, and that is not likely to happen soon. Each obstacle is to be negotiated in its own turn; life is a sequence of episodes – each to be calculated separately, as each has its own balance of gains and losses. Life's roads do not get straighter in the course of being trodden, and turning one corner is not a warranty that right turns will be taken in the future.

And so work has changed its character. More often than not, it is a one-off act: a ploy of a *bricoleur*, a trickster, aimed at what is at hand and inspired and constrained by what is at hand, more shaped than shaping, more the outcome of chasing a chance than the product of planning and design. It bears an uncanny resemblance to the famed cyber-mole who knew how to move around seeking an electrical socket to plug into in order to replenish the energy used up in moving around in search of an electrical socket to plug into in order to replenish the energy . . .

Perhaps the term 'tinkering' would be more apt to grasp the changed nature of work cut out from the grand design of human-kind's universally shared mission and no less grandiose design of a life-long vocation. Stripped of its eschatological trappings and cut off from its metaphysical roots, work has lost the centrality which it was assigned in the galaxy of values dominant in the era of solid modernity and heavy capitalism. Work can no longer offer the secure axis around which to wrap and fix self-definitions, identities and life-projects. Neither can it be easily conceived of as the ethical foundation of society, or as the ethical axis of individual life.

Instead, work has acquired – alongside other life activities – a mainly aesthetic significance. It is expected to be gratifying by and in itself, rather than be measured by the genuine or putative effects it brings to one's brothers and sisters in humanity or to the might of the nation and country, let alone the bliss of future generations. Only a few people – and then only seldom – can claim privilege, prestige or honour, pointing to the importance and common benefit of the work they perform. Hardly ever is work expected to 'ennoble' its performers, to make them 'better human beings', and rarely is it admired and praised for that reason. It is instead measured and evaluated by its capacity to be entertaining and amusing, satisfying not so much the ethical, Promethean vocation of the producer and creator as the aesthetical needs and desires of the consumer, the seeker of sensations and collector of experiences.

The rise and fall of labour

According to the *OED*, the first usage of the word 'labour' in the meaning of 'physical exertion directed to the supply of the material wants of the community' was recorded in 1776. A century later it came to signify in addition 'the general body of labourers and operatives' who take this part in production, and shortly afterwards also the unions and other bodies which linked the two meanings, made the link hold and reforged it into a political issue and instrument of political power. The English usage is remarkable for bringing into sharp view the structure of the 'labour trinity' – the close connection (indeed, the semantic convergence linked to the identity of fate) between the significance assigned to work (that 'bodily and mental toil'), the self-constitution of those who work into a class, and the politics grounded in that self-constitution – in other words, the link between casting physical toil as the principal source of wealth and the well-being of society, and the self-assertion of the labour movement. Together they rose, together they fell.

Most economic historians agree (see, for instance, a recent summary of their findings by Paul Bairoc[10]) that, as far as the levels of wealth and income are concerned, there was little to distinguish between civilizations at the peak of their powers: the riches of Rome in the first century, of China in the eleventh, of India in the seventeenth, were not much different from those of Europe at the threshold of the Industrial Revolution. By some estimates, the income per head in Western Europe in the eighteenth century was no more than 30 per cent higher than that of India, Africa or China of that time. Not much more than one century was, however, enough to transform the ratio beyond recognition. Already by 1870 income per head in industrialized Europe was eleven times higher than in the poorest countries of the world. In the course of the next century or so the factor grew five-fold, reaching fifty by 1995. As the Sorbonne economist Daniel Cohen points out, 'I daresay that the phenomenon of inequality between nations is of recent origin; it is a product of the last two centuries.'[11] And so was the idea of labour as the source of wealth, and the politics born of and guided by that assumption.

The new global inequality and the new self-confidence and feeling of superiority which followed it were as spectacular as they were unprecedented: new notions, new cognitive frames were needed to grasp them and assimilate them intellectually. Such new notions and frames were supplied by the newly born science of political economy, which came to replace the physiocratic and mercantilist ideas that accompanied Europe on its way to the modern phase of its history up to the threshold of the Industrial Revolution.

It was, one may say, 'no accident' that these new notions were coined in Scotland, a country both inside and outside the mainstream of the industrial upheaval, involved and detached at the same time, physically and psychologically close to the country which was to become the epicentre of the emerging industrial order yet staying for a time relatively immune to its economic and cultural impact. The tendencies at full swing in the 'centre' are, as a rule, most promptly spotted and most clearly articulated in places temporarily relegated to the 'fringes'. Living at the outskirts of the civilizational centre means being near enough to see things clearly, yet far enough to 'objectify' them and so to mould and condense the perceptions into concepts. It was not a 'mere coincidence', therefore, that the gospel arrived from Scotland: wealth comes from work, labour being wealth's prime, perhaps sole source.

As Karl Polanyi was to suggest many years later, updating Karl Marx's insight, the starting point of the 'great transformation' which brought the new industrial order into being was the separation of labourers from the sources of their livelihood. That momentous event was part of a more comprehensive departure: production and exchange ceased to be inscribed into a more general, indeed all-embracing, indivisible way of life, and so conditions were created for labour (alongside land and money) to be considered mere commodity and treated as such.[12] We may say that it was the same new disconnectedness that set the labour capacity and its holders free to move, to be moved, and so to be put to different ('better' – more useful or more profitable) uses, recombined, made part of other ('better' – more useful or profitable) arrangements. The separation of productive activities from the rest of life pursuits allowed 'bodily and mental exertion' to congeal into a phenomenon in its own right – a 'thing' which could be treated like all things – that is, to be 'handled', moved, joined with other 'things' or set asunder.

Were not that disconnection to happen, there would be little chance for the idea of labour to be mentally separated from the 'totality' to which it 'naturally' belonged and to be condensed into a self-contained object. In the pre-industrial vision of wealth 'land' was such a totality – complete with those who tilled and harvested it. The new industrial order and the conceptual network which allowed the proclamation of the advent of a distinct – industrial – society, were born in Britain; and Britain stood out from its European neighbours for having destroyed its peasantry, and with it the 'natural' link between land, human toil and wealth. The tillers of the land had first to be made idle, drifting and 'masterless' in order to be seen as mobile containers or carriers of the ready-to-use 'labour power'; and for that power to be named the potential 'source of wealth' in its own right.

That new idleness and uprootedness of labourers appeared to the more reflectively inclined among contemporary witnesses as an emancipation of labour – part and parcel of the exhilarating sensation of the liberation of human abilities in general from vexing and stultifying parochial constraints, force of habit and hereditary inertia. But the emancipation of labour from its 'natural constraints' did not make labour free-floating, unattached or 'masterless' for long; and it hardly rendered it autonomous, self-determining, free to set and follow its own ways. The dismantled, or just no longer workable self-reproducing 'traditional way of life' of which labour was a part prior to its emancipation was to be replaced by another order; this time, however, a predesigned order, a 'built' order, no longer a sediment of aimless meanderings of fate and history's blunders, but a product of rational thought and action. Once it had been discovered that labour was the source of wealth, it was the task of reason to mine, drain and exploit that source more efficiently than ever before.

Some commentators imbued by the new boisterous spirit of the modern age (Karl Marx most prominent among them) saw the passing of the old order as primarily the outcome of deliberate dynamiting: an explosion caused by a bomb planted by capital bent on 'melting the solids and profaning the sacreds'. Others, like de Tocqueville, more sceptical and considerably less enthusiastic, saw that disappearance as a case of implosion rather than explosion: looking back, they spied out the seeds of doom in the heart of the *ancien régime* (always easier to be revealed or guessed in retrospect) and saw the agitation and swagger of the new masters as, essentially, the kicking of a corpse or not much more than pursuing with more vigour and resolve the self-same wonder-cures which the old order tested long before in desperate, yet vain efforts to ward off or at least postpone its own demise. There was little contention, though, as to the prospects of the new regime and the intentions of its masters: the old and by then defunct order was to be replaced by a new one, less vulnerable and more viable than its predecessor. New solids were to be conceived and constructed to fill the void left by the melted ones. Things set afloat were to be anchored again, more securely than before. To express the same intention in the currently fashionable idiom: what had been 'disembedded' would need to be, sooner or later, 're-embedded'.

Tearing up the old local/communal bonds, declaring war on habitual ways and customary laws, shredding and pulverizing *les pouvoirs intermédiaires* – the overall result of all that was the intoxicating delirium of the 'new beginning'. 'Melting the solids' felt like melting iron ore to cast steel pillars. Melted and now fluid realities seemed to be ready to be rechannelled and poured in new moulds, to be given a shape they would never have acquired had they been allowed to flow in the river-beds they themselves carved. No purpose, however ambitious, seemed to exceed human ability to think, discover, invent, plan and act. If the happy society – the society of happy people – was not yet exactly round the next corner, its imminent arrival was already anticipated on the drawing boards of the thinking men, and their contours sketched by the thinking men were given flesh in the offices and command posts of the men of action. The purpose to which men of thought and men of action alike dedicated their labours was the construction of a new order. The newly discovered freedom was to be deployed in the effort to bring about future orderly routine. Nothing was to be left to its own capricious and unpredictable course, to accident and contingency; nothing at all was to be left in its present shape if only that shape could be improved, made more useful and effective.

That new order in which all ends presently loose will be tied up again, while the flotsam and jetsam of past fatalities, the castaways now shipwrecked, marooned or drifting, will be grounded, resettled and fixed in their right places, was to be massive, solid, set in stone or wrought in steel: meant to last. Big was beautiful, big was rational; 'big' stood for power, ambition and courage. The building site of the new industrial order was spattered all over with monuments to that power and ambition, monuments which were or were not indestructible but certainly made to look that way: like giant factories filled wall to wall with bulky machinery and crowds of machine operatives, or dense networks of canals, bridges and rail tracks, punctuated by the majestic railway stations meant to emulate the ancient temples erected for the worship of eternity and for the eternal glory of the worshippers.

The same Henry Ford who declared that 'History is bunk', that 'We don't want tradition' and that 'We want to live in the present and the only history that is worth a tinker's damn is the history we make today', one day doubled his workers' wages, explaining that he wished his employees to buy his cars. That was of course a tongue-in-cheek explanation: the cars bought by Ford's workers made a negligible fraction of the total sales, while the doubling of wages weighed heavily on Ford's production costs. The true reason for the unorthodox step was Ford's wish to arrest the irritatingly high labour mobility. He wanted to tie his employees to Ford enterprises once for all, to make the money invested in their training and drill pay, and pay again, for the duration of the working lives of his workers. And to achieve such effect, he had to immobilize his staff, to keep them where they were preferably until their labour power was used up completely. He had to make them as dependent on employment in *his* factory and selling their labour to *its* owner as he himself depended for his wealth and power on employing them and using their labour.

Ford expressed in a raised voice the thoughts which others cherished yet managed only to whisper; or, rather, he thought out what others in a similar predicament felt, but were unable to express in so many words. The borrowing of Ford's name for the universal model of intentions and practices typical of solid modernity or heavy capitalism was appropriate. Henry Ford's model of a new, rational order set the standard for the universal tendency of his time: and it was an ideal which all or most other entrepreneurs of that era struggled, with mixed success, to achieve. The ideal was to tie together capital and labour in a union which – like a marriage made in heaven – no human power would be allowed, or would dare, to untie.

Solid modernity was, indeed, also the time of heavy capitalism –
of the engagement between capital and labour fortified by the
mutuality of their dependency. Workers depended on being hired
for their livelihood; capital depended on hiring them for its reproduction and growth. Their meeting-place had a fixed address; neither of the two could easily move elsewhere – the massive factory
walls enclosed and kept both partners in a shared prison. Capital
and workers were united, one may say, for richer for poorer, in
sickness and in health, and until death them did part. The plant
was their common habitat – simultaneously the battlefield for trench
warfare and the natural home for hopes and dreams.

What brought capital and labour face to face and tied them
together was the transaction of buying and selling; and so, in order
to stay alive, each needed to be kept in the shape fit for that
transaction: the owners of capital had to be able to go on buying
labour, and the owners of labour had to be alert, healthy, strong
and otherwise attractive enough not to put off the prospective
buyers and not to charge the buyers with the full costs of their
condition. Each side had 'vested interests' in keeping the other side
in the right shape. No wonder that the 'recommodification' of
capital and labour had become the principal function and concern
of politics and the supreme political agency, the state. The state
had to see to it that the capitalists stayed fit to buy labour and
afford its current prices. The unemployed were fully and truly the
'reserve army of labour', and so had to be kept through thick and
thin in a state of readiness, in case they were called back into active
service. The welfare state, a state dedicated to doing just that, was
for that reason genuinely 'beyond left and right', a prop without
which neither capital nor labour could stay alive and healthy, let
alone grow.

Some people saw the welfare state as a temporary measure,
which would work itself out of business once the collective insurance against misfortune made the insured bold and resourceful
enough to develop their potential in full and muster the courage to
take risks – and so allow them, so to speak, to 'stand on their own
feet'. More sceptical observers saw the welfare state as a collectively financed and managed sanitation device – a cleaning-and-
healing operation to be run as long as the capitalist enterprise kept
generating social waste it had neither intention nor resources to
recycle (that is, for a long time to come). There was a general

agreement, though, that the welfare state was a contraption meant to tackle the anomalies, prevent the departures from the norm and defuse the consequences of norm-breaking were it to happen nevertheless. The norm itself, hardly ever put in question, was the direct, face-to-face, mutual engagement of capital and labour, and solving all the important and vexing social issues within the frame of such engagement.

Whoever as a young apprentice took his first job at Ford could be pretty sure to finish his life of work in the same place. The time horizons of heavy capitalism were long-term. For the workers, the horizons were drawn by the prospect of life-long employment inside a company which might or might not be immortal, but whose life-span stretched nonetheless well beyond theirs. For the capitalists, the 'family fortune', which was meant to last beyond the life-span of any single family member, was synonymous with the plants they inherited, built or yet intended to add to the family heirloom.

To put it in a nutshell: the 'long-term' mentality amounted to an expectation born of experience, and by that experience convincingly and ever anew corroborated, that the respective fates of people who buy labour and people who sell it are closely and inseparably intertwined for a long time to come – in practical terms for ever – and that therefore working out a bearable mode of cohabitation is just as much 'in everybody's interest' as is the negotiation of the rules of neighbourly fair play among the house-owners settled in the same estate. That experience took many decades, perhaps more than a century, to entrench. It emerged at the end of the long and tortuous process of 'solidification'. As Richard Sennett suggested in his recent study, it was only after World War II that the original disorder of the capitalist era came to be replaced, at least in the most advanced economies, by 'strong unions, guarantees of the welfare state, and large-scale corporations' which combined to produce an era of 'relative stability'.[13]

The 'relative stability' in question underlay, to be sure, perpetual conflict. As a matter of fact, it made that conflict possible and, in a paradoxical sense well spotted in his time by Lewis Coser, 'functional': for better or worse, the antagonists were tied together by mutual dependency. Confrontation, tests of strength and the ensuing bargaining strengthened the unity of the conflicting parties precisely because none of them could go it alone and both sides knew that their continuous survival depended on finding solutions which they would consider acceptable. As long as the staying in each other's company was assumed to last, the rules of that togetherness were the focus of intense negotiations, sometimes of acrimony, confrontations and showdowns, at other times of truce and compromise. Unions reforged the impotence of individual workers into collective bargaining power and fought with intermittent success to recast the disabling regulations into workers' rights and to refashion them into constraints imposed on the employers' freedom of manoeuvre. As long and in so far as the mutual dependency held, even the impersonal time-schedules hotly resented by the craftsmen herded into early capitalist factories (and causing resistance, which E. P. Thompson vividly documented), and yet more their later 'new and improved' versions in the form of the infamous Frederic Taylor's time-measurements, these, in Sennett's words, acts 'of repression and domination practised by management for the sake of the giant industrial organization's growth', 'had become an arena in which workers could assert their own demands, an arena of empowerment'. Sennett concludes: 'Routine can demean, but it can also protect; routine can decompose labour, but it can also compose a life.'[14]

That situation has changed now, and the crucial ingredient of the multi-sided change is the new 'short-term' mentality which came to replace the 'long-term' one. Marriages 'till death us do part' are decidedly out of fashion and have become a rarity: no more do the partners expect to stay long in each other's company. According to the latest calculation, a young American with a moderate level of education expects to change jobs at least eleven times during his or her working life – and the pace and frequency of change are almost certain to go on growing before the working life of the present generation is over. 'Flexibility' is the slogan of the day, and when applied to the labour market it augurs an end to the 'job as we know it', announcing instead the advent of work on short-term contracts, rolling contracts or no contracts, positions with no in-built security but with the 'until further notice' clause. Working life is saturated with uncertainty.

From marriage to cohabitation

One may retort of course that there is nothing particularly new about this situation: working life has been full of uncertainty since time immemorial. The present-day uncertainty is, however, of a strikingly novel kind. The feared disasters which may play havoc with one's livelihood and its prospects are not of the sort which could be repelled or at least fought against and mitigated through joining forces, standing united and jointly debated, agreed and enforced measures. The most dreadful disasters now strike at random, picking their victims with a most bizarre logic or no visible logic at all, scattering their blows capriciously, so that there is no way to anticipate who is doomed and who will be saved. The present-day uncertainty is a powerful *individualizing* force. It divides instead of uniting, and since there is no telling who will wake up the next day in what division, the idea of 'common interests' grows ever more nebulous and loses all pragmatic value.

Contemporary fears, anxieties and grievances are made to be suffered alone. They do not add up, do not cumulate into a 'common cause', have no specific, let alone obvious, address. This deprives solidary stands of their past status of rational tactics and suggests a life-strategy quite different from the one which led to the establishment of working-class defensive and militant organizations. When talking to people already hit or fearing to be hit by the current changes in the conditions of employment, Pierre Bourdieu heard over and over again that 'In the face of the new forms of exploitation, favoured notably by the deregulation of work and development of temporary employment, the traditional forms of unionist action are felt inadequate.' Bourdieu concludes that recent departures 'have broken the foundations of past solidarities', and that the resulting 'disenchantment goes hand in hand with the demise of the spirit of militancy and political participation'.[15]

Once the employment of labour has become short-term and precarious, having been stripped of firm (let alone guaranteed) prospects and therefore made episodic, when virtually all rules concerning the game of promotions and dismissals have been scrapped or tend to be altered well before the game is over, there is little chance for mutual loyalty and commitment to sprout and take root. Unlike in the times of long-term mutual dependency, there is hardly any stimulus to take acute and serious, let alone critical, interest in the wisdom of the common endeavour and related arrangements which are bound to be transient anyway. The place of employment feels like a camping site which one visits for just a few days, and may leave at any moment if the comforts on offer are not delivered or found unsatisfactory when delivered – rather than like a shared domicile where one is inclined to take trouble and patiently work out the acceptable rules of cohabitation. Mark Granovetter suggested that ours is the time of 'weak ties', while Sennett proposes that 'fleeting forms of association are more useful to people than long-term connections'.[16]

The present-day 'liquefied', 'flowing', dispersed, scattered and deregulated version of modernity may not portend divorce and the final break of communication, but it does augur the advent of light, free-floating capitalism, marked by the *disengagement* and loosening of ties linking capital and labour. One may say that this fateful departure replicates the passage from marriage to 'living together' with all its corollary attitudes and strategic consequences, including the assumption of the temporariness of cohabitation and of the possibility that the association may be broken at any moment and for any reason, once the need or desire dries out. If staying together was a matter of *reciprocal* agreement and *mutual* dependency, disengagement is *unilateral*: one side of the configuration has acquired an autonomy it might have always secretly desired but had never seriously adumbrated before. To an extent never really achieved by the 'absentee landlords' of yore, capital has cut itself loose from its dependency on labour through the new freedom of movement undreamt of in the past. The reproduction and growth of capital, profits and dividends and the satisfaction of stockholders have all become largely independent from the duration of any particular local engagement with labour.

The independence is not, of course, complete, and capital is not as yet as volatile as it would wish and does its best to be. Territorial – local – factors still need to be reckoned with in most calculations, and the 'nuisance power' of local governments may still put vexing constraints on capital's freedom of movement. But capital has become exterritorial, light, unencumbered and disembedded to an unprecedented extent, and its already achieved level of spatial mobility is in most cases quite sufficient to blackmail territory-bound political agencies into submission to its demand. The threat (even unspoken and merely guessed) of cutting local ties and moving elsewhere is something which any responsible government, for its own sake and for the sake of its constituency, must treat in all seriousness, trying to subordinate its policies to the paramount purpose of warding off the threat of capital disinvestment.

To an unprecedented degree politics has today become a tug-of-war between the speed with which capital can move and the 'slowing down' capacities of local powers, and it is the local institutions which more often than not feel like waging a battle they cannot win. A government dedicated to the well-being of its constituency has little choice but to implore and cajole, rather than force, capital to fly in, and once inside, to build sky-scraping offices instead of staying in rented-per-night hotel rooms. And this can be done or can be attempted to be done by (to use the common political jargon of the free-trade era) 'creating better conditions for free enterprise', which means adjusting the political game to the 'free enterprise' rules – that is, using all the regulating power at the government's disposal in the service of deregulation, of dismantling and scrapping the extant 'enterprise constraining' laws and statutes, so that the government's vow that its regulating powers will not be used to restrain capital's liberties become credible and convincing; refraining from any move which may create an impression that the territory politically administered by the government is inhospitable to the usages, expectations and all future undertakings of globally thinking and globally acting capital, or less hospitable to them than the lands administered by the next-door neighbours. In practice, all this means low taxes, fewer or no rules and above all a 'flexible labour market'. More generally, it means a docile population, unable and unwilling to put up an organized resistance to whatever decision the capital might yet take. Paradoxically, governments can hope to keep capital in place only by convincing it beyond reasonable doubt that it is free to move away – at short notice or without notice.

Having shed the ballast of bulky machinery and massive factory crews, capital travels light with no more than cabin luggage – a briefcase, laptop computer and cellular telephone. That new attribute of volatility has made all engagement, and particularly a stable engagement, redundant and unwise at the same time: if entered, it would cramp the movement and detract from the desired competitiveness, cutting out *a priori* the options which may lead to increased productivity. Stock exchanges and boards of management around the world are prompt to reward all steps 'in the right direction' of disengagement, like 'slimming down', 'downsizing' and 'hiving off', while punishing just as promptly any news of staff expansion, increased employment and the company being 'bogged down' in costly long-term projects. The Houdini-like 'escape artist' skills of disappearing acts, the strategy of elision and avoidance and the readiness and ability to run away if need be, that hub of the new policy of disengagement and noncommitment, are today the signs of managerial wisdom and success. As Michel Crozier pointed out a long time ago, being free of awkward bonds, cumbersome commitments and dependencies arresting the freedom of manoeuvre, was always a favourite and effective weapon of domination; but the supplies of that weapon and the capacities to use them seem nowadays doled out less evenly than ever before in modern history. Speed of movement has today become a major, perhaps the paramount, factor of social stratification and the hierarchy of domination.

The main sources of profits – the big profits in particular, and so also of tomorrow's capital – tend to be, on a constantly growing scale, the *ideas* rather than *material objects*. Ideas are produced only once, and then keep on bringing in wealth depending on the number of people attracted as buyers/clients/consumers – not on the number of people hired and engaged in replicating the prototype. When it comes to making the ideas profitable, the objects of competition are the consumers, not the producers. No wonder that the present-day engagement of capital is primarily with the consumers. Only in this sphere can one sensibly speak of 'mutual dependency'. Capital is dependent, for its competitiveness, effectiveness and profitability, on consumers – and its itineraries are guided by the presence or absence of consumers or by the chances of consumers' production, of generating and then beefing up the demand for the ideas on offer. In the planning of travels and prompting capital's dislocations, the presence of a labour force is but a secondary consideration. Consequently, the 'holding power' of a local labour force on capital (more generally, on the conditions of employment and availability of jobs) has shrunk considerably.

Robert Reich[17] suggests that people presently engaged in economic activity can be divided roughly into four broad categories.

'Symbol manipulators', people who invent the ideas and the ways to make them desirable and marketable, form the first category. Those engaged in the reproduction of labour (educators or various functionaries of welfare state) belong to the second. The third category comprises people employed in 'personal services' (the kind of occupations which John O'Neill classified as 'skin trades'), requiring face-to-face encounter with the recipients of service; the sellers of products and the producers of desire for products form the bulk of this category.

Finally, the fourth category includes the people who for the last century and a half formed the 'social substratum' of the labour movement. They are, in Reich's terms, 'routine labourers', tied to the assembly line or (in more up-to-date plants) to the computer networks and electronic automated devices like check-out points. Nowadays, they tend to be the most expendable, disposable and exchangeable parts of the economic system. Neither particular skills, nor the art of social interaction with clients are listed in their job requirements – and so they are easiest to replace; they have few special qualities which would inspire in their employers the wish to keep them at all cost; they command, if anything, only a residual and negligible bargaining power. They know that they are disposable, and so they see little point in developing attachment or commitment to their jobs or entering lasting associations with their workmates. To avoid imminent frustrations, they tend to be wary of any loyalty to the workplace or inscribing their own life purposes into its projected future. This is a natural reaction to the 'flexibility' of the labour market, which when translated into the individual life experience means that long-term security is the last thing one is likely to learn to associate with the job currently performed.

As Sennett found out, visiting a New York bakery a couple of decades after his previous visit, 'the morale and motivation of workers dropped sharply in the various squeeze plays of downsizing. Surviving workers waited for the next blow of the ax rather than exulting in competitive victory over those who were fired.' But he adds another reason for the dwindling of the workers' interest in their work and the workplace and the fading of their wish to invest thought and moral energy in the future of both:

In all forms of work, from sculpting to serving meals, people identify with tasks which challenge them, tasks which are difficult. But
in this flexible workplace, with its polyglot workers coming and
going irregularly, radically different orders coming in each day,
the machinery is the only real standard of order, and so has to be
easy for anyone, no matter who, to operate. Difficulty is counterproductive in a flexible regime. By a terrible paradox, when we
diminish difficulty and resistance, we create the very conditions for
uncritical and indifferent activity on the part of the users.[18]

Around the other pole of the new social division, on the top of
the power pyramid of the light capitalism, circulate those for whom
space matters little if at all – those who are out of place in any place
they may be physically present. They are as light and volatile as the
new capitalist economy which gave them birth and endowed them
with power. As Jacques Attali describes them: 'They do not own
factories, lands, nor occupy administrative positions. Their wealth
comes from a portable asset: their knowledge of the laws of the
labyrinth.' They 'love to create, play and be on the move'. They
live in a society 'of volatile values, carefree about the future, egois-
tic and hedonistic'. They 'take the novelty as good tidings, precariousness as value, instability as imperative, hybridity as richness'.[19]
Though in varying degrees, they all master the art of 'labyrynthine
living': acceptance of disorientation, readiness to live outside space
and time, with vertigo and dizziness, with no inkling of the direction or the duration of travel they embark on.

A few months ago I sat with my wife in an airport bar waiting
for the connecting flight. Two men in their late twenties or early
thirties circled around the next table, each armed with a cellular
telephone. Through about an hour and a half of waiting, they did
not exchange a word with each other, though they both spoke
without interruption – to the invisible conversationalist on the
other end of the phone connection. Which does not mean that they
were oblivious to each other's presence. As a matter of fact, it was
the awareness of that presence which seemed to motivate their
actions. The two men were engaged in competition – as intense,
frenzied and furious as competition could be. Whoever finished the
cellular conversation while the other was still talking, searched
feverishly for another number to press; clearly the number of connections, the degree of 'connectedness', the density of the respective networks which made them into nodes, the quantity of other

nodes they could link to at will, were matters of utter, perhaps even superior, importance to both: indices of social standing, position, power and prestige. Both men spent that hour and a half in what was, in its relation to the airport bar, an outer space. When the flight they were both to take was announced, they simultaneously locked their briefcases with identical synchronized gestures and left, holding their telephones close to their ears. I am sure they hardly noticed me and my wife sitting two yards away and watching their every move. As far as their *Lebenswelt* was concerned, they were (after the pattern of orthodox anthropologists censured by Claude Lévi-Strauss) physically close to us yet spiritually and infinitely remote.

Nigel Thrift in his brilliant essay on what he has chosen to call 'soft' capitalism[20] notices the remarkable change of vocabulary and the cognitive frame which mark the new global and exterritorial elite. To convey the gist of their own actions, they use metaphors of 'dancing' or 'surfing'; they speak no longer of 'engineering', but instead of cultures and networks, teams and coalitions, and of influences rather than of control, leadership and management. They are concerned with looser forms of organization which could be put together, dismantled and reassembled at short notice or without notice: it is such a fluid form of assembly which fits their view of the surrounding world as 'multiple, complex, and fast-moving, and therefore "ambiguous", "fuzzy" and "plastic"', 'uncertain, paradoxical, even chaotic'. Today's business organization has an element of disorganization deliberately built into it: the less solid and the more fluid it is, the better. Like everything else in the world, all knowledge cannot but age quickly and so it is the 'refusal to accept established knowledge', to go by precedents and to recognize the wisdom of the lessons of accumulated experience that are now seen as the precepts of effectiveness and productivity.

The two young men with cellular telephones whom I watched at the airport bar might have been specimens (actual or aspiring) of that new, numerically small elite of the cyberspace residents thriving on the uncertainty and instability of all things worldly, but the style of the dominant tends to become the dominant style – if not by offering an attractive choice, then at any rate by imposing a life-setting in which its imitation becomes simultaneously desirable and imperative, turning into a matter of self-satisfaction and survival. Few people spend their time in airport lounges, and fewer still feel in their natural element there, or at least are sufficiently exterritorial not to feel oppressed or encumbered by the oozing tedium of the place and the noisy and uncouth crowds that fill it. But many, perhaps most, are nomads without leaving their caves. They may still seek shelter in their homes, but would hardly find seclusion there and however hard they may try they would never be truly *chez soi*: the shelters have porous walls, pierced all over by countless wires and easily penetrated by ubiquitous airwaves.

These people are, as most people before them, dominated and 'remotely controlled'; but they are dominated and controlled in a new way. Leadership has been replaced by the spectacle, and surveillance by seduction. Who rules the (air)waves, rules the lived world, decides its shape and contents. No one needs to force or nudge the spectators to attend the spectacle: woe to those who would dare deny them entry. Access to the (mostly electronic) 'information' has become the most zealously defended human right, and the rise of well-being among the population at large is now measured by, among other things, the number of households equipped with (invaded by?) television sets. And what the information informs more than on anything else and whatever that 'anything else' may be is the fluidity of the world its recipients inhabit and the virtue of flexibility of its residents. 'The news', that part of electronic information with most chance of being mistaken for the true representation of the 'world out there', with the strongest pretention to the role of the 'mirror of reality' (and most commonly credited with reflecting that reality faithfully and without distortion), is in Pierre Bourdieu's estimate among the most perishable of the goods on offer; indeed, life expectation of the news is ludicrously short when compared with that of soap-operas, talk-shows or stand-up-comedians' hours. But the perishability of the news as information about the 'real world' is itself a most important item of information: the news broadcasts are the constant, daily repeated celebration of the breathtaking speed of change, accelerated ageing, and perpetuality of new beginnings. [21]

Excursus: a brief history of procrastination

Cras, in Latin, means 'tomorrow'. The word used also to be semantically stretchable, so as to refer, not unlike the famously vague *mañana*, to an undefined 'later' – the future as such. *Crastinus* is what belongs to tomorrow. To *pro*-crastinate, is to place something among the things that belong to tomorrow. To *place* something there, which implies right away that tomorrow is not that thing's natural place, that the thing in question does not belong there of right. By implication, it belongs elsewhere. Where? The present, obviously. In order to land in the tomorrow, the thing needs first to be pulled out from the present or barred access to it. 'To procrastinate' means *not* to take things as they come, *not* to act according to a natural succession of things. Contrary to an impression made common in the modern era, procrastination is not a matter of sloth, indolence, quiescence or lassitude; it is an *active* stance, an attempt to assume control over the sequence of events and make that sequence different from what it would be were one to stay docile and unresisting, To procrastinate is to manipulate the possibilities of the *presence* of a thing by putting off, delaying and postponing its becoming present, keeping it at a distance and deferring its immediacy.

Procrastination as a cultural practice came into its own with the dawn of modernity. Its new meaning and ethical significance derived from the new meaningfulness of time, from time having a history, time *being* history. That meaning derived from time conceived as a passage between the 'present moments' of *different* quality and *varying* value, time considered as travelling towards another present distinct from (and as a rule more desirable than) the present lived through now.

To put it in a nutshell: procrastination derived its modern meaning from time lived as a pilgrimage, as a movement coming closer to a target. In such time, each present is evaluated by something that comes after. Whatever value this present here and now may possess, it is but a premonitory signal of a higher value to come. The use – the task – of the present is to bring one closer to that higher value. By itself, the present time is meaningless and valueless. It is for that reason flawed, deficient and incomplete. The meaning of the present lies ahead; what is at hand is evaluated and given sense by the *noch-nicht-geworden*, by what does not yet exist.

Living a life as a pilgrimage is therefore intrinsically aporetic. It obliges each present to serve something which is-not-yet, and to serve it by closing up the distance, by working towards proximity and immediacy. But were the distance closed up and the goal reached, the present would forfeit everything that made it significant and valuable. The instrumental rationality favoured and privileged by the pilgrim's life prompts the search for such means as may perform the uncanny feat of keeping the end of the efforts forever in sight while never reaching proximity, of bringing the end ever closer while preventing the distance from being brought to zero. The pilgrim's life is a travel-towards-fulfilment, but 'fulfilment' in that life is tantamount to the loss of meaning. Travelling towards the fulfilment gives the pilgrim's life its meaning, but the meaning it gives is blighted with a suicidal impulse; that meaning cannot survive the completion of its destiny.

Procrastination reflects that ambivalence. The pilgrim procrastinates in order to be better prepared to grasp things that truly matter. But grasping them will signal the end of the pilgrimage, and so the end to such life as derives from it its sole meaning. For this reason, procrastination has an in-built tendency to break any time-limit set in advance and to stretch indefinitely – *ad calendas graecas*. Procrastination tends to become its own objective . The most important thing put off in the act of procrastination tends to be the termination of the procrastination itself.

The attitudinal/behavioural precept which laid the foundation of modern society and rendered the modern way of being-in-the-world both possible and inescapable was the principle of *delay of gratification* (of the satisfaction of a need or desire, of the moment of a pleasurable experience, of enjoyment). It is in this avatar that procrastination entered the modern scene (or, more exactly, rendered the scene modern). As Max Weber explained, it was that particular dilatoriness, rather than haste and impatience, that resulted in such spectacular and seminal modern innovations as, on the one hand, accumulation of capital and, on the other, the spread and entrenchment of the work ethic. The desire for improvement gave the effort its spur and momentum; but the caveat 'not yet', 'not just now', directed that effort towards its unanticipated consequence, which came to be known as growth, development, acceleration and, for that matter, modern society.

In the form of the 'delay of gratification' procrastination retained all its inner ambivalence. Libido and Thanatos vied with each other in every act of deferment, and each delay was the triumph of Libido over its mortal enemy. Desire prompted the effort through the hope of gratification, yet the prompting retained its force as long as the coveted gratification remained but a hope. All the motivating powers of desire were vested in its unfulfilment. In the end, in order to stay alive desire had to desire only its own survival.

In the form of the 'delay of gratification', procrastination put ploughing and sowing above harvesting and ingesting the crops, investment above creaming off the gains, saving above spending, self-denial above self-indulgence, work above consumption. Yet it never denigrated the value of the things to which it denied priority nor played down their merit and significance. Those things were the prizes of the self-inflicted abstinence, rewards for the voluntary dilatoriness. The more severe the self-restraint, the greater would be, eventually, the opportunity for self-indulgence. Do save, since the more you save, the more you will be able to spend. Do work, since the more you work, the more you will consume. Paradoxically, the denial of immediacy, the apparent demotion of the goals, rebounded as their elevation and ennoblement. The need to wait magnified the teasing/seductive powers of the prize. Far from degrading the gratification of desires as a motive of life efforts, the precept to postpone it made it into the supreme purpose of life. Delay of gratification kept the producer in the consumer toiling – by keeping the consumer in the producer wide awake and wide-eyed.

Owing to its ambivalence, procrastination fed two opposite tendencies. One led to the *work ethic*, which prodded the means to swap places with the ends and proclaimed the virtue of *work for the work's sake*, the delay of joy to be a value in its own right and a value more exquisite than those other values it was supposed to serve, work ethics pressed the delay to be extended indefinitely. Another tendency led to the aesthetic of consumption, demoting work to a purely subordinate, instrumental role of soil-mulching, an activity that derives all its value from what it is not, but what it prepares the ground for, and to the casting of abstention and renunciation as sacrifices perhaps necessary, but cumbersome and rightly resented, preferably to be reduced to a bare minimum.

Being a double-edged sword, procrastination could serve modern society in both its 'solid' and 'fluid', producer and consumer stage, though it burdened each phase with tensions and unresolved attitudinal and axiological conflicts. The passage to the present-day consumer society therefore signified a shift in emphasis rather than a change of values. And yet it stressed the principle of procrastination to the breaking point. That principle now stands vulnerable, as it has lost the protective shield of the ethical injunction. No longer is the delay of gratification a sign of moral virtue. It is a hardship pure and simple, a problematic burden signalling imperfections in social arrangements, personal inadequacy, or both. Not an exhortation, but a resigned and sad admission of an unpleasant (yet curable) state of affairs.

If the work ethic pressed towards indefinite extension of delay, the aesthetic of consumption presses towards its abolition. We live, as George Steiner put it, in a 'casino culture', and in the casino the never-too-distant call 'Rien ne va plus!' sets the welcome limit to procrastination; if an act is to be rewarded, the reward is instantaneous. In the casino culture the waiting is taken out of wanting, but the satisfaction of the wanting must also be brief, must last only until the next run of the ball, to be as short-lived as the waiting, lest it should smother, rather than replenish and reinvigorate, the desire – that most coveted of rewards in the world ruled by the aesthetic of consumption.

And so the beginning and the end of procrastination meet, the distance between desire and its gratification condenses into the moment of ecstasy – of which, as John Tusa has observed (in the *Guardian* of 19 July 1997), there must be plenty: 'Immediate, constant, diversionary, entertaining, in ever-growing numbers, in ever-growing forms, on ever-growing occasions.' No qualities of things and acts count 'other than instant, constant and unreflecting self-gratification'. Obviously, demand for the gratification to be *instant* militates against the principle of procrastination. But being instant, gratification cannot be constant unless it is also short-lived, barred from lingering beyond the life-span of its diversionary and entertaining power. In the casino culture the principle of procrastination is under attack on two fronts at the same time. Under pressure are the delay of the gratification's *arrival*, as well as the delay of its *departure*.

This is, though, one side of the story. In the society of producers, the ethical principle of delayed gratification used to secure the durability of the work effort. In the society of consumers, on the other hand, the same principle may be still needed in practice to secure the durability of desire. Desire being much more ephemeral, fragile and desiccation-prone than labour, and unlike work not being fortified with institutionalized routines, it is unlikely to survive when the satisfaction is put *ad calendas graecas*. To stay alive and fresh, desire must be time and again, and quite often, gratified – yet gratification spells the end of the desire. A society ruled by the aesthetic of consumption therefore needs a very special kind of gratification – akin to the Derridean *pharmakon*, the healing drug and a poison at the same time, or rather a drug which needs to be apportioned sparingly, never in the full – murderous – dosage. A gratification-not-really-gratifying, never drunk to the bottom, always abandoned half-way . . .

Procrastination serves the consumer culture by its own self-denial. The source of creative effort is no longer the induced desire to delay the gratification of desire, but the induced desire to shorten the delay or abolish it altogether, coupled with the induced desire to shorten the stay of gratification once it comes. Culture waging a war against procrastination is a novelty in modern history. It has no room for taking distance, reflection, continuity, tradition – that *Wiederholung* (recapitulation) that according to Heidegger was the modality of Being as we know it.

Human bonds in the fluid world

The two kinds of space, occupied by the two categories of people, are strikingly different, yet interrelated; they do not converse with each other, yet are in constant communication; they have little in common, yet simulate similarity. The two spaces are ruled by sharply dissimilar logics, mould different life experiences, gestate diverging life itineraries and narratives which use distinct, often opposite definitions of similar behavioural codes. And yet both spaces are accommodated within the same world – and the world they both are part of is the world of vulnerability and precariousness.

The title of a paper given in December 1997 by one of the most incisive analysts of our times, Pierre Bourdieu, was 'Le précarité est aujourd'hui partout'.[22] The title said it all: precariousness, instability, vulnerability is the most widespread (as well as the most painfully felt) feature of contemporary life conditions. The French theorists speak of *précarité*, the German of *Unsicherheit* and *Risikogesellschaft*, the Italians of *incertezza* and the English of *insecurity* – but all of them have in mind the same aspect of the human predicament, experienced in various forms and under different names all over the globe, but felt to be especially unnerving and depressing in the highly developed and affluent part of the planet – for the reason of being new and in many ways unprecedented. The phenomenon which all these concepts try to grasp and articulate is the combined experience of *insecurity* (of position, entitlements and livelihood), of *uncertainty* (as to their continuation and future stability) and of *unsafety* (of one's body, one's self and their extensions: possessions, neighbourhood, community).

Precariousness is the mark of the preliminary condition of all the rest: the livelihood, and particularly the most common sort of livelihood, that which is claimed on the ground of work and employment. That livelihood has already become exceedingly fragile, but goes on growing more brittle and less reliable by the year. Many people, when listening to the notoriously contradictory opinions of learned experts, but more often than not just looking around and pondering the fate of their nearest and dearest, suspect with good enough reason that, however brave are the faces the politicians make and however brave their promises may sound, unemployment in the affluent countries has become 'structural': for every new vacancy there are some jobs that have vanished, and there is simply not enough work for everybody. And technological progress – indeed, the rationalizing effort itself – tends to augur ever fewer, not more jobs.

How brittle and uncertain the lives of those already redundant have become as the result of their redundancy does not take much imagination to adumbrate. The point is, though, that – at least psychologically – all the others are also affected, if for the time being only obliquely. In the world of structural unemployment no one can feel truly secure. Secure jobs in secure companies seem to be the yarn of grandfathers' nostalgia; nor are there many skills and experiences which, once acquired, would guarantee that the job will be offered, and once offered, will prove lasting. No one may reasonably assume to be insured against the next round of 'downsizing', 'streamlining' or 'rationalizing', against erratic shifts of market demand and whimsical yet irresistible, indomitable pressures of 'competitiveness', 'productivity' and 'effectiveness'. 'Flexibility' is the catchword of the day. It augurs jobs without in-built security, firm commitments or future entitlements, offering no more than fixed-term or rolling contracts, dismissal without notice and no right to compensation. No one can therefore feel truly irreplaceable – neither those already outcast nor those relishing the job of casting others out. Even the most privileged position may prove to be only temporary and 'until further notice'.

In the absence of long-term security, 'instant gratification' looks enticingly like a reasonable strategy. Whatever life may offer, let it be offered *hic et nunc* – right away. Who knows what tomorrow may bring? Delay of satisfaction has lost its allure. It is, after all, highly uncertain whether the labour and effort invested today will count as assets as long as it takes to reach reward. It is far from certain, moreover, that the prizes which look attractive today will still be desirable when they at long last come. We all learn from bitter experience that in no time assets may become liabilities and glittering prizes may turn into badges of shame. Fashions come and go with mind-boggling speed, all objects of desire become obsolete, off-putting and even distasteful before they have time to be fully enjoyed. Styles of life which are 'chic' today will tomorrow become targets of ridicule. To quote Bourdieu once more: 'Those who deplore the cynicism which marks men and women of our times, ought not to omit relating it to the social and economic conditions which favour it and demand . . .' When Rome burns and there is little or nothing that one can do to smother the fire, playing the fiddle seems neither particularly silly nor less timely than any other pursuit.

Precarious economic and social conditions train men and women (or make them learn the hard way) to perceive the world as a container full of *disposable* objects, objects for *one-off* use; the whole world – including other human beings. In addition, the world seems to consist of 'black boxes', hermetically sealed, never to be opened by the users, tinkered with, let alone repaired once they go bust. Today's car mechanics are not trained in repairing broken or damaged engines, only in easing out and throwing away the used-up or faulty parts and replacing them with other ready-made and sealed parts picked from the warehouse shelves. Of the inner structure of the 'spare parts' (an expression that tells it all), of the mysterious ways in which they work, they have little or no inkling; they do not consider such understanding and the skills which accompany it to be their responsibility or to lie within their field of competence. As in the garage, so it is in life outside: every 'part' is 'spare' and replaceable, and had better be replaceable. Why would one waste time on labour-consuming repairs, if it takes but a few moments to dump the damaged part and put another in its place?

In the world in which the future is at best dim and misty but more likely full of risks and dangers, setting distant goals, surrendering private interest in order to increase group power and sacrificing the present in the name of a future bliss does not seem an attractive, nor for that matter sensible, proposition. Any chance not taken here and now is a chance missed; not taking it is thus unforgivable and cannot be easily excused, let alone vindicated. Since the present-day commitments stand in the way of the next-day opportunities, the lighter and more superficial they are, the less is the likely damage. 'Now' is the keyword of life strategy, whatever that strategy applies to and whatever else it may suggest. In an insecure and unpredictable world, clever wanderers would do their best to imitate the happy globals who travel light; and they would not shed too many tears when getting rid of anything that cramped the moves. They seldom pause long enough to muse that human bonds are not like engine parts – that they hardly ever come ready-made, that they tend to rot and disintegrate fast if kept hermetically sealed and are not easily replaced once no longer of use.

And so the policy of deliberate 'precarization' conducted by the operators of labour markets finds itself to be aided and abetted (with its effects reinforced) by life policies, whether adopted deliberately or embraced by default. Both converge on the same result: the fading and wilting, falling apart and decomposing of human bonds, of communities and of partnerships. Commitments of the 'till death us do part' type become contracts 'until satisfaction lasts', temporal and transient by definition, by design and by pragmatic impact – and so prone to be broken unilaterally, whenever one of the partners sniffs out more opportunity and better value in opting out of the partnership rather than trying to save it at any – incalculable – cost.

In other words, bonds and partnerships tend to be viewed and treated as things meant to be *consumed*, not produced; they are subject to the same criteria of evaluation as all other objects of consumption. In the consumer market, the ostensibly durable products are as a rule offered for a 'trial period'; return of money is promised if the purchaser is less than fully satisfied. If the partner in partnership is 'conceptualized' in such terms, then it is no longer the task of both partners to 'make the relationship work' – to see it work through thick and thin, 'for richer for poorer', in sickness and in health, to help each other through good and bad patches, to trim if need be one's own preferences, to compromise and make sacrifices for the sake of a lasting union. It is instead a matter of obtaining satisfaction from a ready-to-consume product; if the pleasure derived is not up to the standard promised and expected, or if the novelty wears off together with the joy, one can sue for divorce, quoting consumer rights and the Trade Descriptions Act. One can think of no reason to stick to an inferior or aged pro-duct rather than look for a 'new and improved' one in the shops.

What follows is that the assumed temporariness of partnerships tends to turn into a self-fulfilling prophecy. If the human bond, like all other consumer objects, is not something to be worked out through protracted effort and occasional sacrifice, but something which one expects to bring satisfaction right away, instantane-ously, at the moment of purchase – and something that one rejects if it does not satisfy, something to be kept and used only as long as (and no longer than) it continues to gratify – then there is not much point in 'throwing good money after bad', in trying hard and harder still, let alone in suffering discomfort and unease in order to save the partnership. Even a minor stumble may cause the partner-ship to fall and break down; trivial disagreements turn into bitter conflicts, slight frictions are taken for the signals of essential and irreparable incompatibility. As the American sociologist W. I. Thomas would have said, were he to witness this turn of affairs: if people assume their commitments to be temporary and until fur-ther notice, these commitments do tend to become such in conse-quence of these people's own actions.

The precariousness of social existence inspires a perception of the world around as an aggregate of products for immediate con-sumption. But perceiving the world, complete with its inhabitants, as a pool of consumer items makes the negotiation of lasting hu-man bonds exceedingly hard. Insecure people tend to be irritable; they are also intolerant of anything that stands in the way of their desires; and since quite a few of the desires are bound to be frus-trated, there is seldom a shortage of things and people to be intol-erant of. If instant gratification is the sole way of stifling the gnawing feeling of unsafety (without, let us note, ever quenching the thirst for security and certainty), there is indeed no evident reason to be tolerant toward something or someone of no obvious relevance to the quest of satisfaction, let alone something or someone awkward and reluctant about bringing the gratification one seeks.

There is, though, one more link between the 'consumerization' of a precarious world and the disintegration of human bonds. Unlike production, consumption is a lonely activity, endemically and irredeemably lonely, even at such moments as it is conducted in company with others. Productive (as a rule long-term) efforts require co-operation even if what they call for is just adding up raw muscular forces: if carrying a heavy log from one site to another takes eight men one hour, it does not follow that one man can do the same given eight (or any number of) hours. In the case of more complex tasks which involve the division of labour and call for diverse specialist skills which cannot meet and blend in one person's know-how, the need for co-operation is even more obvious; without it, there would be no chance for any product to emerge. It is the co-operation which makes the scattered and disparate efforts into productive ones. In the case of consumption, though, co-operation is not only unnecessary, but downright superfluous. Whatever is consumed is consumed individually, even if in a crowded hall. In a touch of his versatile genius, Luis Buñuel (in *Phantom of Liberty*) showed eating, that allegedly prototypical accoutrement of gregariousness and sociation, to be (contrary to the common pretence) the most solitary and secret of activities, zealously guarded from other people's inquisition.

The self-perpetuation of non-confidence

Alain Peyrefitte[23] in his retrospective study of the modern/capitalist society of 'compulsive and obsessive development' comes to the conclusion that the most prominent, indeed the constitutive, feature of that society was *confidence*: confidence in oneself, in others, and in institutions. All three constituents of confidence used to be indispensable. They conditioned and sustained each other: take one away, and the other two will implode and collapse. We could describe the modern order-making bustle as an ongoing effort to lay the institutional foundations for confidence: offering a stable framework for the investment of trust and making credible the belief that the presently cherished values will go on being cherished and desired, that the rules of pursuing and attaining these values will go on being observed, stay uninfringed and immune to the flow of time.

Peyrefitte singles out the enterprise-cum-employment as the most important site for the sowing and cultivation of trust. The fact that the capitalist enterprise was also the hotbed of conflicts and confrontations should not mislead us: there is no *défiance* without *confiance*, no contest without trust. If the employees fought for their rights, it was because they had confidence in the 'holding power' of the frame in which, as they hoped and wished, their rights would be inscribed; they trusted the enterprise as the right place to deposit their rights for safekeeping.

This is no more the case, or at least it rapidly ceases to be the case. No rational person would expect to spend her or his whole working life, or at least a large chunk of it, in one company. Most rational people would prefer to entrust their life savings to the notoriously risk-ridden, stock-exchange-playing investment funds and insurance companies than to count on the pensions that the companies for which they work at present could provide. As Nigel Thrift summed it up recently, 'It is very difficult to build trust in organizations which are, at the same time, being "delayered", "downsized" and "re-engineered".'

Pierre Bourdieu[24] shows the link between the collapse of confidence and the fading will for political engagement and collective action: the ability to make future projections, he suggests, is the *conditio sine qua non* of all 'transformative' thought and all effort to re-examine and reform the present state of affairs – but projecting into the future is unlikely to appear in people who lack hold on their present. Reich's fourth category most conspicuously lacks such a hold. Tied as they are to the ground, barred from moving, or arrested if they move at the first of the heavily guarded border posts, they are in a position *a priori* inferior to the capital which moves around freely. Capital is increasingly global; they, however, stay local. For that reason they are exposed, armless, to the inscrutable whims of mysterious 'investors' and 'shareholders', and even more bewildering 'market forces', 'terms of trade' and 'demands of competition'. Whatever they gain today may be taken away tomorrow without warning. They cannot win. Neither – being the rational persons they are or struggle to be – are they willing to risk the fight. They are unlikely to reforge their grievances into a political issue and to turn to the political powers that be for redress. As Jacques Attali forecast a few years ago, 'Power will reside tomorrow in the capacity to block or facilitate the movement along certain routes. The State won't exercise its powers otherwise as through the control of network. And so the impossibility to exercise control over the network will weaken the political institutions irreversibly.'[25]

The passage from heavy to light capitalism and from solid to fluid or liquefied modernity constitutes the framework in which the history of the labour movement has been inscribed. It also goes a long way toward making sense of that history's notorious con-volutions. It would be neither reasonable nor particularly illuminating to explain away the dire straits in which the labour movement has fallen throughout the 'advanced' (in the 'modernizing' sense) part of the world, by reference to the change of public mood – whether brought about by the debilitating impact of the mass media, a conspiracy of the advertisers, the seductive pull of the consumer society or the soporific or distracting effects of a spectacle-and-entertainment society. Laying the blame at the doorstep of blundering or two-faced 'labour politicians' won't help either. The phenomena invoked in such explanations are not at all imaginary, but they would not do as explanations if it were not for the fact that the context of life, the social setting in which people (seldom ever by their own choice) go about their business of life, had changed radically since the times when workers crowded into mass-production factories joined ranks to enforce more humane and rewarding terms for selling their labour, and the theorists and practitioners of the labour movement sensed in those workers' solidarity the inchoate and as yet inarticulate (but inborn and in the long run overwhelming) desire for a 'good society' which would make flesh the universal principles of justice.

5

Community

Differences are born when reason is not fully awake or falls asleep again; this was the unspoken credo which lent credibility to the unclouded trust that post-Enlightenment liberals vested in the human individual's capacity for immaculate conception. We, the humans, are endowed with everything that everybody needs to select the right path which, once selected, would prove to be the same to us all. Descartes's subject and Kant's Man, armed with reason. wouldn't err in their human ways unless pushed or tempted away from the straight, reason-blazed trail. Different choices are the sediment of history blunders – the outcome of a brain damage variously called prejudice, superstition or false consciousness. Unlike the *eindeutig* verdicts of reason which is the property of each single human being, the differences in judgement have collective origins: Francis Bacon's 'idols' reside where people mill and jostle together: in the theatre, in a marketplace, in tribal festivals. To set free the power of human reason meant to liberate the individual from all that.

That credo was forced into the open only by liberalism's critics. There was no shortage of them, charging the liberal interpretation of the Enlightenment's legacy with either getting things wrong or making them wrong. Romantic poets, historians and sociologists joined nationalistic politicians in pointing out that – before humans start flexing their individual brains to write down the best code of cohabitation their reason may suggest – they already have a (collective) history and (collectively obeyed) customs. Our contemporary communitarians say much the same, only using different terms: it is not the 'disembedded' and 'unencumbered' individual, but a language user and a schooled/socialized person who 'self-asserts' and 'self-constructs'. It is not always clear what the critics have in mind: is the vision of the self-contained individual untrue, or is it harmful? Should liberals be censured for preaching false opinion' or for conducting, inspiring or absolving false politics?

It seems, though, that the current liberal-communitarian *querelle* concerns politics, not 'human nature'. The question is not so much whether setting the individual free from received opinions and collective insurance against inconveniences of individual responsibility does or does not happen – but whether it is good or bad. Raymond Williams noted long ago that the remarkable thing about 'community' is that it always has been. There is commotion around the need of community mainly because it is less and less clear whether the realities which the portraits of 'community' claim to represent are much in evidence, and if such realities can be found, will their life-expectancy allow them to be treated with the kind of respect which realities command. The valiant defence of community and the bid to restore it to the favours denied by the liberals would hardly have happened had it not been for the fact that the harness by which collectivities tie their members to a joint history, custom, language or schooling is getting more threadbare by the year. In the liquid stage of modernity, only zipped harnesses are supplied, and their selling point is the facility with which they can be put on in the morning and taken off in the evening (or vice versa). Communities come in many colours and sizes, but if plotted on the Weberian axis stretching from 'light cloak' to 'iron cage', they all come remarkably close to the first pole.

In so far as they need to be defended to survive and they need to appeal to their own members to secure that survival by their individual choices and take for that survival individual responsibility – all communities are *postulated*; projects rather than realities, something that comes *after*, not *before* the individual choice. The community 'as seen in communitarian paintings' would be tangible enough to be invisible and to afford silence; but then communitarians won't paint its likenesses, let alone exhibit them.

This is the inner paradox of communitarianism. To say 'It is nice to be a part of a community' is an oblique testimony of *not* being a part, or being unlikely to remain a part for long unless individual muscles are flexed and individual brains stretched. In order to fulfil the communitarian project, one needs to appeal to the selfsame ('self-disencumbering'?) individual choices whose possibility has been denied. One cannot be a bona fide communitarian without giving the devil his due, without on one occasion admitting the freedom of individual choice denied on another.

In the eyes of logicians, this contradiction may by itself discredit the effort to disguise the communitarian political project as a descriptive theory of social reality. For the sociologist, however, it is rather the ongoing (and perhaps rising) popularity of communitarian ideas that constitutes an important social fact calling for explanation/understanding (while the fact that the disguise itself has been so effectively disguised and did not stand in the way of the communitarians' success would not raise many sociological eyebrows – it is much too common for that).

Sociologically speaking, communitarianism is an all-too-expectable reaction to the accelerating 'liquefaction' of modern life, a reaction first and foremost to the one aspect of life felt perhaps as the most vexing and annoying among its numerous painful consequences – the deepening imbalance between individual freedom and security. Supplies of security provisions shrink fast, while the volume of individual responsibilities (assigned if not exercised in practice) grows on a scale unprecedented for the post-war generations. A most salient aspect of the vanishing act performed by old securities is the new fragility of human bonds. The brittleness and transience of bonds may be an unavoidable price for individuals' *right* to pursue their individual goals, and yet it cannot but be, simultaneously, a most formidable obstacle to pursue them *effectively* – and to the courage needed to pursue them. This is also a paradox – one rooted deeply in the nature of life under liquid modernity. Not for the first time paradoxical situations provoke and inspire paradoxical answers. In the light of the paradoxical nature of liquid-modern 'individualization' the contradictory nature of the communitarian response to the paradox should not amaze: the first is an adequate explanation of the other, while the other is a fitting effect of the first.

What born-again communitarianism responds to is a most genuine and poignant issue of the pendulum shifting radically – perhaps too far away – from the security pole in the dyad of *sine qua non* human values. For this reason, the communitarian gospel can count on a large audience-in-waiting. It speaks in the name of millions: *précarité*, as Pierre Bourdieu insists, *est aujourd'hui partout* – it penetrates every nook and cranny of human existence. In his recent book *Protéger ou disparaître*,[1] an angry manifesto against the indolence and hypocrisy of the present-day power elites in the face of 'la montée des insécurités', Philippe Cohen lists unemployment (nine of ten new vacancies are strictly temporary and short term), uncertain old-age prospects and the hazards of urban life as the main sources of diffuse anxiety about the present, the next day and more distant future: absence of security is what unites all three, and the main appeal of communitarianism is the promise of a safe haven, the dream destination for sailors lost in a turbulent sea of constant, unpredictable and confusing change.

As Eric Hobsbawm caustically remarked, 'Never was the word "community" used more indiscriminately and emptily than in the decades when communities in sociological sense became hard to find in real life.'[2] 'Men and women look for groups to which they can belong, certainly and forever, in a world in which all else is moving and shifting, in which nothing else is certain.'[3] Jock Young supplies a succinct summary to Hobsbawm's observation: 'Just as community collapses, identity is invented.'[4] We may say that the 'community' of the communitarian gospel is not the pre-established and securely grounded *Gemeinschaft* known from social theory (and famously dressed up as a 'law of history' by Ferdinand Tönnies), but a cryptonym for the zealously sought yet elusive 'identity'. And as Orlando Patterson (quoted by Eric Hobsbawm) observed, while people are called to *choose* between competitive identity reference groups their choice is predicated on the strongly held belief that the chooser has absolutely no choice but to choose the specific group to which he or she 'belongs'.

The community of the communitarian gospel is a home writ large (the *family* home, not a *found* home or a *made* home, but a home *into which one is born*, so that one could not trace one's origin, one's 'reason to exist', in any other place): and a kind of home, to be sure, which for most people these days is more a beautiful fairy-tale than a matter of personal experience. (Family homesteads, once securely wrapped by a dense web of routinized habits and customary expectations, have had their breakwaters dismantled and are these days wide open to the tides buffeting the rest of life.) Being outside the realm of experience helps: the benign cosiness of home cannot be put to a test, and its attractions, as long as they are imagined, may stay unsullied by the less prepossessing aspects of enforced belonging and non-negotiable obligations – the darker colours are largely absent in the palette of imagination.

Being a home writ large also helps. Those locked inside an ordinary, brick-and-mortar home could be struck time and time again by an uncanny impression of being in prison rather than in a safe haven; the freedom of the street beckoned from the outside, tantalizingly inaccessible just as the dreamt-of security of the imagined home tends to be today. If the seductive security of *chez soi* is, however, projected on a big enough screen, no 'outside' liable to spoil the fun is left. The ideal community is a *compleat mappa mundi*: a total world, supplying everything one may need to lead a meaningful and rewarding life. By focusing on what pains the homeless most, the communitarian remedy of the passage (masquerading as return) to a total and totally consistent world is made to look like a truly radical solution of all, present and future, troubles; other worries look small and insignificant by comparison.

That communal world is complete in so far as all the rest is irrelevant; more exactly, hostile – a wilderness full of ambushes and conspiracies and bristling with enemies wielding chaos as their main weapon. The inner harmony of the communal world shines and glitters against the background of the obscure and tangled jungle which starts on the other side of the turnpike. It is there, to that wilderness, that people huddling in the warmth of shared identity dump (or hope to banish) the fears which prompted them to seek communal shelter. In Jock Young's words, 'The desire to demonize others is based on the ontological uncertainties' of those inside.[5] An 'inclusive community' would be a contradiction in terms. Communal fraternity would be incomplete, perhaps unthinkable but certainly unviable, without that inborn fratricidal inclination.

Nationalism, mark 2

The community of the communitarian gospel is either an ethnic community or a community imagined after the pattern of an ethnic one. This choice of archetype has its good reasons.

First, the 'ethnicity', unlike any other foundation of human unity, has the advantage of 'naturalizing history', of presenting the cultural as 'a fact of nature', freedom as 'understood (and accepted) necessity'. Ethnic belonging spurs into action: one must *choose* loyalty to one's nature – one needs to try hard and with no time to rest to live up to the set model and thus make a contribution to its preservation. The model itself, however, is not a matter of choice. The choice is not between different referents of belonging, but between belonging and rootlessness, home and homelessness, being and nothingness. This is precisely the dilemma which the communitarian gospel wishes (needs) to hammer home.

Second, the nation-state promoting the principle of ethnic unity overriding all other loyalties was the only 'success story' of community in modern times or, rather, the sole entity which made the bid to a community status with any degree of conviction and effect. The idea of ethnicity (and ethnic homogeneity) as the legitimate basis of unity and self-assertion has been thereby given a historical grounding. Contemporary communitarianism naturally hopes to capitalize on that tradition; given the present-day wobbliness of state sovereignty and the evident need for someone to take over the banner falling out of the state's hands, the hope is not entirely unwarranted. Yet it is easy to observe that drawing parallels between the accomplishment of the nation-state and communitarian ambitions has its limits. The nation-state, after all, owed its success to the *suppression of* self-asserting communities; it fought tooth and nail against 'parochialism', local customs or 'dialects', promoting a unified language and historical memory at the expense of communal traditions; the more determined the state-initiated and state-supervised *Kulturkämpfe*, the fuller the nation-state success in the production of a 'natural community'. Moreover, nation-states (unlike the present-day communities-in-waiting) did not sit down to the task bare-handed and would not think of relying just on the power of indoctrination. Their effort had a powerful support in the legal enforcement of official language, school curricula and the unified system of law, which the communities-in-waiting lack and are nowhere near acquiring.

It was argued well before the recent rise of communitarianism that there was a precious gem inside the ugly and prickly carapace of modern nation-building. Isaiah Berlin suggested that there are human and ethically praiseworthy sides to the modern 'homeland' apart from its cruel and potentially gory side. Fairly popular is the distinction made between patriotism and nationalism. More often than not, the patriotism of that opposition is the 'marked' member of the couple, the unsavoury realities of nationalism being cast as the 'unmarked' member: patriotism, more postulated than empirically given, is what nationalism (if tamed, civilized and ethically ennobled) could be but is not. Patriotism is described through the negation of the most disliked and shameful traits of known nationalisms. Leszek Kołakowski[6] suggests that, while the nationalist wants to assert the tribal existence through aggression and hatred of others, believes that all the mishaps of his own nation are the outcome of a strangers' plot and holds a grudge against all other nations for failing to admire properly and otherwise give its due to his own tribe, the patriot is marked by 'benevolent tolerance of cultural variety and particularly of ethnic and religious minorities', as well as by his readiness to tell his own nation things it would not savour or enjoy hearing. Though this distinction is fine and morally and intellectually laudable, its value is somewhat weakened by the fact that what is opposed here is not so much two options equally likely to be embraced, as a noble idea and an ignoble reality. Most people who wished their appointed brethren to be patriots would in all likelihood decry the features ascribed here to the patriotic stance as evidence of two-facedness, national betrayal or worse. Such features – tolerance of difference, hospitality to minorities and courage to tell the truth, however unpleasant – are most widespread in the lands where 'patriotism' is not a 'problem'; in societies secure enough in their republican citizenship not to worry about patriotism as a problem, let alone to view it as an urgent task.

Bernard Yack, the editor of *Liberalism without Illusions* (University of Chicago Press, 1996), was not therefore out of order when in his polemics against Maurizio Viroli, the author of *For Love of Country: An Essay on Patriotism and Nationalism* (Oxford University Press, 1995), he paraphrased Hobbes to coin an aphorism. 'Nationalism is patriotism misliked and patriotism, nationalism liked.'[7] Indeed, there are reasons to conclude that there is little else to distinguish between nationalism and patriotism, except our enthusiasm for their manifestations or its absence or the degree of shame-facedness or guilty conscience with which we admit or deny them. It is the naming that makes the difference, and the difference made is mainly rhetorical, distinguishing not the substance of talked-about phenomena, but the ways we talk about sentiments or passions that are otherwise essentially similar. But it is the nature of sentiments and passions and their behavioural and political consequences that count and affect the quality of human cohabitation, not the words we use to narrate them. Looking back at the deeds of which the patriotic stories tell, Yack concludes that whenever lofty patriotic feelings have 'risen to the level of shared passion' 'it has been a fierce rather than gentle passion that patriots have displayed', and that patriots could display over the centuries 'many memorable and useful virtues, but gentleness and sympathy towards outsiders are not prominent among them'.

There is no denying, though, the significance of the difference in rhetorics, nor its occasionally poignant pragmatic reverberations. One rhetoric is made to the measure of the discourse of 'being', another to that of 'becoming'. 'Patriotism' on the whole pays tribute to the modern creed of the 'unfinishedness', the pliability (more to the point, the 'reformability') of humans: it may therefore declare with a clear conscience (whether or not the promise is kept in practice) that the call to 'close ranks' is an open and standing invitation: that joining ranks is a matter of choices made, and that all that is required is that one makes the right choice and remains loyal to it through thick and thin for ever after. 'Nationalism', on the other hand, is more like the Calvinist version of salvation or St Augustine's idea of free will: it puts little trust in choice – you are either 'one of us' or you are not, and in either case you can do little, perhaps nothing at all, to change it. In the nationalist narrative, 'belonging' is a fate, not a chosen destiny or a life project. It may be a matter of biological heredity, as in the now rather outmoded and unpractised racist version of nationalism, or of cultural heredity, as in the presently fashionable 'culturalist' variant of nationalism – but in either case the matter has been decided well before this or another person started to walk and talk, so that the sole choice left to the individual is between embracing the verdict of fate with both arms and in good faith and rebelling against the verdict and so becoming a traitor to one's calllng.

This difference between patriotism and nationalism tends to reach beyond mere rhetoric into the realm of political practice. Following Claude Lévi-Strauss's terminology, we may say that the first formula is more likely to inspire 'anthropophagic' strategies ('eating up' the strangers so that they are assimilated by the body of the eater and become identical with its other cells, having lost their own distinctiveness), while the second associates more often than not with the 'anthropoemic' strategy of 'vomiting' and 'spitting out' those 'unfit to be us', either isolating them by incarcerating them inside the visible walls of the ghettos or the invisible (though no less tangible for this reason) walls of cultural prohibitions, or by rounding them up, deporting them or forcing them to run away, as in the practice currently given the name of ethnic cleansing. It would be prudent, however, to remember that the logic of thought is seldom binding on the logic of deeds, that there is therefore no one-to-one relation between rhetorics and practices, and so each of the two strategies may be wrapped in either of the two rhetorics.

Unity – through similarity or difference?

'We' of the patriotic/nationalist creed means people *like us*; 'they' – means people who are *different from us*. Not that 'we' are identical in every respect; there are differences between 'us' alongside the common features, but the similarities dwarf, defuse and neutralize their impact. The aspect in which we are all alike is decidedly more significant snd consequential than everything that sets us apart from one another; significant enough to outweigh the impact of the differences when it comes to taking a stand. And not that 'they' differ from us in every respect; but they differ in one respect which is more important than all the others, important enough to preclude a common stand and render genuine solidarity unlikely whatever the similarities that make us alike. It is a typically either/or situation: the boundaries dividing 'us' from 'them' are clearly drawn and easy to spot, since the certificate of 'belonging' contains just one rubric, and the questionnaire which those applying for the identity card are required to fill in contains but one question and a 'yes or no' answer.

Let us note that the question of which of the differences is 'crucial' – that is, which one is the kind of difference that matters more than any similarity and makes all common feature seem small and insignificant (the difference that makes the hostility-generating division an open-and-shut case well before the start of the meeting in which the eventuality of unity could be discussed) –

is minor and above all derivative, most often an afterthought, rather than the starting point of argument. As Frederick Barth explained, borders do not acknowledge and register the already existing estrangement; they are drawn, as a rule, before the estrangement is brought about. First there is a conflict, a desperate attempt to set 'us' apart from 'them'; then the traits keenly spied out among 'them' are taken to be the proof and the source of a strangehood that bears no conciliation. Human beings being as they are multi-faceted creatures having many attributes, it is not difficult to find such traits once the search has started in earnest.

Nationalism locks the door, pulls out the door-knockers and disables the doorbells, declaring that only those who are inside have the right to be there and settle there for good. Patriotism is, at least on the face of it, more tolerant, hospitable and forthcoming – it passes the buck to those who ask admission. And yet the ultimate result is, more often than not, remarkably similar. Neither the patriotic nor the nationalist creed admits the possibility that people may belong together while staying attached to their differences, cherishing and cultivating them or that their togetherness, far from requiring similarity or promoting it as the value to be coveted and pursued, actually *benefits* from the variety of life-styles, ideals and knowledge while adding more strength and substance to what makes them what they are – and that means, to what makes them different.

Bernard Crick quotes from the *Politics* of Aristotle his idea of a 'good *polis*', articulated in defiance of Plato's dream of one truth, one unified standard of righteousness, binding all:

> There is a point at which a polis, by advancing in unity, will cease to be a polis; but will none the less come near to losing its essence, and will thus be a worse polis. It is as if you were to turn harmony into mere unison, or to reduce a theme to a single beat. The truth is that the polis is an aggregate of many members.

In his commentary, Crick advances the idea of a kind of unity which neither patriotism nor nationalism is eager to support and more often than not would actively resent: a kind of unity which assumes that civilized society is inherently pluralistic, that living together in such a society means negotiation and conciliation of 'naturally different' interests, and that 'It is normally better to

conciliate differing interests than to coerce and oppress them perpetually:'[8] in other words, that the pluralism of modern civilized
society is not just a 'brute fact' which can be disliked or even
detested but (alas) not wished away, but a good thing and fortu-
nate circumstance, as it offers benefits much in excess of the discomforts and inconveniences it brings, widens horizons for humanity
and multiplies the chances of life altogether more prepossessing
than the conditions any of its alternatives may deliver. We may say
that, in a stark opposition to either the patriotic or the nationalistic
faith, the most promising kind of unity is one which is *achieved*,
and achieved daily anew, by confrontation, debate, negotiation
and compromise between values, preferences and chosen ways of
life and self-identifications of many and different, but always self-
determining, members of the *polis*.

This is, essentially, the *republican* model of unity, of an emergent unity which is a joint achievement of the agents engaged in
self-identification pursuits, a unity which is an outcome, not an *a
priori* given condition, of shared life, a unity put together through
negotiation and reconciliation, not the denial, stifling or smother-
ing out of differences.

This, I wish to propose, is the sole variant of unity (the only
formula of togetherness) which the conditions of liquid modernity render compatible, plausible and realistic. Once the beliefs,
values and styles have all been 'privatized' – decontextualized or
'disembedded', with the sites offered for re-embedding reminiscent
more of motel accommodation than of a permanent (mortgage
loan repaid) home – identities cannot but look fragile, temporary
and 'until further notice', and devoid of all defences except the
skills and determination of the agents to hold them tight and
protect them from erosion. The volatility of identities, so to speak,
stares the residents of liquid modernity in the face. And so does the
choice that logically follows it: to learn the difficult art of living
with difference or to bring about, by hook or by crook, such
conditions as would make that learning no longer necessary. As
Alain Touraine put it recently, the present state of society signals
'the end of definition of the human being as a social being, defined
by his or her place in society which determines his or her behaviour
or action', and so the defence by social actors of their 'cultural and
psychological specificity' cannot but be conducted with 'consciousness that the principle of their combination can be found within

the individual, and no longer in social institutions or universalistic principles'.[9]

The news concerning the condition about which theorists theorize and philosophers philosophize is daily hammered home by the joint forces of the popular arts, whether appearing under their proper name of fiction or disguised as 'true stories'. As the viewers of the film *Elizabeth I* are informed, even being the Queen of England is a matter of self-assertion and self-creation; being a daughter of Henry VIII takes a lot of individual initiative backed by cunning and determination. To force the quarrelsome and incalcitrant courtiers to kneel and bow, and above all to listen and obey, the future Gloriana needs to buy a lot of paint for make-up and change her hair-style, the head-dress and the rest of her attire. There is no assertion but self-assertion, no identity but made-up identity.

It all boils down, to be sure, to the strength of the agent in question. The defence weapons are not uniformly available, and it stands to reason that weaker, poorly armed individuals would seek in the power of numbers redress for their individual impotence. Given the varying width of the universally experienced gap between the condition of the 'individual *de jure*' and the chance to obtain the 'individual *de facto*' status, the same fluid modern environment may – and will – favour a variety of survival strategies. The 'we', as Richard Sennett insists, is nowadays 'an act of self-protection. The desire for community is defensive . . . To be sure, it is almost a universal law that "we" can be used as a defense against confusion and dislocation.' But – and this is a most crucial but – when that desire for community 'is expressed as rejection of immigrants and other outsiders', it is because

> current politics based on the desire for refuge takes aim more at the weak, those who travel the circuits of the global labour market, rather than at the strong, those institutions which set poor workers in motion or make use of their relative deprivation. The IBM programmers . . . in one important way transcended this defensive sense of community, when they ceased blaming their Indian peers and their Jewish president.[10]

'In one important way,' perhaps – but, let me add, in one only, and not necessarily the most significant either. The impulse to withdraw from risk-ridden complexity into the shelter of uniformity is universal; it is only the ways to act on that impulse that differ, and they tend to differ in direct proportion to the means and resources available to the actors. The better-off, like the IBM programmers, comfortable in their cyberspatial enclave but much less immune to the vagaries of fate in the difficult to 'virtualize', physical sector of the social world, can afford the costs of high-tech moats and draw-bridges to keep the dangers at arm's length. Guy Nafilyah, the head of a leading developer company in France, observed that 'The Frenchmen are uneasy, they are afraid of neighbours, except those who resemble them.' Jacques Patigny, the president of the National Association of the Accommodation Renters, concurs, and sees the future in 'peripheral closure and filtering of access' to residential areas by magnetic cards and guards. The future belongs to 'archipelagos of islands dotted along the axes of communication'. The cut-off and fenced-off, truly exterritorial residential areas equipped with intricate intercom systems, ubiquitous video-surveillance cameras and heavily armed guards on twenty-four-hours-a-day beats are cropping up all around Toulouse, as they have done already some time ago in the USA and as they do in ever growing numbers all over the affluent part of the fast globalizing world.[11] The heavily guarded enclaves bear a remarkable resemblance to the ethnic ghettoes of the poor. They differ, though, in one seminal respect: they have been freely chosen as a privilege one is expected to pay an arm and leg for. And the security men who guard the access have been legally hired and so carry their guns with the full approval of the law.

Richard Sennett offers a psycho-sociological gloss to the trend:

> The image of the community is purified of all that may convey a feeling of difference, let alone conflict, in who 'we' are. In this way the myth of community solidarity is a purification ritual ... What is distinctive about this mythic sharing in communities is that people feel they belong to each other, and share together, *because they are the same* ... The 'we' feeling, which expresses the desire to be similar, is a way for men to avoid the necessity of looking deeper into each other.[12]

Like so many other modern undertakings of public powers, the dream of purity has been in the era of liquid modernity deregulated and privatized; acting on that dream has been left to private – local, group – initiative. The protection of personal safety is now a personal matter, and local authorities and local police are at hand to help with their advice, while land developers would gladly take over the worry from those who are able to pay for their services. Measures undertaken personally – singly or severally – need to be on a par with the urge which prompted their search. According to the common rules of mythical reasoning, the metonymical is reforged into the metaphorical: the wish to repel and push back the ostensible dangers adjacent to the endangered body is transmogrified into the urge to make the 'outside' similar, 'alike' or identical with the outside, to remake the 'out there' after the likeness of the 'in here'; the dream of the 'community of similarity' is, essentially, a projection of *l'amour de soi*.

It is also a frantic bid to avoid confrontation with vexing questions without a good answer: the question whether that self, frightened and lacking in self-confidence, is worth loving in the first place, and whether it deserves therefore to serve as the design for refurbishing its habitat and as the standard to assess and measure the acceptable identity. In a 'community of similarity' such unpleasant questions won't, we hope, be asked, and so the credibility of the safety obtained through purification will never be put to the test.

In another place (*In Search of Politics*, Polity Press, 1999) I have discussed the 'unholy trinity' of uncertainty, insecurity and unsafety, each one generating anxiety all the more acute and painful for being unsure of its provenance; whatever its origin, the accumulating steam desperately seeks an outlet, and with the access to the sources of uncertainty and insecurity blocked or out of reach, all the pressure shifts elsewhere, to fall ultimately on the tantalizingly thin and friable valve of bodily, domestic and environmental safety. As a result, the 'safety problem' tends to be chronically overloaded with worries and cravings it can neither carry away nor unload. The unholy alliance results in the perpetual thirst for more safety, a thirst which no practical measures can quell since they are bound to leave the primary and perpetually prolific sources of uncertainty and insecurity, those main suppliers of anxiety, untouched and intact.

Security at a price

Going through the writings of the born-again apostles of the communitarian cult, Phil Cohen concluded that the communities they extol and recommend as the cure for their contemporaries' life troubles are more like orphanages, prisons or mad houses than sites of potential liberation. Cohen is right; but the potential for liberation was never the communitarians' concern; the troubles which it was hoped the would-be communities would heal were sediments of the liberation's excesses, of a liberation potential too big for comfort. In the long and inconclusive search for the right balance between freedom and security, communitarianism stood fast on the side of the latter. It also accepted that the two cherished human values are at odds and cross-purposes, that one cannot have more of one without surrendering a bit, perhaps even a large chunk, of another. One possibility which the communitarians will not admit is that broadening and entrenching human freedoms may add to the sum total of human security, that freedom and security may grow together, let alone that each may grow only if growing together with the other.

The vision of community, let me repeat, is that of an island of homely and cosy tranquillity in a sea of turbulence and inhospitality. It tempts and seduces, prompting the admirers to refrain from looking too closely, since the eventuality of ruling the waves and taming the sea has already been deleted from the agenda as a proposition both suspect and unrealistic. Being the only shelter offers the vision an added value, and that value goes on being added to as the stock exchange where other life values are traded grows ever more capricious and unpredictable.

As a safe investment (or, rather, an investment less blatantly risky than others), the value of the community shelter has no serious competitors except, perhaps, the body of the investor – now, unlike in the past, the element of the *Lebenswelt* with an ostensibly longer (indeed, *incomparably* longer) life-expectation than that of any of its trappings and casings. As before, the body remains mortal and so transient, but its mortality-bound brevity seems like eternity when compared with the volatility and ephemerality of all reference frames, orientation points, classifications and evaluations which liquid modernity puts on and takes off the display windows and shop-shelves. Family workmates, class, neighbours are all too fluid to imagine their permanence and credit them with the capacity of reliable reference frames. The hope that 'we will meet again tomorrow', the belief which used to offer all the reasons needed to think ahead, to act long-term and to weave the steps, one by one, into a carefully designed trajectory of the temporary, incurably mortal life, has lost much of its credibility; the probability that what one will meet tomorrow will be one's own body immersed in quite different or radically changed family, class, neighbourhood and the company of other workmates is nowadays much more credible and so a safer bet.

In an essay which reads today like a letter sent to posterity from the land of solid modernity, Émile Durkheim suggested that only 'Actions which have a lasting quality are worthy of our volition, only pleasures which endure are worthy of our desires.' This was indeed the lesson which solid modernity hammered into the heads of its denizens with good results, but it sounds outlandish and hollow to contemporary ears – though perhaps less bizarre than the practical advice Durkheim derived from that lesson. Having asked what seemed to him a purely rhetorical question, 'Of what value are our individual pleasures, which are so empty and short?', he hastened to put his readers' qualms to rest, pointing out that, fortunately, we are not abandoned to the chase after such pleasures – 'because societies are infinitely more long-lived than individuals', 'They permit us to taste satisfactions which are not merely ephemeral.' Society, in Durkheim's view (quite credible at his time) is that body 'under whose protection' to shelter from the horror of one's own transience.'[13]

The body and its satisfactions have not become *less* ephemeral since the time when Durkheim sang the glory of durable social institutions. The snag, though, is that everything else – and those social institutions most prominently – has now become *more* ephemeral yet than the 'body and its satisfactions'. Length of life is a comparative notion, and the mortal body is now perhaps the longest-living entity around (in fact, the sole entity whose life-expectation tends to increase over the years). The body, one may say, has become the last shelter and sanctuary of continuity and duration; whatever 'long-term' may mean, it can hardly exceed the limits drawn by bodily mortality. It is becoming safety's last line of trenches, trenches which are exposed to constant enemy bombardment, or the last oasis among wind-swept moving sands. Hence the rabid, obsessive, feverish and overwrought concern with the defence of the body. The boundary between the body and the world outside is among the most vigilantly policed of contemporary frontiers. The body orifices (the points of entry) and the body surfaces (the places of contact) are now the primary foci of terror and anxiety generated by the awareness of mortality. No longer do they share the load with other foci (except, perhaps, the 'community').

The body's new primacy is reflected in the tendency to shape the image of community (the community of certainty-cum-security dreams, the community as the greenhouse of safety) after the pattern of the ideally protected body: to visualize it as an entity homogeneous and harmonious on the inside, thoroughly cleansed of all foreign, ingestion-resistant substances, all points of entry closely watched, controlled and guarded, but heavily armed on the outside and encased in impenetrable armour. The boundaries of the postulated community, like the outer limits of the body, are to divide the realm of trust and loving care from the wilderness of risk, suspicion and perpetual vigilance. The body and the postulated community alike are velvety on the inside and prickly and thorny on the outside.

Body and community are the last defensive outposts on the increasingly deserted battlefield on which the war for certainty, security and safety is waged daily with little, if any, respite. They need now to perform the tasks once divided among many bastions and stockades. More depends on them now than they are able to carry, and so they are likely to deepen, rather than to allay, the fears which prompted the seekers of security to run to them for shelter.

The new loneliness of body and community is the result of a wide set of seminal changes subsumed under the rubric of liquid modernity. One change in the set is, however, of particular importance: the renunciation, phasing out or selling off by the state of all the major appurtenances of its role as the principal (perhaps even monopolistic) purveyor of certainty and security, followed by its refusal to endorse the certainty/security aspirations of its subjects.

After the nation-state

In modern times, the nation was 'another face' of the state and the principal weapon in its bid for sovereignty over the territory and its population. A good deal of the nation's credibility and its attraction as the warrant of safety and durability has been derived from its intimate association with the state, and – through the state – with the actions aimed at laying the certainty and security of citizens on a durable and trustworthy, since collectively insured, foundation. Under the new conditions little can be gained by the nation from its close links with the state. The state may not expect much from the mobilizing potential of the nation which it needs less and less as the mass conscript armies held together by the feverishly beefed-up patriotic frenzy are replaced by the elitist and coldly professional high-tech units, while the wealth of the country is measured not so much by the quality, quantity and morale of its labour force, as by the country's attractiveness to coolly mercenary forces of global capital.

In a state that is no longer the secure bridge leading beyond the confinement of individual mortality, a call to sacrifice individual well-being, let alone individual life, for the preservation or the undying glory of the state sounds vacuous and increasingly bizarre, if not amusing. The centuries-long romance of nation with state is drawing to an end; not so much a divorce as a 'living together' arrangement is replacing the consecrated marital togetherness grounded in unconditional loyalty. Partners are now free to look elsewhere and enter other alliances; their partnership is no longer the binding pattern for proper and acceptable conduct. We may say that the nation, which used to offer the substitute for the absent community at the era of *Gesellschaft*, now drifts back to the left-behind *Gemeinschaft* in search of a pattern to emulate and to model itself after. The institutional scaffolding capable of holding the nation together is thinkable increasingly as a do-it-yourself job. It is the dreams of certainty and security, not their matter-of-fact and routinized provision, that should prompt the orphaned individuals to huddle under the nation's wings while chasing the stubbornly elusive safety.

Of salvaging the certainty-and-security services of the state there seem to be little hope. The freedom of state politics is relentlessly eroded by the new global powers armed with the awesome weapons of exterritoriality, speed of movement and evasion/escape ability; retribution for violating the new global brief is swift and merciless. Indeed, the refusal to play the game by the new global rules is the most mercilessly punishable crime, which the state powers, tied to the ground by their own territorially defined sovereignty, must beware of committing and avoid at all cost.

More often than not, the punishment is economic. Insubordinate governments, guilty of protectionist policies or generous public provisions for the 'economically redundant' sectors of their populations and of recoiling from leaving the country at the mercy of 'global financial markets' and 'global free trade', would be refused loans or denied reduction of their debts; local currencies would be made global lepers, speculated against and pressed to devalue; local stocks would fall head down on the global exchanges; the country would be cordoned off by economic sanctions and told to be treated by past and future trade partners as a global pariah; global investors would cut their anticipated losses, pack up their belongings and withdraw their assets, leaving local authorities to clean up the debris and bail out the victims out of their added misery.

Occasionally, though, the punishment would not be confined to the 'economic measures'. Particularly obstinate governments (but not too strong to resist for long) would be taught an exemplary lesson intended to warn and frighten their potential imitators. If the daily, routine demonstration of the global forces' superiority appeared insufficient to force the state to see reason and to co-operate with the new 'world order', the military might would be deployed: the superiority of speed over slowness, of the ability to escape over the need to engage, of exterritoriality over locality, all would be spectacularly manifested with the help, this time, of armed forces specialized in hit-and-run tactics and the strict separation of 'lives to be saved' and lives unworthy of saving.

Whether as an ethical act the way the war against Yugoslavia was conducted was right and proper is open to discussion. That war made sense, though, as the 'promotion of global economic order by other than political means'. The strategy selected by the attackers worked well as the spectacular display of the new global hierarchy and the new rules of the game which sustain it. If not for its thousands of quite real 'casualties' and a country cast into ruin and deprived of livelihood and self-regenerative ability for many years to come, one would be tempted to decribe it as a *sui generis* 'symbolic war'; the war itself, its strategy and tactics was (consciously or subconsciously) a symbol of the emergent power relationship. The medium was indeed the message.

As a teacher of sociology, I kept repeating to my students, year in, year out, the standard version of the 'history of civilization' as marked by a gradual yet relentless rise of sedentariness and the eventual victory of the settled over the nomads; it went without further argument that the defeated nomads were, in their essence, the regressive and anti-civilizational force. Jim MacLoughlin has recently unpacked the meaning of that victory, sketching a brief history of the treatment accorded to the 'nomads' by the sedentary populations within the orbit of modern civilization.[14] Nomadism, he points out, was seen and treated as 'characteristics of "barbarous" and underdeveloped societies'. Nomads were defined as primitive, and, from Hugo Grotius on, there was a parallel drawn between 'primitive' and 'natural' (that is, uncouth, raw, pre-cultural, uncivilized): 'the development of laws, cultural progress and the enhancement of civilization were all intimately linked to the evolution and improvement of man–land relations over time and across space'. To make a long story short: progress was identified with the abandonment of nomadism in favour of the sedentary way of life. All that, to be sure, happened at the time of heavy modernity, when domination implied direct and tight engagement and meant territorial conquest, annexation and colonization. The founder and the main theorist of 'diffusionism' (a view of history once highly popular in the empires' capitals), Friedrich Ratzel, the preacher of the 'rights of the stronger' which he thought were ethically superior as much as inescapable in view of the rarity of civilizational genius and commonality of passive immitation, grasped precisely the mood of the time when he wrote at the threshold of the colonialist century that

> The struggle for existence means a struggle for space . . . A superior people, invading the territory of its weaker savage neighbours, robs them of their land, forces them back into corners too small for their support, and continues to encroach even upon their meagre possession, till the weaker finally loses the last remnants of its domain, is literally crowded off the earth . . . The superiority of such expan-

sionists consists primarily in their greater ability to appropriate, thoroughly utilize and populate territory.

Clearly, no more. The game of domination in the era of liquid modernity is not played between the 'bigger' and the 'smaller', but between the quicker and the slower. Those who are able to accelerate beyond the catching power of their opponents rule. When velocity means domination, the 'appropriation, utilization and population of territory' becomes a handicap – a liability, not an asset. Taking over under one's own jurisdiction and even more the annexation of someone else's land imply capital-intensive, cumbersome and unprofitable chores of administration and policing, responsibilities, commitments – and, above all, cast considerable constraint on one's future freedom to move.

It is far from clear whether more hit-and-run-style wars will be undertaken, in view of the fact that the first attempt ended up in immobilizing the victors – burdening them with the cumbersome jobs of ground occupation, local engagements and managerial and administrative responsibilities quite out of tune with liquid modernity's techniques of power. The might of the global elite rests on its ability to escape local commitments, and globalization is meant precisely to avoid such necessities, to divide tasks and functions in such a way as to burden local authorities, and them only, with the role of guardians of law and (local) order.

Indeed, one can see many signals of the tide of 'second thoughts' swelling in the camp of the victors: the strategy of the 'global police force' is subject once more to an intense critical scrutiny. Among the functions which the global elite would rather leave to the nation-states-turned-local-police-precincts a growing number of influential voices would include the efforts to solve gory neighbourly conflicts; the solution to such conflicts, we hear, should be also 'decongested' and 'decentralized', reallocated down in the global hierarchy, human rights or no human rights, and passed over 'where it belongs', to the local warlords and the weapons they command thanks to the generosity or 'well understood economic interest' of global companies and of governments intent on promoting globalization. For instance, Edward N. Luttwak, Senior Fellow at the American Center for Strategic and International Studies and for many years a reliable barometer of changing Pentagon moods, has appealed in the July–August 1999 issue of *Foreign*

Affairs (described by the *Guardian* as 'the most influential period-
ical in print') to 'give war a chance'. Wars, according to Luttwak,
are not altogether bad, since they lead to peace. Peace, though, will
come only 'when all belligerents become exhausted or when one
wins decisively'. The worst thing (and NATO did just such a thing)
is to stop them midway, before the shoot-out ends in mutual exhaustion or the incapacitation of one of the warring parties. In
such cases conflicts are not resolved, but merely temporarily frozen, and the adversaries use the time of truce to rearm, redeploy
and rethink their tactics. So, for your own and their sake, do not
interfere 'in other people's wars'.

Luttwak's appeal may well fall on many willing and grateful
ears. After all, as the 'promotion of globalization by other means'
goes, abstaining from intervention and allowing the war of attrition to reach its 'natural end' would have brought the same benefits without the nuisance of direct engagement in 'other people's
wars', and particularly in their awkward and unwieldy consequences. To placate the conscience aroused by the imprudent decision to wage war under a humanitarian banner, Luttwak points
out the obvious inadequacy of military involvement as a means to
an end: 'Even a large-scale disinterested intervention can fail to
achieve its ostensibly humanitarian aim. One wonders whether the
Kosovars would have been better off had NATO simply done
nothing.' It would probably have been better for the NATO forces
to go on with their daily drills and leave the locals to do what the
locals had to do.

What caused the second thoughts and prompted the victors to
regret the interference (officially proclaimed a success) was their
failure to escape the selfsame eventuality which the hit-and-run
campaign was meant to ward off: the need for invasion and for the
occupation and administration of conquered territory. By the para-
troopers' landing and settling in Kosovo the belligerents had been
prevented from shooting themselves to death, but the task of keeping them at a safe distance from the shooting range brought the
NATO forces 'from heaven to earth' and embroiled them with
responsibility for the messy realities on the ground. Henry Kissinger,
a sober and perceptive analyst and the grandmaster of politics
understood (in a somewhat old-fashioned way) as the art of
the possible, warned against another blunder of shouldering the
responsibility for the recovery of the lands devastated by the

bombers' war.[15] That plan, Kissinger points out, 'risks turning into an open-ended commitment toward ever deeper involvement, casting us in the role of gendarme of a region of passionate hatreds and where we have few strategic interests'. And 'involvement' is precisely what the wars aimed to 'promote globalization by other means' are meant to avoid! Civil administration, Kissinger adds, would inevitably entail conflicts, and it will fall on the administrators, as their costly and ethically dubious task, to resolve them by force.

Thus far, there are few, if any, signs that the occupying forces may acquit themselves in the conflict-resolution task any better than those whom they bombed out and replaced on account of their failure. In a sharp opposition to the fate of the refugees in whose name the bombing campaign was launched, the daily lives of returnees seldom get into the headlines, but the news which does occasionally reach the readers and listeners of the media is ominous. 'A wave of violence and continued reprisals against Serbs and the Roma minority in Kosovo threatens to undermine the province's precarious stability and leave it ethnically cleansed of Serbs only a month after NATO's troops took control'; reports Chris Bird from Pristina.[16] NATO forces on the ground seem lost and helpless in the face of raging ethnic hatreds, which looked so easy to ascribe to the malice aforethought of but one villain, and so to resolve, when watched from the TV cameras installed on ultrasonic bombers.

Jean Clair, alongside many other observers, expects the immediate outcome of the Balkan war to be a profound and durable destabilization of the whole area, and the implosion rather than maturation of young and vulnerable, or still unborn, democracies of the Macedonian, Albanian, Croatian or Bulgarian type.[17] (Daniel Vernet supplied his survey of the views expressed on that subject by high-class Balkan political and social scientists with the title 'The Balkans face a risk of agony without end'.[18]) But he also wonders how the political void opened by cutting the roots of the nation-states' viability will be filled. Global market forces, jubilant at the prospect of no longer being stemmed and obstructed, would probably step in, but they would not wish (or manage, if they wished) to deputize for the absent or disempowered political authorities. Nor would they necessarily be interested in the resurrection of a strong and confident nation-state in full command of its territory.

'Another Marshal plan' is the most commonly suggested answer to the present quandary. It is not just the generals who are notorious for constantly fighting the last victorious war. But one cannot pay one's way out of every predicament, however large the sums laid aside for the purpose. The Balkan predicament is starkly different from that of the rebuilding by nation-states after War World II of their sovereignty together with the livelihood of their citizens. What we are facing in the Balkans after the Kosovo war is not only the task of material reconstruction almost from scratch (the Jugoslavs' livelihood has been all but destroyed) but also the seething and festering interethnic chauvinisms which have emerged from the war reinforced. The inclusion of the Balkans in the network of global markets would not do much to assuage intolerance and hatred, since it will add to, rather than detract from that insecurity which was (and remains) the prime source of boiling tribal sentiments. There is, for instance, a real danger that the weakening of Serbian power to resist will serve as a standing invitation to its neighbours to engage in a new round of hostilities and ethnic cleansings.

Given the NATO politicians' unprepossessing and off-putting record of clumsy handling of the delicate and complex issues typical of the Balkan 'belt of mixed populations' (as Hannah Arendt perceptively called it), one can fear a further series of costly blunders. One would not be wide of the mark either when suspecting the imminence of a moment at which European leaders, having made sure that no new wave of refugees and asylum-seekers is threatening their affluent electorate, will lose their interest in the unmanageable lands as they already have so many times before – in Somali, Sudan, Rwanda, East Timor and Afghanistan. We may then be back at square one, after a detour strewn with corpses. Antonina Jelyazkova, the director of the International Institute for Minority Studies, expressed this well (as quoted by Vernet): 'One cannot solve the question of minorities with bombs. The blows let loose the devil on both sides.'[19] Taking the side of nationalistic vindications, NATO actions beefed up further the already frenzied nationalisms of the area and prepared the ground for the future repetitions of genocidal attempts. One of the most gruesome consequences is that the mutual accommodation and friendly coexistence of languages, cultures and religions of the area have been made less likely than ever before. Whatever the intentions, the outcomes go against the grain of what a truly ethical undertaking would have us expect.

The conclusion, preliminary as it is, is inauspicious. The attempts to mitigate the tribal aggression through the new 'global
police actions' have thus far proved inconclusive at best, and more
likely counterproductive. The overall effects of the relentless globalization have been sharply unbalanced: the injury of renewed
tribal strife has come first, while the medicine needed to heal it is,
at best, at the test (more likely the trial-and-error) stage. Globalization appears to be much more successful in adding new vigour to
intercommunal enmity and strife than in promoting the peaceful
coexistence of communities.

Filling the void

For the multinationals (that is, global companies with scattered
and shifting local interests and allegiancies), 'the ideal world' 'is
one of no states, or at least of small rather than larger states', Eric
Hobsbawm observed. 'Unless it has oil, the smaller the state, the
weaker it is, and the less money it takes to buy a government.'

> What we have today is in effect a dual system, the official one of the
> 'national economies' of states, and the real but largely unofficial one
> of transnational units and institutions . . . [U]nlike the state with its
> territory and power, other elements of the 'nation' can be and easily
> are overriden by the globalization of the economy. Ethnicity and
> language are the two obvious ones. Take away state power and
> coercive force, and their relative insignificance is clear.[20]

As the globalization of the economy proceeds by leaps and bounds,
'buying governments', to be sure, is ever less necessary. The glaring
inability of governments to balance the books with the resources
they control (that is, the resources which they can be sure would
stay inside the realm of their jurisdiction whatever way of balan-
cing the books they chose) would suffice to make the government
not just surrender to the inevitable, but actively and keenly to
collaborate with the 'globals'.
     Anthony Giddens used the metaphor of the apocryphal 'jugger-
naut' to grasp the mechanism of world-wide 'modernization'. The
same metaphor fits well the present-day globalization of the
economy: it is increasingly difficult to separate the actors and their
passive objects, as most national governments vie with each other

to implore, cajole or seduce the global juggernaut to change track and roll first to the lands they administer. The few among them who are too slow, dim-witted, myopic or just vainglorious to join in the competition will either find themselves in dire trouble having nothing to boast about when it comes to wooing their 'voting with the wallets' electors, or be promptly condemned and ostracized by the compliant chorus of 'world opinion' and then showered with bombs or with threats of showering with bombs in order to restore their good sense and prompt them to join or rejoin the ranks.

If the principle of nation-states' sovereignty is finally discredited and removed from the statute-books of international law, if the states' power of resistance is effectively broken so that it needs no longer to be seriously reckoned with in the global powers' calculations, the replacement of the 'world of nations' by the supranational order (a global political system of checks-and-balances to constrain and regulate the global economic forces) is but one – and from today's perspective not the most certain – of the possible scenarios. The world-wide spread of what Pierre Bourdieu has dubbed 'the policy of precarization' is equally, if not more, likely to ensue. If the blow delivered to state sovereignty proves fatal and terminal, if the state loses its monopoly of coercion (which Max Weber and Norbert Elias alike considered to be its most distinctive feature and, simultaneously, the *sine qua non* attribute of modern rationality or civilized order), it does not necessarily follow that the sum total of violence, including violence with potentially genocidal consequences, will diminish; violence may be only 'deregulated', descending from the state to the 'community' (neo-tribal) level.

In the absence of the institutional frame of 'arboretic' structures (to use Deleuze/Guattari's metaphor), sociality may well return to its 'explosive' manifestations, spreading rhizomically and sprouting formations of varying degree of durability, but invariably unstable, hotly contested and devoid of foundation to rely on – except the passionate, frenetic actions of their adherents. The endemic instability of the foundations would need to be compensated for. An active (whether willing or enforced) complicity in the crimes which only the continuous existence of an 'explosive community' may exonerate and effectively exempt from punishment is the most suitable candidate to fill the vacancy. Explosive communities need violence to be born and need violence to go on living. They need enemies who threaten their extinction and enemies to be collectively persecuted, tortured and mutilated, in order to make every member of the community into an accessory to what, in case the battle were lost, would most certainly be declared a crime against humanity, prosecuted and punished.

In a long series of challenging studies (*Des Choses cachées depuis la fondation du monde*; *Le Bouc émissaire*; *La Violence et le sacré*) René Girard developed a comprehensive theory of the role of violence in the birth and perseverance of community. A violent urge is always seething just under the calm surface of peaceful and friendly co-operation; it needs to be channelled beyond the boundaries of community to cut off the communal island of tranquillity, where violence is prohibited. Violence, which would otherwise call the bluff of communal unity, is thereby recycled into the weapon of communal defence. In this recycled form it is indispensable; it needs to be restaged ever again in the form of a sacrificial rite, for which a surrogate victim is selected according to rules that are hardly ever explicit, yet nevertheless strict. 'There is a common denominator that determines the efficacy of all sacrifices.' This common denominator is

> internal violence – all the dissensions, rivalries, jealousies, and quarrels within the community that the sacrifices are designed to suppress. The purpose of the sacrifice is to restore harmony to the community, to reinforce the social fabric.

What unites the numerous forms of ritualistic sacrifice is its purpose of keeping alive the memory of the communal unity and its precariousness. But to perform this role the 'surrogate victim', the object sacrificed at the altar of communal unity, must be properly selected – and the rules of selection are as demanding as they are precise. To be suitable for the sacrifice, the potential object 'must bear a sharp resemblance to the human categories excluded from the ranks of the "sacrificeable" ' (that is, the humans assumed to be the 'insiders of the community') 'while still maintaining a degree of difference that forbids all possible confusion'. The candidates must be outside, but not too far; similar to 'us rightful community members' yet unmistakably different. The act of sacrificing these objects is meant, after all, to draw tight unsurpassable boundaries between the 'inside' and 'outside' of the community. It goes without saying that the categories from which victims are regularly selected are

> beings who are outside or on the fringes of society; prisoners of war, slaves, pharmakos . . . exterior or marginal individuals, incapable of establishing or sharing the social bonds that link the rest of the inhabitants. Their status as foreigners or enemies, their servile condition, or simply their age prevents these future victims from fully integrating themselves into the community.

The absence of social link with the 'legitimate' members of the community (or prohibition to establish such link) has an added advantage: victims 'can be exposed to violence without risk of vengeance';[21] one can punish them with impunity – or so one may hope, while voicing quite opposite expectations, painting the murderous capacity of the victims in the most lurid of colours and issuing reminders that the ranks must be kept closed and that the vigour and vigilance of community must be maintained at the highest pitch.

Girard's theory goes a long way towards making sense of the violence that is profuse and rampant at the frayed frontiers of communities, particularly communities whose identities are uncertain and contested, or, more to the point, of the common use of violence as the boundary-drawing device when the boundaries are absent, porous or blurred. Three comments seem in order, however.

First: if regular sacrifice of 'surrogate victims' is a ceremony of renewal of the unwritten 'social contract', it can play this role thanks to its other aspect – that of the collective remembrance of an historical or mythical 'event of creation', of the original compact entered on the battlefield soaked with enemy blood. If there was no such event, it needs to be retrospectively construed by the assiduous repetitiveness of the sacrifice rite. Genuine or invented, however, it sets a pattern for all the candidates for community status – the would-be communities not yet in position to replace the gory 'real thing' with benign ritual and the murder of real victims with the killing of surrogate ones. However sublimated may be the form of the ritualized sacrifice which transforms communal life into a continuous replay of the miracle of 'independence day', the pragmatic lessons drawn by all aspiring communities prompt deeds short on subtlety and liturgical elegance.

Second: the idea of a community committing the 'original murder' in order to render its existence safe and secure and tighten up the ranks is in Girard's own terms incongruent; before the original murder had been committed there would hardly have been the ranks to be tightened and a communal existence to be made secure. (Girard himself implies that much, when explaining in his chapter 10 the ubiquitous symbolics of severance in the sacrificial liturgy: 'The birth of the community is first and foremost an act of separation.') The vision of calculated deportation of inner violence beyond the community borders (community killing outsiders in order to keep peace among the insiders) is another case of the tempting but ill-founded expedient of taking a function (whether genuine or imputed) for the causal explanation. It is, rather, the original murder itself that brings community to life, by setting the demand for solidarity and the need to close the ranks. It is the legitimacy of the original victims which calls for communal solidarity and which tends to be reconfirmed year by year in the sacrificial rites.

Third: Girard's assertion that 'sacrifice is primarily an act of violence without risk of vengeance' (p. 13) needs to be complemented by the observation that to make the sacrifice effective the absence of risk must be carefully hidden or better still emphatically denied. From the original murder the enemy must have emerged not quite dead, but undead, a zombie ready to rise from the grave at any moment. A really dead enemy, or dead enemy incapable of resurrection, is unlikely to inspire enough fear to justify the need of unity – and sacrificial rites are conducted regularly in order to remind everybody around that the rumours of the enemy's ultimate demise are themselves the enemy propaganda and so the oblique, yet vivid proof that the enemy is alive, kicking and biting.

In a formidable series of studies of the Bosnian genocide, Arne Johan Vetlesen points out that in the absence of reliable (we would hope durable and secure) institutional foundations – an uninvolved, lukewarm or indifferent bystander becomes the community's most formidable and hated enemy: 'From the viewpoint of an agent of genocide, bystanders are people possessing a potential . . . to halt the on-going genocide.'[22] Let me add that whether the bystanders will or will not act on that potential, their presence as 'bystanders' (people doing nothing to destroy the joint enemy) is a challenge to the sole proposition from which the explosive community derives its *raison d'être*: that it is an 'either us or them' situation, that the destruction of 'them' is indispensable for 'our' survival and killing 'them' is the *conditio sine qua non* of 'us' staying alive. Let me add as well that since the membership of the community is in no way 'preordained' or institutionally assured, the 'baptism by (spilt) blood' – a personal participation in collective crime – is the sole way of joining and the sole legitimation of continuous membership. Unlike state-administered genocide (and, most prominently, unlike the Holocaust), the kind of genocide which is the birth-ritual of explosive communities cannot be entrusted to the experts or delegated to specialized offices and units. It matters less how many 'enemies' are killed; it matters more how numerous are the killers.

It also matters that the murder is committed openly, in the daylight and in full vision, that there are witnesses to the crime who know the perpetrators by name – so that retreat and hiding from retribution ceases to be a viable option and the community born of the initiatory crime remains the only refuge for the perpetrators. Ethnic cleansing, as Arne Johan Vetlesen found in his study of Bosnia,

> seizes upon and *maintains* the existing conditions of proximity between perpetrator and victim and in fact creates such conditions if they are not present and prolongs them as a matter of principle when they seem to wane. In this super-personalized violence, whole families were forced to be witnesses to torture, rape and killings . . .[23]

Again unlike in the case of the old-style genocide, and above all the Holocaust as their 'ideal type', witnesses are indispensable ingredients in the mixture of factors of which an explosive community is born. An explosive community can reasonably (though often deceptively) count on a long life only in so far as the original crime remains unforgotten and so its members, aware that the proofs of their crime are aplenty, stay together and solidary – cemented as they are by the joint vested interest in closing ranks in order to contest the criminal and punishable nature of their crime. The best way to meet these conditions is periodically, or continuously, to revive the memory of the crime and the fear of punishment through adding new crimes to the old. Since explosive communities are normally born in pairs (there would be no 'us' if not for 'them'), and since genocidal violence is a crime eagerly resorted to by whichever of the two members of the pair happens to be momentarily stronger, there would be normally no shortage of opportunity to find a suitable pretext for a new 'ethnic cleansing' or genocidal attempt. Violence which accompanies explosive sociality and is the way of life of the communities it sediments is therefore inherently self-propagating, self-perpetuating and self-reinforcing. It generates Gregory Bateson's 'schizmogenetic chains', which staunchly resist all efforts to cut them short, let alone to reverse them.

A feature which renders explosive communities of the kind analysed by Girard and Vetlesen particularly fierce, riotous and gory, endowing them with considerable genocidal potential, is their 'territorial connection'. That potential can be traced to another paradox of the era of liquid modernity. Territoriality is intimately linked to the spatial obsessions of solid modernity; it feeds on them and in its turn contributes to their preservation or restitution. Explosive communities, on the contrary, are at home in the era of liquefied modernity. The blend of explosive sociality with territorial aspirations is bound to result therefore in many a monstrous, abortive and 'unfit' mutation. The alternation of 'fagic' and 'emic' strategies in the conquest and defence of space (which as a rule was the prime stake in the conflicts of solid modernity) appears starkly out of place (yet more importantly, 'out of time') in a world dominated by the light/fluid/software variety of modernity; in such a world, it breaks the norm instead of following the rule.

The besieged sedentary populations refuse to accept the rules and stakes of the new 'nomadic' power game, an attitude which the up-and-coming global nomadic elite finds exceedingly difficult (as well as utterly repulsive and undesirable) to comprehend and cannot but perceive as the sign of retardation and backwardness. When it comes to confrontation, and particularly military confrontation, the nomadic elites of the liquid modern world view the territorially oriented strategy of sedentary populations as 'barbaric' by comparison with their own 'civilized' military strategy. It is now the nomadic elite which sets the tune and dictates the criteria by which territorial obsessions are classified and judged. The table has been turned – and the old tested weapon of 'chrono-politics', once used by triumphant settled populations to expel the nomads to barbaric/savage prehistory, is now deployed by the victorious nomadic elites in their struggle with whatever has remained of the territorial sovereignty and against those still dedicated to its defence.

In their reprobation of territorial practices nomadic elites can count on popular support. The outrage widely felt at the sight of massive expulsions named 'ethnic cleansing' gathers an added vigour from the fact that they look uncannily like a magnified version of tendencies which are manifested daily, though on a smaller scale, close to home – all over the urban spaces of the lands conducting the civilizing crusade. Fighting the 'ethnic cleansers', we exorcize our own 'inner demons', which prompt us to ghettoize the unwanted 'foreigners', to applaud the tightening of the asylum laws, to demand the removal of obnoxious strangers from the city streets and to pay any price for the shelters surrounded by surveillance cameras and armed guards. In the Jugoslav war the stakes on both sides were remarkably similar, though what was on one side a declared objective was an eagerly, though clumsily, held secret on the other. The Serbs wished to evict from their territory a recalcitrant and awkward Albanian minority, while the NATO countries, so to speak, 'responded in kind': their military campaign was triggered primarily by the wish of other Europeans to keep Albanians in Serbia and so nip in the bud the threat of their reincarnation as awkward and unwanted migrants.

Cloakroom communities

The link between the explosive community in its specifically liquid modern incarnation and territoriality is, however, by no means necessary and certainly not universal. Most contemporary explosive communities are made to the measure of liquid modern times even if their spread can be territorially plotted; they are, if anything, exterritorial (and tend to be all the more spectacularly successful the freer they are from territorial constraints) – just like the identities they conjure up and keep precariously alive in the brief interval between explosion and extinction. Their 'explosive' nature chimes well with the identities of the liquid modern era: similarly to such identities, the communities in question tend to be volatile, transient and 'single-aspect' or 'single-purpose'. Their life-span is short while full of sound and fury. They derive power not from their expected duration, but, paradoxically, from their precarious-

ness and uncertain future, from the vigilance and emotional investment which their brittle existence vociferously demands.

The name 'cloakroom community' grasps well some of their characteristic traits. Visitors to a spectacle dress *for the occasion*, abid-
ing by a sartorial code distinct from those codes they follow daily –
the act which simultaneously sets apart the visit as 'a special occasion' and makes the visitors look, for the duration of the event,
much more uniform than they do in the life outside the theatre
building. It is the evening performance which brought them all here
– different as their interests and pastimes during the day could have
been. Before entering the auditorium they all leave the coats or
anoraks they wore in the streets in the playhouse cloakroom (by
counting the number of hooks and hangers used, one can judge how
full is the house and how assured is the immediate future of the
production). During the performance all eyes are on the stage; so is
everybody's attention. Mirth and sadness, laughter and silence, rounds
of applause, shouts of approval and gasps of surprise are synchronized – as if carefully scripted and directed. After the last fall of the
curtain, however, the spectators collect their belongings from the
cloakroom and when putting their street clothes on once more return to their ordinary mundane and different roles, a few moments
later again dissolving in the variegated crowd filling the city streets
from which they emerged a few hours earlier.

Cloakroom communities need a spectacle which appeals to similar interests dormant in otherwise disparate individuals and so
bring them all together for a stretch of time when other interests –
those which divide them instead of uniting – are temporarily laid
aside, put on a slow burner or silenced altogether. Spectacles as the
occasion for the brief existence of a cloakroom community do not
fuse and blend individual concerns into 'group interest'; by being
added up, the concerns in question do not acquire a new quality,
and the illusion of sharing which the spectacle may generate would
not last much longer than the excitement of the performance.

Spectacles have come to replace the 'common cause' of the heavy/
solid/hardware modernity era – which makes a lot of difference to
the nature of new-style identities and goes a long way towards
making sense of the emotional tensions and aggression-generating
traumas which from time to time accompany their pursuit.

'Carnival communities' seems to be another fitting name for the
communities under discussion. Such communities, after all, offer

temporary respite from the agonies of daily solitary struggles, from the tiresome condition of individuals *de jure* persuaded or forced to pull themselves out of their troublesome problems by their own bootstraps. Explosive communities are *events* breaking the monotony of daily solitude, and like all carnival events they let off the pent-up steam and allow the revellers better to endure the routine to which they must return the moment the frolicking is over. And like philosophy in Ludwig Wittgenstein's melancholy musings, they 'leave everything as it was' (that is, if one does not count the wounded victims and the moral scars of those who escaped the lot of 'collateral casualties').

'Cloakroom' or 'carnival', the explosive communities are as indispensable a feature of the liquid modernity landscape as the essentially solitary plight of the individuals *de jure* and their ardent, yet on the whole vain efforts to rise to the level of individuals *de facto*. The spectacles, the pegs and hangers in the cloakroom and the crowd-pulling carnival fairs are many and varied, catering for any sort of taste. The Huxleyan brave new world has borrowed from the Orwellian 1984 the stratagem of 'five minutes of (collectivized) hatred', shrewdly and ingeniously complementing it by the expedient of the 'five minutes of (collectivized) adoration'. Each day the first-page press and first-minute TV headlines wave a new banner under which to gather and march (virtual) shoulder to (virtual) shoulder. They offer a virtual 'common purpose' around which virtual communities may entwine, pushed and pulled alternately by the synchronized feeling of panic (sometimes of a moral, but more often than not of immoral or amoral kind) and ecstasy.

One effect of cloakroom/carnival communities is that they effectively ward off the condensation of 'genuine' (that is, comprehensive and lasting) communities which they mime and (misleadingly) promise to replicate or generate from scratch. They scatter instead of condense the untapped energy of sociality impulses and so contribute to the perpetuation of the solitude desperately yet vainly seeking redress in the rare and far-between concerted and harmonious collective undertakings.

Far from being a cure for the sufferings born of the unbridged and seemingly unbridgeable gap between the fate of the individual *de jure* and the destiny of the individual *de facto*, they are the symptoms and sometimes causal factors of the social disorder specific to the liquid modernity condition.

Afterthought

On Writing; On Writing Sociology

The need in thinking is what makes us think.

Theodor W. Adorno

Quoting the Czech poet Jan Skácel's opinion on the plight of the poet (who, in Skácel's words, only discovers the verses which 'were always, deep down, there'), Milan Kundera comments (in *L'Art du roman*, 1986): 'To write, means for the poet to crush the wall behind which something that "was always there" hides.' In this respect, the task of the poet is not different from the work of history, which also *discovers* rather than *invents*: history, like poets, uncovers, in ever new situations, human possibilities previously hidden.

What history does matter-of-factly is a challenge, a task and a mission for the poet. To rise to this mission, the poet must refuse to serve up truths known beforehand and well worn, truths already 'obvious' because they have been brought to the surface and left floating there. It does not matter whether such truths 'assumed in advance' are classified as revolutionary or dissident, Christian or atheist – or how right and proper, noble and just they are or have been proclaimed to be. Whatever their denomination, those 'truths' are not this 'something hidden' which the poet is called to uncover; they are, rather, parts of the wall which the poet's mission is to crush. Spokesmen for the obvious, self-evident and 'what we all believe, don't we?' are *false poets*, says Kundera.

But what, if anything, does the poet's vocation have to do with the sociologist's calling? We sociologists rarely write poems. (Some of us who do take for the time of writing a leave of absence from our professional pursuits.) And yet, if we do not wish to share the fate of 'false poets' and resent being 'false sociologists', we ought to come as close as the true poets do to the yet hidden human possibilities; and for that reason we need to pierce the walls of the obvious and self-evident, of that prevailing ideological fashion of the day whose commonality is taken for the proof of its sense. Demolishing such walls is as much the sociologist's as the poet's calling, and for the same reason: the walling-up of possibilities belies human potential while obstructing the disclosure of its bluff.

Perhaps the verses which the poet seeks 'were always there'. One cannot be so sure, though, about the human potential discovered by history. Do humans – the makers and the made, the heroes and the victims of history – indeed carry forever the same volume of possibilities waiting for the right time to be disclosed? Or is it rather that, as human history goes, the opposition between discovery and creation is null and void and makes no sense? Since history is the endless process of human creation, is not history for the same reason (and by the same token) the unending process of human self-discovery? Is not the propensity to disclose/create ever new possibilities, to expand the inventory of possibilities already discovered and made real, the sole human potential which always has been, and always is, 'already there'? The question whether the new possibility has been created or 'merely' uncovered by history is no doubt welcome nourishment to many a scholastic mind; as for history itself, it does not wait for an answer and can do quite well without one.

Niklas Luhmann's most seminal and precious legacy to fellow sociologists has been the notion of *autopoiesis* – self-creation (from Greek ποιείη, do, create, give form, be effective, the opposite of πασχειη – of suffering, being an object, not the source, of the act) – meant to grasp and encapsulate the gist of the human condition. The choice of the term was itself a creation or discovery of the link (inherited kinship rather than chosen affinity) between history and poetry. Poetry and history are two parallel currents ('parallel' in the sense of the non-Euclidean universe ruled by Bolyai and Lobachevski's geometry) of that autopoiesis of human potentialities, in which creation is the sole form discovery can take, while self-discovery is the principal act of creation.

Sociology, one is tempted to say, is a third current, running in parallel with those two. Or at least this is what it should be if it is to stay inside that human condition which it tries to grasp and make intelligible; and this is what it has tried to become since its inception, though it has been repeatedly diverted from trying by mistaking the seemingly impenetrable and not-yet-decomposed walls for the ultimate limits of human potential and going out of its way to reassure the garrison commanders and the troops they command that the lines they have drawn to set aside the off-limits areas will never be transgressed.

Alfred de Musset suggested almost two centuries ago that 'great artists have no country'. Two centuries ago these were militant words, a war-cry of sorts. They were written down amidst deafening fanfares of youthful and credulous, and for that reason arrogant and pugnacious, patriotism. Numerous politicians were discovering their vocation in building nation-states of one law, one language, one world-view, one history and one future. Many poets and painters were discovering their mission in nourishing the tender sprouts of national spirit, resurrecting long-dead national traditions or conceiving of brand-new ones that never lived before and offering the nation as not-yet-fully-enough-aware-of-being-a-nation the stories, the tunes, the likenesses and the names of heroic ancestors – something to share, love and cherish in common, and so to lift the mere living together to the rank of belonging together, opening the eyes of the living to the beauty and sweetness of belonging by prompting them to remember and venerate their dead and to rejoice in guarding their legacy. Against that background, de Musset's blunt verdict bore all the marks of a rebellion and a call to arms: it summoned his fellow writers to refuse co-operation with the enterprise of the politicians, the prophets and the preachers of closely guarded borders and gun-bristling trenches. I do not know whether de Musset intuited the fratricidal capacities of the kind of fraternities which nationalist politicians and ideologists-laureate were determined to build, or whether his words were but an expression of the intellectual's disgust at and resentment of narrow horizons, backwaters and parochial mentality. Whatever the case then, when read now, with the benefit of hindsight, through a magnifying glass stained with the dark blots of ethnic cleansings, genocides and mass graves, de Musset's words

seem to have lost nothing of their topicality, challenge and ur-
gency, nor have they lost any of their original controversiality.
Now as then, they aim at the heart of the writers' mission and
challenge their consciences with the question decisive for any
writer's *raison d'être*.

A century and a half later Juan Goytisolo, probably the greatest
among living Spanish writers, takes up the issue once more. In a
recent interview ('Les batailles de Juan Goytisolo' in *Le Monde* of
12 February 1999), he points out that once Spain had accepted, in
the name of Catholic piety and under the influence of the Inquisition, a highly restrictive notion of national identity, the country
became, towards the end of the sixteenth century, a 'cultural desert'.
Let us note that Goytisolo writes in Spanish, but for many years
lived in Paris and in the USA, before finally settling in Morocco.
And let us note that no other Spanish writer has had so many of his
works translated into Arabic. Why? Goytisolo has no doubt about
the reason. He explains: 'Intimacy and distance create a privileged
situation. Both are necessary.' Though each for a different reason,
both these qualities make their presence felt in his relations to his
native Spanish and acquired Arabic, French and English – the
languages of the countries which in succession became his chosen
substitute homes.

Since Goytisolo spent a large part of his life away from Spain,
the Spanish language ceased for him to be the all-too-familiar tool
of daily, mundane and ordinary communication, always at hand
and calling for no reflection. His intimacy with his childhood language was not – could not be – affected, but now it has been
supplemented with distance. The Spanish language became the
'authentic homeland in his exile', a territory known and felt and
lived through from the inside and yet – since it also became remote
– full of surprises and exciting discoveries. That intimate/distant
territory lends itself to the cool and detached scrutiny *sine ira et
studio*, laying bare the pitfalls and the yet untested possibilities
invisible in vernacular uses, showing previously unsuspected plas-
ticity, admitting and inviting creative intervention. It is the combination of intimacy and distance which allowed Goytisolo to
realize that the unreflexive immersion in a language – just the kind
of immersion which exile makes all but impossible – is fraught
with dangers: 'If one lives only in the present, one risks disappearing together with the present.' It was the 'outside', detached look at

his native language which allowed Goytisolo to step beyond the constantly vanishing present and so enrich his Spanish in a way otherwise unlikely, perhaps altogether inconceivable. He brought back into his prose and poetry ancient terms, long fallen into disuse, and by doing so blew away the store-room dust which had covered them, wiped out the patina of time and offered the words new and previously unsuspected (or long forgotten) vitality.

In *Contre-allée*, a book published recently in co-operation with Catherine Malabou, Jacques Derrida invites his readers to think *in travel* – or, more exactly, to 'think travel'. That means to think that unique activity of departing, going away from *chez soi*, going far, towards the unknown, risking all the risks, pleasures and dangers that the 'unknown' has in store (even the risk of not returning).

Derrida is obsessed with 'being away'. There is some reason to surmise that the obsession was born when the twelve-year-old Jacques was in 1942 sent down from the school which by the decree of the Vichy administration of North Africa was ordered to purify itself of Jewish pupils. This is how Derrida's 'perpetual exile' started. Since then, Derrida has divided his life between France and the United States. In the US he was a Frenchman; in France, however hard he tried, time and time again the Algerian accent of his childhood kept breaking through his exquisite French *parole*, betraying a *pied noir* hidden under the thin skin of the Sorbonne professor. (This is, some people think, why Derrida came to extol the superiority of writing and composed the aetiological myth of priority to support the axiological assertion.) Culturally, Derrida was to remain 'stateless'. This did not mean, though, having no cultural homeland. Quite the contrary: being 'culturally stateless' meant having more than one homeland, building a home of one's own on the crossroads between cultures. Derrida became and remained a *métèque*, a cultural hybrid. His 'home on the crossroads' was built of language.

Building a home on cultural crossroads proved to be the best conceivable occasion to put language to tests it seldom passes elsewhere, to see through its otherwise unnoticed qualities, to find out what language is capable of and what promises it makes it can never deliver. From that home on the crossroads came the exciting and eye-opening news about the inherent plurality and undecidability of sense (in *L'Écriture et la différence*), about the endemic

impurity of origins (in *De la grammatologie*), and about the perpetual unfulfilment of communication (in *La Carte postale*) – as
Christian Delacampagne noted in *Le Monde* of 12 March 1999.

Goytisolo's and Derrida's messages are different from that of de
Musset: it is not true, the novelist and the philosopher suggest in
unison, that great art has no homeland – on the contrary, art, like
the artists, may have many homelands, and most certainly has
more than one. Rather than homelessness, the trick is to be at
home in many homes, but to be in each inside and outside at
the same time, to combine intimacy with the critical look of an
outsider, involvement with detachment – a trick which sedentary
people are unlikely to learn. Learning the trick is the chance of the
exile: *technically* an exile – one that is *in*, but not *of* the place. The
unconfinedness that results from this condition (that *is* this condition) reveals the homely truths to be man-made and un-made, and
the mother tongue to be an endless stream of communication
between generations and a treasury of messages always richer than
any of their readings and forever waiting to be unpacked anew.

George Steiner has named Samuel Beckett, Jorge Luis Borges
and Vladimir Nabokov as the greatest among contemporary writers. What unites them, he said, and what made them all great, is
that each of the three moved with equal ease – was equally 'at
home' – in several linguistic universes, not one. (A reminder is in
order. 'Linguistic universe' is a pleonastic phrase: the universe in
which each one of us lives is and cannot but be 'linguistic' – made
of words. Words lit the islands of visible forms in the dark sea of
the invisible and mark the scattered spots of relevance in the formless mass of the insignificant. It is words that slice the world into
the classes of nameable objects and bring out their kinship or
enmity, closeness or distance, affinity or mutual estrangement –
and as long as they stay alone in the field they raise all such
artefacts to the rank of reality, the only reality there is). One needs
to live, to visit, to know intimately more than one such universe to
spy out human invention behind any universe's imposing and apparently indomitable structure and to discover just how much
human cultural effort is needed to divine the idea of nature with its
laws and necessities; all that is required in order to muster, in the
end, the audacity and the determination to join in that cultural
effort *knowingly*, aware of its risks and pitfalls, but also of the
boundlessness of its horizons.

To create (and so also to discover) always means breaking a rule; following a rule is mere routine, more of the same – not an act of creation. For the exile, breaking rules is not a matter of free choice, but an eventuality that cannot be avoided. Exiles do not know enough of the rules reigning in their country of arrival, nor do they treat them unctuously enough for their efforts to observe them and conform to be perceived as genuine and approved. As to their country of origin, going into exile has been recorded there as their original sin, in the light of which all that the sinners later may do may be taken down and used against them as evidence of their rule-breaking. By commission or by omission, rule-breaking becomes a trademark of the exiles. This is unlikely to endear them to the natives of any of the countries between which their life itineraries are plotted. But, paradoxically, it also allows them to bring to all the countries involved gifts they need badly even without knowing it, such gifts as they could hardly expect to receive from any other source.

Let me clarify. The 'exile' under discussion here is not necessarily a case of physical, bodily mobility. It may involve leaving one country for another, but it need not. As Christine Brook-Rose put it (in her essay 'Exsul'), the distinguishing mark of all exile, and particularly the writer's exile (that is the exile articulated in words and thus made a communicable *experience*) is the refusal to be integrated – the determination to stand out from the physical space, to conjure up a place of one's own, different from the place in which those around are settled, a place unlike the places left behind and unlike the place of arrival. The exile is defined not in relation to any particular physical space or to the oppositions between a number of physical spaces, but through the autonomous stand taken towards space as such. 'Ultimately', asks Brooke-Rose,

> is not every poet or 'poetic' (exploring, rigorous) novelist an exile of sorts, looking in from outside into a bright, desirable image in the mind's eye, of the little world created, for the space of the writing effort and the shorter space of the reading? This kind of writing, often at odds with publisher and public, is the last solitary, non-socialized creative art.

The resolute determination to stay 'nonsocialized'; the consent to integrate solely with the condition of non-integration; the resistance – often painful and agonizing, yet ultimately victorious – to the overwhelming pressure of the place, old or new; the rugged defence of the right to pass judgement and choose; the embracing of ambivalence or calling ambivalence into being – these are, we may say, the constitutive features of 'exile'. All of them – please note – refer to attitude and life strategy, to spiritual rather than physical mobility.

Michel Maffesoli (in *Du nomadisme: Vagabondages initiatiques*, 1997) writes of the world we *all* inhabit nowadays as a 'floating territory' in which 'fragile individuals' meet 'porous reality'. In this territory only such things or persons may fit as are fluid, ambiguous, in a state of perpetual becoming, in a constant state of self-transgression. 'Rootedness', if any, can there be only dynamic: it needs to be restated and reconstituted daily – precisely through the repeated act of 'self-distantiation', that foundational, initiating act of 'being in travel', on the road. Having compared all of us - the inhabitants of the present-day world – to nomads, Jacques Attali (in *Chemins de sagesse*, 1996) suggests that, apart from travelling light and being kind, friendly and hospitable to strangers whom they meet on their way, nomads must be constantly on the watch, remembering that their camps are vulnerable, have no walls or trenches to stop intruders. Above all, nomads, struggling to survive in the world of nomads, need to grow used to the state of continuous disorientation, to the travelling along roads of unknown direction and duration, seldom looking beyond the next turn or crossing; they need to concentrate all their attention on that small stretch of road which they need to negotiate before dusk.

'Fragile individuals', doomed to conduct their lives in a 'porous reality', feel like skating on thin ice; and 'in skating over thin ice', Ralph Waldo Emerson remarked in his essay 'Prudence', 'our safety is in our speed'. Individuals, fragile or not, need safety, crave safety, seek safety, and so then try, to the best of their ability, to maintain a high speed whatever they do. When running among fast runners, to slow down means to be left behind; when running on thin ice, slowing down also means the real threat of being drowned. Speed, therefore, climbs to the top of the list of survival values.

Speed, however, is not conducive to thinking, not to thinking far ahead, to long-term thinking at any rate. Thought calls for pause and rest, for 'taking one's time', recapitulating the steps already taken, looking closely at the place reached and the wisdom (or imprudence, as the case may be) of reaching it. Thinking takes one's mind away from the task at hand, which is always the running and keeping speed whatever else it may be. And in the absence of thought, the skating on thin ice which is the *fate* of fragile individuals in the porous world may well be mistaken for their *destiny*.

Taking one's fate for destiny, as Max Scheler insisted in his *Ordo amoris*, is a grave mistake: 'destiny of man is not his fate . . . [T]he assumption that fate and destiny are the same deserves to be called fatalism.' Fatalism is an error of judgement, since in fact fate has 'a natural and basically comprehensible origin'. Moreover, though fate is not a matter of free choice, and particularly of the individual free choice, it '*grows up* out of the life of a man or a people'. To see all that, to note the difference and the gap between fate and destiny, and to escape the trap of fatalism, one needs resources not easily attainable when running on thin ice: a 'time off' to think, and a distance allowing a long view. 'The image of our destiny', Scheler warns, 'is thrown into relief only in the recurrent traces left when we turn away from it.' Fatalism, though, is a self-corroborating attitude: it makes the 'turning away', that *conditio sine qua non* of thinking, look useless and unworthy of trying.

Taking distance, taking time – in order to separate destiny and fate, to emancipate destiny from fate, to make destiny free to confront fate and challenge it: this is the calling of sociology. And this is what sociologists may do, if they consciously, deliberately and earnestly strive to reforge the calling they have joined – their fate – into their destiny.

'Sociology is the answer. But what was the question?' states, and asks, Ulrich Beck in *Politik in der Risikogesellschaft*. A few pages previously Beck had seemed to articulate the question he seeks: the chance of a democracy that goes beyond 'expertocracy', a kind of democracy which 'begins where debate and decision making are opened about whether we *want* a life under the conditions that are being presented to us . . . '

This chance is under a question mark not because someone has deliberately and malevolently shut the door to such a debate and prohibited an informed decision-taking; hardly ever in the past was the freedom to speak out and to come together to discuss matters of common interest as complete and unconditional as it is now. The point is, though, that more than a formal freedom to talk and pass resolutions is needed for the kind of democracy which Beck thinks is our imperative, to start in earnest. We also need to know what it is we need to talk about and what the resolutions we pass ought to be concerned with. And all this needs to be done in our type of society, in which the authority to speak and resolve issues is the reserve of experts who own the exclusive right to pronounce on the difference between reality and fantasy and to set apart the possible from the impossible. (Experts, we may say, are almost by definition people who 'get the facts straight', who take them as they come and think of the least risky way of living in their company.)

Why this is not easy and unlikely to become easier unless something is done Beck explains in his *Risikogesellschaft: auf dem Weg in eine andere Moderne*. He writes: 'What food is for hunger, eliminating risks, *or interpreting them away*, is for the consciousness of risks.' In a society haunted primarily by material want, such an option between 'eliminating' misery and 'interpreting it away' did not exist. In our society, haunted by risk rather than want it does exist – and is daily taken. Hunger cannot be assuaged by denial; in hunger, subjective suffering and its objective cause are indissolubly linked, and the link is self-evident and cannot be belied. But risks, unlike material want, are not subjectively experienced; at least, they are not 'lived' directly unless mediated by knowledge. They may never reach the realm of subjective experience – they may be trivialized or downright denied before they arrive there, and the chance that they will indeed be barred from arriving *grows* together with the extent of the risks.

What follows is that *sociology is needed today more than ever before*. The job in which sociologists are the experts, the job of restoring to view the lost link between objective affliction and subjective experience, has become more vital and indispensable than ever, while less likely than ever to be performed without their professional help, since its performance by the spokesmen and practitioners of other fields of expertise has become utterly improbable. If all experts deal with practical problems and all expert knowledge is focused on their resolution, sociology is one branch of expert knowledge for which the practical problem it struggles to resolve is *enlightenment aimed at human understanding*. Sociology is perhaps the sole field of expertise in which (as Pierre Bourdieu pointed out in *La Misère du monde*) Dilthey's famed distinction between *explanation* and *understanding* has been overcome and cancelled.

To understand one's fate means to be aware of its difference from one's destiny. And to understand one's fate is to know the complex network of causes that brought about that fate and its difference from that destiny. To *work* in the world (as distinct from being 'worked out and about' by it) one needs to know how the world works.

The kind of enlightenment which sociology is capable of delivering is addressed to freely choosing individuals and aimed at enhancing and reinforcing their freedom of choice. Its immediate objective is to reopen the allegedly shut case of explanation and so to promote understanding. It is the self-formation and self-assertion of individual men and women, the preliminary condition of their ability to decide whether they want the kind of life that has been presented to them as their fate, that as a result of sociological enlightenment may gain in vigour, effectiveness and rationality. The cause of the autonomous society may profit together with the cause of the autonomous individual; they can only win or lose together.

To quote from *Le Délabrement de l'Occident* of Cornelius Castoriadis,

> An autonomous society, a truly democratic society, is a society which questions everything that is pre-given and by the same token *liberates the creation of new meanings*. In such a society, all individuals are free to create for their lives the meanings they will (and can).

Society is truly autonomous once it 'knows, must know, that there are no "assured" meanings, that it lives on the surface of chaos, that it itself is a chaos seeking a form, but a form that is never fixed once for all'. The absence of guaranteed meanings – of absolute truths, of preordained norms of conduct, of pre-drawn borderlines between right and wrong, no longer needing attention, of guaranteed rules of successful action – is the *conditio sine qua non* of, simultaneously, a truly autonomous society and truly free indi-

viduals; autonomous society and the freedom of its members condition each other. Whatever safety democracy and individuality
may muster depends not on fighting the endemic contingency and
uncertainty of human condition, but on recognizing it and facing
its consequences point-blank.

If orthodox sociology, born and developed under the aegis of
solid modernity, was preoccupied with the conditions of human
obedience and conformity, the prime concern of sociology made to
the measure of liquid modernity needs to be the promotion of
autonomy and freedom; such sociology must therefore put individual self-awareness, understanding and *responsibility* at its
focus. For the denizens of modern society in its solid and managed
phase, the major opposition was one between conformity and
deviance; the major opposition in modern society in its present-day
liquefied and decentred phase, the opposition which needs to be
faced up to in order to pave the way to a truly autonomous society,
is one between taking up responsibility and seeking a shelter where
responsibility for one's own action need not be taken by the actors.

That other side of the opposition, seeking shelter, is a seductive
option and realistic prospect. Alexis de Tocqueville (in the second
volume of his *De la démocratie en Amérique*) noted that if selfish-
ness, that bane haunting humankind in all periods of its history,
'desiccated the seeds of all virtues', then individualism, a novel and
typically modern affliction, dries up only 'the source of public
virtues'; the individuals affected are busy 'cutting out small companies for their own use' while leaving the 'great society' to its own
fate. The temptation to do so has grown considerably since de
Tocqueville jotted down his observation.

Living among a multitude of competing values, norms and
life-styles, without a firm and reliable guarantee of being in the
right, is hazardous and commands a high psychological price. No
wonder that the attraction of the second response, of hiding from
the requisites of responsible choice, gathers in strength. As Julia
Kristeva puts it (in *Nations without Nationalism*), 'It is a rare
person who does not invoke a primal shelter to compensate for
personal disarray.' And we all, to a greater or lesser extent, sometimes more and sometimes less, find ourselves in that state of
'personal disarray'. Time and again we dream of a 'great simplification'; unprompted, we engage in regressive fantasies of which
the images of the prenatal womb and the walled-up home are

prime inspirations. The search for a primal shelter is 'the other' of responsibility, just like deviance and rebellion were 'the other' of conformity. The yearning for a primal shelter has come these days to replace rebellion, which has now ceased to be a sensible option; as Pierre Rosanvallon points out (in a new preface to his classic *Le Capitalisme utopique*), there is no longer a 'commanding authority to depose and replace. There seems to be no room left for a revolt, as social fatalism *vis-à-vis* the phenomenon of unemployment testifies.'

Signs of malaise are abundant and salient, yet, as Pierre Bourdieu repeatedly observes, they seek in vain a legitimate expression in the world of politics. Short of articulate expression, they need to be read out, obliquely, from the outbursts of xenophobic and racist frenzy – the most common manifestations of the 'primal shelter' nostalgia. The available and no less popular alternative to neotribal moods of scapegoating and militant intolerance – the exit from politics and withdrawal behind the fortified walls of the private – is no longer prepossessing and, above all, no longer an adequate response to the genuine source of the ailment. And so it is at this point that sociology, with its potential for explanation that promotes understanding, comes into its own more than at any other time in its history.

According to the ancient but never bettered Hippocratic tradition, as Pierre Bourdieu reminds the readers of *La Misère du monde*, genuine medicine begins with the recognition of the invisible disease – 'facts of which the sick does not speak or forgets to report'. What is needed in the case of sociology is the 'revelation of the structural causes which the apparent signs and talks disclose only through distorting them [*ne dévoilent qu'en les voilant*]'. One needs to see through – explain and understand – the sufferings characteristic of the social order which 'no doubt pushed back the great misery (though as much as it is often said), while . . . at the same time multiplying the social spaces . . . offering favourable conditions to the unprecedented growth of all sorts of little miseries.'

To diagnose a disease does not mean the same as curing it – this general rule applies to sociological diagnoses as much as it does to medical verdicts. But let us note that the illness of society differs from bodily illnesses in one tremendously important respect: in the the case of an ailing social order, the absence of an adequate diagnosis (elbowed out or silenced by the tendency to 'interpret away' the risks spotted by Ulrich Beck) is a crucial, perhaps decisive, part of the disease. As Cornelius Castoriadis famously put it, society is ill if it stops questioning itself; and it cannot be otherwise, considering that – whether it knows it or not – society is autonomous (its institutions are nothing but human-made and so, potentially, human-unmade), and that suspension of self-questioning bars the awareness of autonomy while promoting the illusion of heteronomy with its unavoidably fatalistic consequences. To restart questioning means to take a take a long step towards the cure. If in the history of human condition discovery equals creation, if in thinking about the human condition explanation and understanding are one – so in the efforts to improve human condition diagnosis and therapy merge.

Pierre Bourdieu expressed this perfectly in the conclusion of *La Misère du monde*: 'To become aware of the mechanisms which make life painful, even unliveable, does not mean to neutralize them; to bring to light the contradictions does not mean to resolve them.' And yet, sceptical as one can be about the social effectiveness of the sociological message, the effects of allowing those who suffer to discover the possibility of relating their sufferings to social causes cannot be denied; nor can we dismiss the effects of effects of becoming aware of the social origin of unhappiness 'in all its forms, including the most intimate and most secret of them'.

Nothing is less innocent, Bourdieu reminds us, than *laissez-faire*. Watching human misery with equanimity while placating the pangs of conscience with the ritual incantation of the TINA ('there is no alternative') creed, means complicity. Whoever willingly or by default partakes of the cover-up or, worse still, the denial of the human-made, non-inevitable, contingent and alterable nature of social order, notably of the kind of order responsible for unhappiness, is guilty of immorality – of refusing help to a person in danger.

Doing sociology and writing sociology is aimed at disclosing the possibility of living together differently, with less misery or no misery: the possibility daily withheld, overlooked or unbelieved. Not-seeing, not-seeking and thereby suppressing this possibility is itself part of human misery and a major factor in its perpetuation. Its disclosure does not by itself predetermine its use; also, when known, possibilities may not be trusted enough to be put to the test of reality. Disclosure is the beginning, not the end of the war against human misery. But that war cannot be waged in earnest, let alone with a chance of at least partial success, unless the scale of human freedom is revealed and recognized, so that freedom can be fully deployed in the fight against the social sources of all, including the most individual and private, unhappiness.

There is no choice between 'engaged' and 'neutral' ways of doing sociology. A non-committal sociology is an impossibility. Seeking a morally neutral stance among the many brands of sociology practised today, brands stretching all the way from the outspokenly libertarian to the staunchly communitarian, would be a vain effort. Sociologists may deny or forget the 'world-view' effects of their work, and the impact of that view on human singular or joint actions, only at the expense of forfeiting that responsibility of choice which every other human being faces daily. The job of sociology is to see to it that the choices are genuinely free, and that they remain so, increasingly so, for the duration of humanity.

Notes

Chapter 1   Emancipation

1   Herbert Marcuse, 'Liberation from the affluent society', quoted after *Critical Theory and Society: A Reader*, ed. Stephen Eric Bronner and Douglas MacKay Kellner (London: Routledge, 1989), p. 277.

2   David Conway, *Classical Liberalism: The Unvanquished Ideal* (New York: St Martin's Press, 1955), p. 48.

3   Charles Murray, *What it Means to be a Libertarian: A Personal Interpretation* (New York: Broadway Books, 1997), p. 32. See also Jeffrey Friedman's pertinent comments, in 'What's wrong with libertarianism', *Critical Review*, Summer 1997, pp. 407–67.

4   From *Sociologie et philosophie* (1924). Here quoted in Anthony Giddens's translation, in *Émile Durkheim: Selected Writings* (Cambridge: Cambridge University Press, 1972), p. 115.

5   Erich Fromm, *Fear of Freedom* (London: Routledge, 1960), pp. 51, 67.

6   Richard Sennett, *The Corrosion of Character: The Personal Consequences of Work in the New Capitalism* (New York: W. W. Norton & Co., 1998), p. 44.

7   Giles Deleuze and Felix Guattari, *Anti-Oedipus: Capitalism and Schizophrenia*, trans. Robert Hurley (New York: Viking Press, 1977), p. 42.

8   Alain Touraine, 'Can we live together, equal and different?', *European Journal of Social Theory*, November 1998, p. 177.

9   Frankfurt am Main: Suhrkamp, 1986. English trans. Mark Ritter, Ulrich Beck, *Risk Society: Towards a New Modernity* (London: Sage,

1992).
10 Beck, *Risk Society*, p. 137.
11 In Ulrich Beck, *Ecological Enlightenment: Essays on the Politics of the Risk Society*, trans. Mark A. Ritter (New Jersey: Humanity Press, 1995), p. 40.
12 Theodor Adorno, *Negative Dialectics*, trans. E. B. Ashton (London: Routledge, 1973), p. 408.
13 Theodor Adorno, *Minima Moralia: Reflections from Damaged Life*, trans. E. F. N. Jephcott (London: Verso, 1974), pp. 25–6.
14 Adorno, *Negative Dialectics* p. 220.
15 Adorno, *Minima Moralia*, p. 68.
16 Adorno, *Minima Moralia*, pp. 33–4.
17 Theodor Adorno and Max Horkheimer, *Dialectics of Enlightenment*, trans. John Cumming (London: Verso, 1986), p. 213.
18 Adorno and Horkheimer, *Dialectics of Enlightenment*, pp. 214–15.
19 *Leo Strauss on Tyranny, including the Strauss–Kojève Correspondence*, ed. Victor Gourevitch and Michael S. Roth (New York: Free Press, 1991), pp. 212, 193, 145, 205.

Chapter 2 Individuality

1 Nigel Thrift, 'The rise of soft capitalism', *Cultural Values*, 1/1, April 1997, pp. 29–57. Here Thrift creatively develops concepts coined and defined in Kenneth Jowitt, *New World Disorder* (Berkeley: University of California Press, 1992), and Michel Serres, *Genesis* (Ann Arbor: University of Michigan Press, 1995).
2 Alain Lipietz, 'The next transformation', in *The Milano Papers: Essays in Societal Alternatives*, ed. Michele Cangiani (Montreal: Black Rose Books, 1996), pp. 116–17.
3 See V. I. Lenin, 'Ocherednye zadachi sovetskoi vlasti', *Sochinenia*, 27, February–July 1918; Moscow: GIPL, 1950, pp. 229–30.
4 Daniel Cohen, *Richesse du monde, pauvretés des nations* (Paris: Flammarion, 1997), pp. 82–3.
5 Max Weber, *The Theory of Social and Economic Organization*, trans. A. R. Henderson and Talcott Parsons (New York: Hodge, 1947), pp. 112–14.
6 Gerhard Schulze, 'From situations to subjects: moral discourse in transition', in *Constructing the New Consumer Society*, ed. Pekka Sulkunen, John Holmwood, Hilary Radner and Gerhard Schulze (New York: Macmillan, 1997), p. 49.
7 Turo-Kimmo Lehtonen and Pasi Mäenpää, 'Shopping in the East-Central Mall', in *The Shopping Experience*, ed. Pasi Falk and Colin Campbell (London: Sage, 1997), p. 161.

8   David Miller, *A Theory of Shopping* (Cambridge: Polity Press, 1998), p. 141

9   Zbyszko Melosik and Tomasz Szkudlarek, *Kultura, Tozsamosc i Demokracja: Migotanie Znaczen* (Kraków: Impuls, 1998), p. 89.

10 Marina Bianchi, *The Active Consumer: Novelty and Surprise in Consumer Choice* (London: Routledge, 1998), p. 6.

11 Hilary Radner, 'Producing the body: Jane Fonda and the new public feminine', in *Constructing the New Consumer Society*, ed. Sulkunen *et al.*, pp. 116, 117, 122.

12 An appropriate, well-aimed corollary to Tony Blair's bewilderment was provided by Dr Spencer Fitz-Gibbon's letter to the *Guardian*: 'It's interesting that Robin Cook is a bad guy now his extra marital promiscuity has been revealed. Yet not long ago he was involved in the sale of equipment to the dictatorship in Indonesia, a regime which had massacred 200,000 people in occupied East Timor. If the British media and public displayed the same degree of outrage over genocide as over sex, the world would be a safer place.'

13 See Michael Parenti, *Inventing Reality: The Politics of the Mass Media* (New York: St Martin's Press, 1986), p. 65. In Parenti's words, the message underlying the massive and ubiquitous commercials, whatever they try to sell, is that 'In order to live well and live properly, consumers need corporate producers to guide them.' As a matter of fact the corporate producers can count on the army of counsellors, personal advisors and writers of 'teach yourself' books to hammer home much the same message of personal incompetence.

14 Harvie Ferguson, *The Lure of Dreams: Sigmund Freud and the Construction of Modernity* (London: Routledge, 1996), p. 205.

15 Harvie Ferguson, 'Watching the world go round: Atrium culture and the psychology of shopping', in *Lifestyle Shopping: The Subject of Consumption*, ed. Rob Shields (London: Routledge, 1992), p. 31.

16 See Ivan Illich, 'L'Obsession de la santé parfaite', *Le Monde diplomatique*, March 1999, p. 28.

17 Quoted from Barry Glassner, 'Fitness and the postmodern self', *Journal of Health and Social Behaviour*, 30, 1989.

18 See Albert Camus, *The Rebel*, trans. Anthony Bower (London: Penguin, 1971), pp. 226–7.

19 Gilles Deleuze and Felix Guattari, *Oedipus Complex: Capitalism and Schizophrenia*, trans. Robert Hurley (New York: Viking Press, 1977), p. 5.

20 Efrat Tseëlon, 'Fashion, fantasy and horror', *Arena*, 12, 1998, p. 117.

21 Christopher Lasch, *The Culture of Narcissim* (New York: W. W. Norton and Co., 1979), p. 97.

22 Christopher Lasch, *The Minimal Self* (London: Pan Books, 1985), pp. 32, 29, 34.
23 Jeremy Seabrook, *The Leisure Society* (Oxford: Blackwell, 1988) p. 183.
24 Thomas Mathiesen, 'The viewer society: Michel Foucault's 'Panopticon' revisited', *Theoretical Criminology*, 1/2, 1997, pp. 215–34.
25 Paul Atkinson and David Silverman, 'Kundera's *Immortality*: the interview society and the invention of the self', *Qualitative Inquiry*, 3, 1997, pp. 304–25.
26 Harvie Ferguson, 'Glamour and the end of irony', *The Hedgehog Review*, Fall 1999, pp. 10–16.
27 Jeremy Seabrook, *The Race for Riches: The Human Costs of Wealth* (Basingstoke: Marshall Pickering, 1988), pp. 168–9.
28 Yves Michaud, 'Des Identités flexibles', *Le Monde*, 24 October 1997.

Chapter 3   Time/Space

1 Quoted from Chris McGreal, 'Fortress town to rise on Cape of low hopes', the *Guardian*, 22 January 1999.
2 See Sarah Boseley, 'Warning of fake stalking claims', the *Guardian*, 1 February 1999, quoting the report signed by Michel Pathé, Paul E. Mullen and Rosemary Purcell.
3 Sharon Zukin, *The Culture of Cities* (Oxford: Blackwell, 1995), pp. 39, 38.
4 Richard Sennett, *The Fall of Public Man: On the Social Psychology of Capitalism* (New York: Vintage Books, 1978), pp. 39ff.
5 Sennett, *The Fall of Public Man*, p. 264.
6 Liisa Uusitalo, 'Consumption in postmodernity', in *The Active Consumer*, ed. Marina Bianchi (London: Routledge, 1998), p. 221.
7 Turo-Kimmo Lehtonen and Pasi Mäenpää, 'Shopping in the East-Centre Mall', in *The Shopping Experience*, ed. Pasi Falk and Colin Campbell (London: Sage, 1997), p. 161.
8 Michel Foucault, 'Of other spaces', *Diacritics*, 1, 1986, p. 26.
9 Richard Sennett, *The Uses of Disorder: Personal Identity and City Life* (London: Faber & Faber, 1996), pp. 34–6.
10 See Steven Flusty, 'Building paranoia', in *Architecture of Fear*, ed. Nan Elin (New York: Princeton Architectural Press, 1997), pp. 48–9. Also Zygmunt Bauman, *Globalization: The Human Consequences* (Cambridge: Polity Press, 1998), pp. 20–1.
11 See Marc Augé, *Non-lieux: Introduction à l'anthropologie de la surmodernité* (Paris: Seuil, 1992). Also Georges Benko, 'Introduction: modernity, postmodernity and social sciences', in *Space and*

Social Theory: Interpreting Modernity and Postmodernity, ed. Georges Benko and Ulf Strohmayer (Oxford: Blackwell, 1997), pp. 23–4.

12   Jerzy Kociatkiewicz and Monika Kostera, 'The anthropology of empty space', *Qualitative Sociology*, 1, 1999, pp. 43, 48.
13   Sennett, *The Uses of Disorder*, p. 194.
14   Zukin, *The Culture of Cities*, p. 263.
15   Sennett, *The Fall of Public Man*, pp. 260ff.
16   Benko, 'Introduction', p. 25.
17   See Rob Shields, 'Spatial stress and resistance: social meanings of spatialization', in *Space and Social Theory*, ed. Benko and Strohmayer, p. 194.
18   Michel de Certeau, *The Practice of Everyday Life*, (Berkeley: University of California Press, 1984); Tim Crosswell, 'Imagining the nomad: mobility and the postmodern primitive', in *Space and Social Theory*, pp. 362–3.
19   See Daniel Bell, *The End of Ideology* (Cambridge, Mass.: Harvard University Press, 1988), pp. 230–5.
20   Daniel Cohen, *Richesse du monde, pauvretés des nations* (Paris: Flammarion, 1997), p. 84.
21   Nigel Thrift, 'The rise of soft capitalism', *Cultural Values*, April 1997, pp. 39–40. Thrift's essays can only be described as eye-opening and seminal, but the concept of 'soft capitalism' used in the title and throughout the text seems a misnomer – and a misleading characterization. There is nothing 'soft' about software capitalism of light modernization. Thrift points out that 'dancing' and 'surfing' are among the best metaphors to approximate to the nature of capitalism in its new avatar. The metaphors are well chosen, since they suggest weightlessness, lightness and facility of movement. But there is nothing 'soft' about daily dancing and surfing. Dancers and surfers, and particularly those on the overcrowded ballroom floor and on a coast buffeted by a high tide, need to be tough, not soft. And they are tough – as few of their predecessors, able to stand still or move along clearly marked and well-serviced tracks, ever needed to be, Software capitalism is no less hard and tough than its hardware ancestor used to be. And liquid is anything but soft. Think of a deluge, flood or broken dam.
22   See Georg Simmel, 'A chapter in the philosophy of value', in *The Conflict in Modern Culture and Other Essays*, trans. K. Peter Etzkorn (New York: Teachers College Press, 1968), pp. 52–4.
23   As reported in Eileen Applebaum and Rosemary Batt, *The New American Workplace* (Ithaca: Cornell University Press, 1993). Here quoted after Richard Sennett, *The Corrosion of Character: The Per-*

sonal Consequences of Work in the New Capitalism (New York: W. W. Norton & Co., 1998), p. 50.
24 Sennett, *The Corrosion of Character*, pp. 61–2.
25 Anthony Flew, *The Logic of Mortality* (Oxford: Blackwell, 1987), p. 3.
26 See Michael Thompson, *Rubbish Theory: The Creation and Destruction of Value* (Oxford: Oxford University Press, 1979), particularly pp. 113–19.
27 Leif Lewin, 'Man, society, and the failure of politics', *Critical Review*, Winter–Spring 1998, p. 10. The criticized quotation comes from Gordon Tullock's preface to William C. Mitchell and Randy T. Simmons, *Beyond Politics: Markets, Welfare, and the Failure of Bureaucracy* (Boulder, Col.: Westview Press, 1994), p. xiii.
28 Guy Debord, *Comments on the Society of the Spectacle*, trans. Malcolm Imrie (London: Verso, 1990), pp. 16, 13.

Chapter 4   Work

1 In the preface, written in his capacity as the Chairman of the Commission on the Year 2000, to his *The Year 2000*, ed. Hermann Hahn and Anthony J. Wiener. Here quoted from I. F. Clarke, *The Pattern of Expectation, 1644–2001* (London: Jonathan Cape, 1979), p. 314.
2 Pierre Bourdieu, *Contre-feux: Propos pour servir à la résistance contre l'invasion néo-liberale* (Paris: Liber, 1998), p. 97.
3 Alain Peyrefitte, *Du 'Miracle' en économie: Leçons au Collège de France* (Paris: Odile Jacob, 1998), p. 230.
4 Kenneth Jowitt, *New World Disorder* (Berkeley: University of California Press, 1992), p. 306.
5 Guy Debord, *Comments on the Society of the Spectacle*, trans. Malcolm Imrie (London: Verso, 1990), p. 9.
6 Peter Drucker, *The New Realities*, London: Heinemann, 1989), pp. 15, 10.
7 Ulrich Beck, *Risk Society: Towards a New Modernity*, trans. Mark Ritter (London: Sage, 1992), p. 88.
8 See David Ruelle, *Hasard et chaos* (Paris: Odile Jacob, 1991), pp. 90, 113.
9 Jacques Attali, *Chemins de sagesse: Traité du labyrinthes* (Paris: Fayard, 1996), pp. 19, 60, 23.
10 See Paul Bairoch, *Mythes et paradoxes de l'histoire économique* (Paris: La Découverte, 1994).
11 Daniel Cohen, *Richesse du monde, pauvretés des nations* (Paris: Flammarion, 1998), p. 31.

12 See Karl Polanyi, *The Great Transformation* (Boston: Beacon Press, 1957), particularly pp. 56–7 and ch. 6.
13 Richard Sennett, *The Corrosion of Character: The Personal Consequences of Work in the New Capitalism* (New York: W. W. Norton & Co., 1998), p. 23.
14 Sennett, *The Corrosion of Character*, pp. 42–3.
15 *La Misère du monde*, ed. Pierre Bourdieu (Paris: Seuil, 1993), pp. 631, 628.
16 Sennett, *The Corrosion of Character*, p. 24.
17 Robert Reich, *The Work of Nations* (New York: Vintage Books, 1991).
18 Sennett, *The Corrosion of Character*, pp. 50, 82.
19 Attali, *Chemins de sagesse*, pp. 79–80, 109.
20 Nigel Thrift, 'The rise of soft capitalism', *Cultural Values*, April 1997, p. 52.
21 Pierre Bourdieu, *Sur la télévision* (Paris: Liber, 1996), p. 85.
22 Bourdieu, *Contre-feux*, pp. 95–101.
23 Alain Peyrefitte, *La Société de confiance: Essai sur les origines du développement* (Paris: Odile Jacob, 1998), pp. 514–16.
24 Bourdieu, *Contre-feux*, p. 97.
25 Attali, *Chemins de sagesse*, p. 84.

Chapter 5 Community

1 Philippe Cohen, *Protéger ou disparaître: les élites face à la montée des insécurités* (Paris: Gallimard, 1999), pp. 7–9.
2 Eric Hobsbawm, *The Age of Extremes* (London: Michael Joseph, 1994), p. 428.
3 Eric Hobsbawm, 'The cult of identity politics', *New Left Review*, 217 (1998), p. 40.
4 Jock Young, *The Exclusive Society* (London: Sage, 1999), p. 164.
5 Young, *The Exclusive Society*, p. 165
6 Leszek Kołakowski, 'Z lewa, z prawa', *Moje słuszne poglady na wszystko* (Kraków: Znak, 1999), pp. 321–7.
7 See Bernard Yack, 'Can patriotism save us from nationalism? Rejoinder to Virioli', *Critical Review*, 12/1–2 (1998), pp. 203–6.
8 See Bernard Crick, 'Meditation on democracy, politics, and citizenship', unpublished manuscript.
9 Alain Touraine, 'Can we live together, equal and different?', *European Journal of Social Theory*, 2/1998, p. 177.
10 Richard Sennett, *The Corrosion of Character: The Personal Consequences of Work in the New Capitalism* (London: W. W. Norton,

1998), p. 138.

11   See Jean-Paul Besset and Pascale Krémer, 'Le Nouvel Attrait pour les résidences "sécurisées" ', *Le Monde*, 15 May 1999, p. 10.

12   Richard Sennett, 'The myth of purified community', *The Uses of Disorder: Personal Identity and City Style* (London: Faber & Faber, 1996), pp. 36, 39.

13   Quoted after *Émile Durkheim: Selected Writings*, ed. Anthony Giddens (Cambridge: Cambridge University Press, 1972), pp. 94, 115.

14   See Jim MacLaughlin, 'Nation-building, social closure and anti-traveller racism in Ireland', *Sociology*, February 1999, pp. 129–51. Also for Friedrich Rabel quotation.

15   See Jean Clair, 'De Guernica à Belgrade', *Le Monde*, 21 May 1999, p. 16.

16   *Newsweek*, 21 June 1999.

17   See Chris Bird, 'Serbs flee Kosovo revenge attacks', *Guardian*, 17 July 1999.

18   See Daniel Vernet, 'Les Balkans face au risque d'une tourmente sans fin', *Le Monde*, 15 May, p. 18.

19   Vernet, 'Les Balkans face au risque d'une tourmente sans fin'.

20   Eric Hobsbawm, 'The nation and globalization', *Constellations*, March 1998, pp. 4–5.

21   René Girard, *La Violence et le sacré* (Paris: Grasset, 1972). Here quoted after Patrick Gregory's English translation, *Violence and the Sacred* (Baltimore: Johns Hopkins University Press, 1979), pp. 8, 12, 13.

22   Arne Johan Vetlesen, 'Genocide: a case for the responsibility of the bystander', July 1998 (manuscript).

23   Arne Johan Vetlesen, 'Yugoslavia, genocide and modernity', January 1999 (manuscript).

Afterthought: On Writing; On Writing Sociology

1   This essay has been first published in *Theory, Culture and Society*, 2000, 1.

Index